T. S. Eliot, Dant

MW01222690

T. S. Eliot, Dante, and the Idea of Europe

Edited by

Paul Douglass

T. S. Eliot, Dante, and the Idea of Europe,
Edited by Paul Douglass

This book first published 2011

Cambridge Scholars Publishing

12 Back Chapman Street, Newcastle upon Tyne, NE6 2XX, UK

British Library Cataloguing in Publication Data
A catalogue record for this book is available from the British Library

ISBN (10): 1-4438-2878-5, ISBN (13): 978-1-4438-2878-9

Table of Contents

PART II: DANTE'S GHOST AND ELIOT'S MODERNISM

PART III: ELIOT, DANTE, AND THE IDEA OF EUROPE

ACKNOWLEDGMENTS

The editor wishes to thank Richard Berengarten for his "Invocation," which alludes to the tradition of the guide embodied in Dante's relationship to Virgil and Eliot's to Dante; and also for the concluding "Benediction," which invites us to "join hands through poetry." The assistance of Stefano Maria Casella was indispensable to the assembling of this volume. The editor is also deeply grateful for the counsel and guidance of Jewel Spears Brooker, Dominic Manganiello, Temur Kobakhidze, and John Xiros Cooper. The same and more must be said of Massimo Bacigalupo, who provided not only counsel and guidance, but editorial skill and finesse that served to improve the entire volume. Molto grazie, Massimo.

GUIDE TO ABBREVIATIONS USED IN CITATIONS

The following abbreviations have been used in citing works of T. S. Eliot. Works not frequently cited are cited by title in parenthetical references and may be found in the "Works Cited" list at the end of the volume.

CPP	*Complete Poems and Plays*: 1909-1950. New York: Harcourt Brace, 1952.
IMH	*Inventions of the March Hare*. Ed. Christopher Ricks. New York: Harcourt, 1996.
Letters	*The Letters of T. S. Eliot.* 2 vols. Vol. 1 Ed. Valerie Eliot. New York: Harcourt, 1993. Vol. 2 Ed. Valerie Eliot and Hugh Haughton. London: Faber and Faber, 2009.
NTDC	*Notes Towards the Definition of Culture*. London: Faber, 1948.
OPP	*On Poetry and Poets*. London: Faber, 1986 [1957].
SE	*Selected Essays*. Third Enlarged ed. London and Boston: Faber, 1980 [1951].
SW	*The Sacred Wood. Essays on Poetry and Criticism.* London: Methuen, 1980 [1920].
TCC	*To Criticize the Critic and other Writings*. London: Faber, 1978 [1965].
UPUC	*The Use of Poetry and the Use of Criticism*. London: Faber, 1975 [1933].
VMP	*The Varieties of Metaphysical Poetry*. Ed. Ronald Schuchard. London: Faber, 1993.

A Note on the Citation of Dante's Works

In many cases, quotations from Dante are part of quotations from Eliot, and in those cases the reference is given to the appropriate passage in Eliot's *Selected Essays*. When Dante is quoted without reference to T. S. Eliot's work, the following translations are referenced, unless another reference is given in the parenthetical note. All works cited in this edition are included in the "Works Cited" list at the end of the volume.

The Divine Comedy of Dante Alighieri: Inferno. Trans. Allen Mandelbaum. New York: Bantam, 1980.

The Divine Comedy of Dante Alighieri: Paradiso. Trans. Allen Mandelbaum. New York: Bantam, 1984.

The Divine Comedy of Dante Alighieri: Purgatorio. Trans. Allen Mandelbaum. New York: Bantam, 1982.

Vita Nuova. Trans. Mark Musa. New York: Oxford University Press, 1992.

INVOCATION:
AND MY GUIDE TOOK ME

RICHARD BERENGARTEN

And my guide took me by the hand and led me
into a darkness that was not a darkness and
into a silence that was not a silence and paused
and said in a voice as quiet as running water
You have come from a country where poetry

is so trammelled up in clever elegance
that only opacity is praised and prized
but if you will listen and open up your hands
I shall teach you a poetry transparent and pure
as the wind and as impossible to pin down as light

INTRODUCTION

PAUL DOUGLASS

DANTE'S INFLUENCE ON EUROPEAN LITERATURE was enhanced greatly by T. S. Eliot, who in a sense renovated Dante for modern literature. The essays in this volume explore Dante's influence through a focus on Eliot. In asking what Eliot made of Dante, and what Dante meant to Eliot, the writers here assess the legacy of Modernism by engaging its "classicist" roots, covering a wide spectrum of topics radiating from the central node of Dante's presence in the poetry and criticism of Eliot. The essays included reflect upon Eliot's aesthetic, philosophical, and religious convictions in relation to Dante, his influence upon literary Modernism through his embracing and championing of the Florentine, and his efforts to promote a strong sense of European unity founded upon a shared cultural past. The writers in the present volume offer a stimulating convergence of concisely-argued views on Dante's importance for Eliot, and the meaning of that connection for the poetry and criticism of his and our time.

There has been a continuing interest in this important topic from the 1930s, when Mario Praz published an essay in *The Southern Review* on Eliot and Dante. In addition to numerous articles, books written about Eliot's work have been obliged to mention Dante, and the subject has been approached from a great variety of angles in many essays in English and Italian letters, leading up to Steve Ellis's historical study, *Dante and English Poetry: Shelley to T. S. Eliot* (1983). Dominic Manganiello brought Ellis's and others' work into focus with his ambitious *T. S. Eliot and Dante* (1989), which has served as the foundation for further exploration. Examples of recent trends in this area of literary study include Brian Moloney's "T. S. Eliot's Dante" (1997), A. Walton Litz's "Dante, Pound, Eliot: The Visionary Company" (1998), James Wilhelm's "Two Visions of the Journey of Life: Dante as Guide for Eliot and Pound" (2004), and J. H. Copley's "Plurilingualism and the Mind of Europe in T. S. Eliot and Dante" (2005). Twenty years on from Manganiello's milestone work, it seems a good time for scholarship to confront new temporal and cultural challenges, especially T. S. Eliot's role in the formation of a "European Union," but also other issues, including Eliot as a postcolonial writer in relation to Dante, and his influence upon his contemporaries and later-emerging writers not treated in previous waves of criticism.

The first section of this book deals with aesthetic and philosophical issues related to Eliot's engagement with Dante. Distinguished Eliot scholar and editor Jewel Spears Brooker focuses on Eliot's early struggle to decide between philosophy and poetry, a struggle personified in F. H. Bradley—whose philosophical work was the subject of Eliot's PhD thesis—and in Dante, whose work informed Eliot's earliest poetry. Eliot's most detailed discussion of the connection between philosophy and poetry is contained in his 1926 Clark Lectures at Cambridge University, published as *Varieties of Metaphysical Poetry*. Here he defines the "philosophic poet" in Bradleyean terms as one who "enlarges immediate experience" by "drawing within the orbit of feeling and sense what had existed only in thought" (*VMP* 55, 51). Brooker explores Eliot's linking of Bradley and Dante, his claims for Dante's verse, and his attempt to model his own verse after Dante's, taking special note of the fact that Eliot's Cambridge lectures occurred at a turning point in his life, immediately before his conversion to Anglo-Catholicism, an event pointing to his landmark essay on Dante and his openly Dantesque sequence in "Ash-Wednesday."

Viorica Patea follows Brooker with a discussion of Eliot's belief in a lost unity of "sensibility" and language in Europe, and how the work of Dante informs his poetics. Preoccupied with the nineteenth-century disjunction of thought from sense, and object from subject, Eliot's theory of a unified sensibility, Patea argues, is strikingly similar to Henri Corbin's "mundus imaginalis" and Jung's archetypal imagination—but owes most of all to Dante's visual and allegoric imagination. Eliot scholar Nancy Gish complements Patea's exploration of Eliot's idea of sensibility with an essay on "Altered Consciousness," building on the work of *The Protean Self*, by Robert J. Lifton, who defines the modern form of self as "fluid and many-sided." In the late nineteenth and early twentieth centuries, Pierre Janet had defined this multiplicity as "désagrégation," translated as both "dissociation" and "disintegration." Eliot, who knew Janet's work, used both terms. In *The Waste Land*, he represents a fragmentation of consciousness so severe as to be disintegrative, and yet, paradoxically, to define a form of cohesion. Gish explores the importance of allusions to Dante in published and draft forms of "Gerontion," arguing that Gerontion is the epitome of a major figure of Eliot's earliest work: the mad old man, who represents what Eliot saw as the disintegration of European consciousness since Dante.

The last two essays of this first section deal with symbols of unity, eternity, and repleteness in Eliot's work from the perspective of Dante's practice and influence. P. S. Sri argues that Eliot often attempts an East-West ideo-synthesis, combining Dante's symbolism with that of Hindu-Buddhism. As Sri says, Eliot employs, on one hand, the Western single rose as a symbol of completion and unity, and on the other hand, the thousand-petalled lotus (*sahasrara*) of Eastern mysticism. Eliot's work should thus be credited as a true quest for the universal and eternal, common to both the East and the West. In a similar vein, Temur Kobakhidze depicts the recurring images and motifs of Eliot's major works as a quest for a "musical structure" based not only on the pattern of a rotating circle and a still point, but also on the corresponding numerical designation of the process of circulation and of the circle itself—the number four. Focusing particularly on *Four Quartets*, Kobakhidze suggests that images of quaternity and the square owe much to *Paradiso* 33, but that Eliot chooses a reverse way: for him the aspiration to grasp the inconceivable is movement towards the centre.

The second part of *Eliot, Dante, and the Idea of Europe* takes up the subject of Eliot's relation to and influence upon literary Modernism, including especially Ezra Pound. The first three essays trace the Dantean legacy in Eliot's earliest and later periods. Arianna Antonielli traces the influence of Dante to Eliot's earliest poetical work in *Inventions of the March Hare*, juvenilia which nonetheless reflects Eliot's recurrent themes, symbols and images, already inspired by Dante's "clear visual images," by "the lucidity" of his style and "his extraordinary force of compression." David Summers believes that the trajectory of Eliot's major poems follows a distinctly Dantesque pattern. The earliest poems, especially "Prufrock" and *The Waste Land*, comprise variations on a Modernist *Inferno*. The poems that come after his conversion to Anglo-Catholicism, Summers argues, demonstrate an ardent search for a modern "purgatorial mode" of meditative poetry, but a *Paradiso* is distinctly lacking from Eliot's work. Summers explains Eliot's failure to write the obvious culmination to his poetic and spiritual pilgrimage as a feature of his membership in the Modernist movement, despite his overt commitment to a reactionary religious and political philosophy.

Andrija Matic also finds in Eliot's earlier and later poems a changing relation to Dante's legacy that is the product of his Modernist connections. He argues that in the early poems (up to "The Hollow Men"), almost all of Eliot's borrowings from or allusions to Dante have ironic purposes or dimensions which contribute to the polysemic structure of the poetry. In the period after Eliot's conversion to Anglo-Catholicism, the poems (particularly "Animula," "Ash-Wednesday," and passages of *Four Quartets*) deal with religious and philosophical ideas, without apparent irony. Also interesting, Matic says, is the reduction or intertextual characteristics. Even so, the later works contain passages based on Dante's imagery that cannot be fully understood without appreciating Eliot's ironic juxtaposition of meanings. His ironic stance is yet another instance of his Modernist sensibility.

Ezra Pound is perhaps the epitome of the Modernist Dantesque voice , and the two essays that conclude this section deal with Eliot's relationship to Pound through Dante. Stefano Maria Casella argues that Dante emerges as one of the fundamental elements of Eliot's and Pound's creative activity, a fact exemplified in the second part of Eliot's "Little Gidding" and in Pound's Canto 72, in which each poet attempts writing "à la maniére de" Dante. These two poems stand out as the longest and loftiest instances of Dantesque imitations, and different as they are (the former is written in English, the latter in Italian), they elicit a close comparison with their models, including mainly Dante, but also Virgil and Homer. Eliot and Pound both engaged in a strenuous effort to reassert Dante's unceasing modernity. For his part, Massimo Bacigalupo considers Pound's and Eliot's endeavors to "regain paradise" following in Dante's footsteps, and places their Dantesque project in the context of American modernism and more generally of America's peculiar relation to European literature and culture.

The final section of *T. S. Eliot, Dante, and the Idea of Europe* builds upon the preceding discussions to assess Eliot's role in the formation of a modern sense of European unity. It begins with Randy Malamud's "Dante as Guide to Eliot's Competing Traditions," which argues that Eliot valorizes Dante as the voice of Europe: Eliot's poetry "invites a reader-response approach: he who most clearly hears Dante amid the cacophony of voices in his poetry, and who chooses Dante as the guide through this terrain, will be the better reader." Exploring Eliot's extensive commentary on Dante and Shakespeare, Malamud says that Eliot engages his readers in an "overarching methodological exercise that involves detecting various traditions, learning how to appreciate these traditions, and finding guides who will help us navigate them." The tension between Dante and Shakespeare in Eliot's poetry and prose more generally plays out as Europe vs. England. When Margate failed to cure his emotional ailments, Eliot found refuge and healing in continental Europe; so, too, his poetry often dismisses Englishness in favor of European perspectives and experiences.

Paul Douglass's essay on Dante and Matthew Arnold argues that as Eliot sought to break in to the world of English letters, he followed Arnold by seeking to define himself as a European writer, one whose foundation was the multilingual literature of that continent—especially focusing on the work of Dante. Thus, despite his repeated rejection of much of Arnold's work, Eliot sought a modern expression of Dante's simplicity and profundity, the power of what Arnold called the "touchstone" line: "The accent of high seriousness, born of absolute sincerity..."—which is precisely what Eliot located in Dante. John Xiros Cooper deepens and complicates the sense of Eliot's desire to support an idea of European unity by taking up Eliot's three radio talks to Germany in the summer of 1945, published in German in 1946 and in English as an appendix to *Notes Towards the Definition of Culture* in 1948. As part of the wider denazification strategy after 1945, these talks have been read as simply meeting an ideological need at that historical juncture. But Cooper argues that they bear a clear connection to the rhetorical program of *Four Quartets* and to Eliot's activities as a European intellectual in the 1930s through his editorship of the *Criterion*. The three radio broadcasts look not only back in time, but forward to the Treaty of Rome in 1957. Eliot's radio talks were aimed primarily at a German intelligentsia traumatized by the barbarisms of war, but they also set down cultural conditions for the movement towards European integration and, eventually, the creation of the European Union. Eliot's particular contribution was to discuss the unity of European culture not simply as an abstract idea, but to begin to think of practical institutions to bring about the more pragmatic form of integration as a union of distinct cultures. The balance between region and nation, the local and the universal, was further developed in the closing chapters of *Notes Towards the Definition of Culture*. In this task, Dante was an important predecessor, a figure of European standing and the "least provincial" of poets, whose grounding in the local was nonetheless the foundation of his global influence.

Taking an entirely different view of Eliot's European identity, Mafruha Mohua argues that in 1925, when T. S. Eliot was invited to deliver the 1926 Clark Lectures at Trinity College, he was going through the "blackest moment of [his] life," a profound religious crisis, perceptible in the lectures as personal turmoil. Although the aim of the lectures was to present a theory of metaphysical poetry, Eliot also examines the idea of the European tradition, represented by Dante and the poets of the Italian Trecento, and the disintegration of that tradition, represented by Donne and the seventeenth century. Dante's generation, balancing the classical tradition of Plato and Aristotle and the Catholic tradition of St. Aquinas and Richard of St. Victor, is portrayed by Eliot as representing the apex of European civilization. The seventeenth century, on the other hand, is presented as a chaotic period that marks the beginning of the disintegration of European civilization. What has not been noted is that this disintegration appears to be the result of a non-classical and non-European influence from the Islamic tradition of Al-Andalus. Mafruha shows that Eliot's conception of the superiority of Dante and the Trecento is derived from his belief in the importance of a unified and common religio-philosophical system which is wholly classical and, consequently, European. The seventeenth century, under the influence of the "Mohammedanized," and romantic, Society of Jesus, produced a generation of writers who, according to Eliot, colluded in the "destruction of European civilization." According to Mafruha, Eliot's approval of Dante and his disapproval of Donne reveal a politics of reading which exhibits a neo-imperialist attitude towards the "other" and the fear of a contamination of European culture through an Eastern strain.

While Mafruha sees Eliot's formation of a European identity as stemming from his reaction against perceived outside influences that would adulterate its culture, Patrick Query believes that Eliot's verse plays are equally an expression of this desire to form an idea of Europe, with full awareness of the problem of Otherness and diversity, though admittedly seen from within the fold of a Europe that has been insulated from Muslim influence. The lessons about the local and indigenous which Eliot seems to have learned from his study of Dante are visible behind his move toward becoming a writer for the stage. In the 1930s, although he continued to write poems, Eliot's great concerns were the search for a workable modern drama in verse and for a unified vision of European identity, and Query argues that as these two projects developed—and faltered—together, they brought Eliot as close to an articulation of the (then, as now) elusive unity in diversity as any modern European writer has come. The failure of either vision to materialize as Eliot hoped provides a small but useful point from which to reassess the relationship between literary expression and the European idea.

It is fitting that the last word in this volume should fall to the writer who brought the topic of T. S. Eliot and Dante to coalescence over twenty years ago in *T. S. Eliot and Dante* (1989). One of the most compelling responses to the Eliot-inspired embrace of Dante by twentieth-century writers has come recently from the pen of American writer Wendell Berry. The vital European tradition appears to form the core of Berry's contemporary American literary project. On receiving the T. S. Eliot Award for Creative Writing in 1994, Berry paid tribute to Eliot's "pilgrimage of works" from "The Love Song of J. Alfred Prufrock" to *The Elder Statesman*. Eliot, according to Berry, presented "dismembered" personalities who move out of the shadows of the wasteland and into the light of what Berry calls "a love far greater… than their own." Manganiello argues that Berry's own fragmented figures in novels such as *Remembering* (1988) and *Jayber Crow* (2000) follow a similar trajectory to become transfigured pilgrims in a divine comedy. The exchanges of love and compassion that restore fractured family relationships in Eliot's *The Elder Statesman* are echoed in Berry's work, which Manganiello argues is founded on Dantesque themes that reaffirm the importance of "Europe's Epic" and therefore an "idea of Europe" propounded by Eliot.

PART I:

DANTE AND ELIOT—AESTHETIC AND PHILOSOPHICAL CONVERGENCES

CHAPTER ONE

ENLARGING IMMEDIATE EXPERIENCE: BRADLEY AND DANTE IN ELIOT'S AESTHETIC

JEWEL SPEARS BROOKER

> [A]n enlargement of immediate experience...is a general function of poetry.... [I]t elevates sense for a moment to regions ordinarily attainable only by abstract thought,...[it] clothes the abstract, for a moment, with all the painful delight of flesh.
>
> —T. S. Eliot, *Varieties of Metaphysical Poetry* (54-55)

ON NEW YEAR'S EVE 1914, T. S. Eliot, a twenty-six year old American who had just finished his first term at Oxford University, found himself alone and depressed in the city of London. He was in the middle of a six-week Christmas break, the first part of which he had spent at the seashore. In a letter to his Harvard classmate and fellow poet Conrad Aiken, Eliot muses about the contrast between life in Oxford and in London.

> In Oxford, I have the feeling that I am not quite alive—that my body is walking about with a bit of my brain inside it, and nothing else.... Oxford is very pretty, but I don't like to be dead. I don't think I should stay there another year...but I should not mind being in London.... How much more self-conscious one is in a big city!...Just at present this is an inconvenience, for I have been going through one of those nervous sexual attacks which I suffer from when alone in a city.... this is the worst since Paris.... One walks about the street with one's desires, and one's refinement rises up like a wall whenever opportunity approaches. (*Letters* 1:81-82)

This self-portrait includes a series of parallel binaries. In Oxford, he is a self-conscious robot with a brain; in London, a self-conscious animal filled with desire. In Oxford, dead; in London, alive. He is repelled by Oxford professors with their pregnant wives and book-lined rooms, but intrigued by London street people with their quirks and smirks. In Oxford, he is sexually numb; in London, sexually charged. In retrospect, this split between feeling and intellect, desire and refinement, can be seen as part of his DNA. His family, one of America's most distinguished, was self-consciously dynastic, enlightened, public-spirited, and respectable, all characteristics that facilitated a gap between surface and depth, public and private, self-discipline and promiscuity.

Painfully aware of his bifurcated self, Eliot longed for escape, a longing expressed in his poetry in two ways, the first a proclivity to descend beneath consciousness and the second a mystical longing to merge with the Absolute. The first can be seen in Prufrock's identification with the lowest forms of life. "I should have been a pair of ragged claws / Scuttling across the floors of silent seas" (*CPP* 5). The second can be seen in his identification with saints and martyrs in early poems such as "The Love Song of St. Sebastian." Eliot was an intelligent person pre-occupied with the intelligence trap, remembering with mixed feelings the irrecoverable pre-analytical moments in which he simply existed. He knew that intellect and feeling were incompatible bedfellows, but he also knew that rejecting either one made him less than human. He knew too that one cannot transcend duality by diving into the body in search of immediate experience. To be conscious of unity is to have lost it; to try to recover it is to transform it into its opposite, that is, into an idea.

The gap between body and brain in a major motif in the four great poems Eliot wrote between 1909 and 1911—"The Love Song of J. Alfred Prufrock," "Portrait of a Lady," "Rhapsody on a Windy Night," and "Preludes." "Rhapsody on a Windy Night," for example, consists of a Bergsonian dialogue between mind and matter, between images inside his head and images outside on the streets of Paris. The situation of the persona is strikingly similar to the one described in the New Year's Eve letter to Aiken—i.e., a young man walking through the streets of a city between midnight and 4 am, tormented by memory and desire. Because the street lights are widely spaced, he moves in and out of darkness and light. As he walks through the dark, "Midnight shakes the memory / As a madman shakes a dead geranium" (*CPP* 14). As he enters illuminated areas, street lamps reveal prostitutes hesitating in doorways, cats flattening themselves in gutters. The poem ends not with any rapprochement between mind and world, but with a disturbing image of fatal severance—"The last twist of the knife" (*CPP* 16).

In a poignant letter to his brother, written in January 1936, Eliot looks back on the intellectual and spiritual journey that led him to the Church of England. He mentions his unsuccessful attempt to turn himself into a philosophy professor and adds that he now understands that his graduate studies had been part of a "religious preoccupation."[1] The religious preoccupation, essentially a quest for wholeness, included the problem of the divided self. During his university years, the problem can be seen in the conflict between his attraction to poetry and to philosophy, a conflict exacerbated by a year in Paris during which he attended lectures by Henri Bergson. When Eliot returned to Harvard, he decided to focus on philosophy, a field preoccupied with a parallel problem, the limitations of dualism.[2] As part of his Ph.D. project, he immersed himself in the ideas of F. H. Bradley, whose idealism promised transcendence of emotion and intellect in a more comprehensive complex of feeling. He discovered, however, that philosophy promised more than it could deliver, and so he abandoned it. With Dante as his guide, he returned to poetry. He did not toss out what he had gained from such mentors as Bradley, however, but garnered all of his resources in a renewed effort to achieve in poetry a unification of emotion and intellect. In 1926, in his Clark Lectures at Cambridge, he attempted to put his personal struggle into historical context and to formulate a theory that would integrate his philosophical and poetical studies. In discussing the function of art, he claimed that poetry, especially that of Dante, was more promising than philosophy, that poetry at its best could deliver an "enlargement of immediate experience" (*VMP* 54-55).

Eliot did not pick up the idea of "immediate experience" from literary criticism, but from philosophy. It refers to a major concept in the philosophy of Bradley, on whose work Eliot in 1914 decided to write his dissertation. Bradley offered a strenuous critique of dualism and a theory for overcoming it. He did so, first, by collapsing both subject and object into a larger whole he calls Experience; and second, by adding a third level to the process of knowing, an element that transcends subject and object, appearance and reality, by incorporating both into that larger whole. "There is but one Reality, and its being consists in experience. In this one whole all appearances come together" (*Appearance and Reality* 403). Bradley's critique of dualism and his analysis of Experience is very helpful in understanding Eliot's work as a poet. It illuminates his quest for wholeness, his dissatisfaction with the solutions offered by philosophy, and his return to poetry. Bradley's notion of Experience is not something Eliot abandoned, but something he both critiqued and carried forward as a foundation for his appreciation of poetry.

---

[1] Unpublished letter. Houghton Library, Harvard University.

[2] For an exploration of this issue, see Arthur O. Lovejoy. *The Revolt Against Dualism: An Inquiry Concerning the Existence of Ideas*. 1929. (LaSalle, IL: Open Court, 1955).

Bradley divides Experience into three categories: "immediate experience," "intellectual experience," and "transcendent experience," the first two of which are almost identical to the body and mind facing off in Eliot's early poems and letters, and the third of which tenuously suggests not only a truce, but a comprehensive peace. Immediate experience is experience that is not mediated through the intellect, a sensuous knowing and being in one which is prior to the development of logical or temporal or spatial categories. This is how Bradley defines it.

> We in short have experience in which there is no distinction between my awareness and that of which it is aware. There is an immediate feeling, a knowing and being in one, with which knowledge begins; and, though this...is transcended, it nevertheless remains throughout as the present foundation of my known world. And if you remove this direct sense of my momentary contents and being, you bring down the whole of consciousness in one common wreck. For it is in the end ruin to divide experience into something on one side experienced as an object, and on the other side, something, not experienced at all. (*Essays on Truth and Reality* 159-60)

An example of immediate experience would be the ground swell of desire on the midnight street, desire in which, at first, there no distinction between self, on the one side, and the girl in the doorway, on the other. This directly experienced many-in-one is not the walker's experience, for he as subject and girl as object do not yet exist. When he becomes aware of "his" desire and of her beckoning eye, then immediate experience has dissolved into the realm of self and not-self.

It is the nature of immediate experience to fall apart, to make way for perception in terms of self and not-self. Experience that is first mediated through the senses inexorably rises to consciousness. The intellect, which had existed heretofore as an undifferentiated part of pure experience, takes control and begins to direct the elements which, like itself, had been part of immediate experience. Reality can no longer be apprehended directly, as a unity; it can only be apprehended in terms of relations and must be approached through the tortuous streets of thought. This is the level of dualism—of self and other, knower and known, mind and matter. In Bradley's view, all of these dualisms are abstractions from reality; all are unreal.

There is, in Bradley's view, a third level, a transcendent experience, which permits a return of sorts to the wholeness and unity of immediate experience. Immediate experience exists before relations, but transcendent experience exists after or above relations. Immediate experience dissolves of itself into relational experience, but relational experience resists resolution into the higher monistic experience. The villain is the discursive intellect, and the transcendence of relations such as self and not-self becomes a matter of reforming the intellect from a servant of division to a partner in the achievement of wholeness. Whereas immediate experience is characterized by a *knowing* and feeling in one which comes before intellection, transcendent experience is characterized by a *thinking* and feeling in one which comes after and which is achieved through reason. Obviously enough, it is this level of experience which Eliot refers to as "a direct sensuous apprehension of thought, or a recreation of thought into feeling" (*SE* 286). One of Bradley's favorite terms for transcendent experience is "felt thought," a term Eliot appropriated in contrasting seventeenth- and nineteenth-century poets. "Tennyson and Browning are poets, and they think; but they do not feel their thought as immediately as the odour of a rose" (*SE* 287).

There is no doubt that Eliot in 1914 and 1915 accepted the idea that intellectual experience is enclosed in an envelope of pure feeling. In the first chapter of his dissertation, he explains Bradley's immediate and transcendent experience and then states his concurrence. "If anyone object that mere experience at the beginning and complete experience at the end are hypothetical limits, I can say not a word in refutation, for this would be just the reverse side of what opinions I hold" *(Knowledge and Experience* 31). For a materialist, such an objection would be reasonable, for both immediate experience and transcendent experience can only be known as hypotheses; for an idealist, however, the before and after are also real. Together, they whisper that although one cannot move backward into the immediate experience of pure feeling, one can inch forward into a unity beyond the fragmentation that comes with self-consciousness.

By the end of his fall term at Oxford, Eliot had finished the first draft of a dissertation in which he described and to some extent defended Bradley's epistemology. Given the promise of Bradley's categories, one might think that Eliot would have found peace within. But not so. He finished his draft before Christmas and yet, on New Year's Eve confessed to Aiken that he was torn between refinement and desire; moreover, less than a week later, on January 6, 1915 he shared his thoughts about philosophy with a fellow student, Norbert Weiner. First, Eliot defines philosophy as "chiefly literary criticism," words about words, as Deconstructionists were to maintain many decades later; second, he claims that philosophy "is a perversion of reality" and has little to do with real life; third, he describes himself as a relativist and a sceptic, unconvinced by either realism or idealism; and fourth, he confesses that despite his admiration for Bradley, he finds himself more muddled than ever, conceding that in writing the dissertation, "[M]y relativism made me see so many sides to questions that I became hopelessly involved, and wrote a thesis perfectly unintelligible to anyone but myself" (*Letters* 1:89). Bradley described the intellectual prison, but did not give him a working key; Bradley led him to believe in an envelope of pure feeling, but on one end, it was irrecoverably lost; on the other, it was unreachable.

Given such reservations, why did Eliot not abandon philosophy at the beginning of 1915? Why finish the year at Oxford? Why revise the dissertation? Why continue down a dead-end road? The answer, contained in letters to his mother, is that he did it out of a sense of duty, primarily to his parents. His mother urged him to finish, and he promised her he would, and he did. But it is clear from his letters to his fellow students that he had concluded that philosophy did not satisfy his needs. The decision to abandon philosophy was complicated by his decision in June 1915 to marry a woman he had known for only a few weeks. The responsibility of caring for her, the fact that England was at war and London under bombardment, and a sharp reduction in financial support from his father made Eliot's determination to become a man of letters particularly perilous. But as indicated in the January letter to Weiner, he realized that relativism undercuts all philosophic conclusions, and concluded that the wisest course was "to avoid philosophy and devote oneself to either *real* art or *real* science" (*Letters* 1:89).

By 1915, Eliot had for several years been deeply involved with "*real* art," both as a student of comparative literature and as a struggling poet. Moreover, partially through reading Dante, he had come to believe that poetry could deliver what philosophy could not. He explains this in his 1926 lectures at Cambridge, the overall subject of which is the relationship between philosophy and poetry, between thought and feeling. The finest poetry, he claims, does not exclude thought, but fuses it into a complex that is experienced as feeling. "It is a function of poetry...to draw within the orbit of feeling and sense what had existed before only in thought" (*VMP* 50-51). The best philosophical poetry is that in which an "idea, or what is ordinarily apprehensible as an intellectual statement, is translated in sensible form; so that the world of sense is actually enlarged" (*VMP* 54). Good poetry, in other words, takes abstractions, thoughts, ideas and transforms them so that they are experienced, at least momentarily, as feelings rather than thoughts, in the body instead of the brain. Genuine poetry enables one to smell his thoughts as immediately as he smells steaks in passageways or roses in gardens. Poetry at its best "elevates sense for a moment to regions ordinarily attainable only by abstract thought,...[it] clothes the abstract, for a moment, with all the painful delight of flesh" (*VMP* 55). In moving thought into the realm of feeling, poetry facilitates a momentary victory over dualism. This brief but real experience of immediacy Eliot experienced as a sort of biblical first fruit—that is, something valuable both in itself and as a pledge of a harvest to come. This experience of immediacy—at once a taste and a foretaste—explains why Eliot migrated from philosophy to poetry. And, by his own testimony in the Clark Lectures, it was Dante who showed the way.

Eliot's appreciation of Dante, then, did not happen in an intellectual bubble. His comments connecting Dante to an "enlargement of immediate experience" are a clear indication that his understanding of Dante's power to move and persuade was indebted to his (Eliot's) absorption of Bradley's triadic concept of experience. In a long, analytical essay on Dante (1929), Eliot supports his claim that the great Florentine's ability to fuse intellect and sensation makes him the philosophic poet *par excellence.* Two major points in Eliot's argument connect Dante with Bradley. The first relates to Dante's images, which transform ideas into sensations—in Bradleyean terms, turn intellectual experience into immediate experience or transcendent experience. The second relates to the overall structure of the *Divine Comedy*. Eliot describes the three canticles—*Inferno*, *Purgatorio*, *Paradiso*—in language that suggests a parallel with Bradley's three stages of experience. Damnation is something that can be apprehended immediately, through the senses. Purgation, on the other hand, must be apprehended first through the intellect, for its underlying idea is theological and philosophical. Beatitude is a state that can only be grasped in terms of a fusion of intellect and feeling, a transcendent whole of feeling that is beyond words.

In the 1929 essay, Eliot explains that in reading Dante he discovered that "genuine poetry can communicate before it is understood" (*SE* 238), that it can be enjoyed before it is understood. Great poetry, in other words, delivers pre-intellectual experience—in Bradley's language, it delivers immediate experience, at least momentarily. It delivers shock, surprise, and horror. The reason for this is that Dante translates abstractions into images which project meaning visually. He had a "*visual* imagination"; he was able "to make us see what he saw" (*SE* 243). More amazingly, he was able to make us see what he thought, to see his ideas without even knowing that they are ideas. Eliot contrasts Dante's images, similes for the most part, with Shakespeare's, for the most part, metaphors. Dante's can be perceived by the senses, whereas Shakespeare's need to be filtered through the mind. To make his point, Eliot compares a passage from *Inferno* 15 with one from *Antony and Cleopatra*. In the passage from the *Inferno*, lost souls are peering at Dante and Virgil in the dim light.

> *e sì ver noi aguzzevan le ciglia,*
> *come vecchio sartor fa nella cruna.*
> [And sharpened their vision (knitted their brows) at us, like an old tailor peering at the eye of his needle.]
> (*Inferno* 15.20-21; *SE* 243-44)[3]

This simile does not invite the reader to think; it enables him to see. In the passage from *Antony and Cleopatra*, the speaker is describing the dead queen.

> [S]he looks like sleep,
> As she would catch another Antony
> In her strong toil of grace. (*Antony and Cleopatra* 5.2; *SE* 244)

Whereas the image from the *Inferno* is simple, the image from *Antony and Cleopatra* is complex; one is anchored in sensation; the other in thought. Dante enables the reader to see eyes straining to see; Shakespeare nudges him to think about fascination so strong that even death could not extinguish it (*SE* 244).

In regard to the structure of the *Divine Comedy*: Eliot discusses the three canticles in terms that suggest direct parallels with Bradley's three levels of experience. His comments on the *Inferno*, which he calls the easiest to read, suggest a parallel with immediate experience; on the *Purgatorio*, which he calls the hardest, a parallel with intellectual experience; and on the *Paradiso*, which he calls more difficult than the *Inferno*, a parallel with transcendent experience.

The *Inferno* is easiest to read because it consists largely of "a succession of phantasmagoric but clear images" (*SE* 246) that originate in the body and can be grasped directly by the senses on the very first reading. The meaning of the sins—gluttony, for example—is visible, is conveyed in the image as image. No explanation is needed. For the most part, these images are material, concrete, and visible, their very physicality sensuously conveying an idea of their essence. The image of Francesca caught in the web of mimetic desire is palpable, felt before either the reader or Dante the pilgrim understands the meaning attached to it. As Eliot says, "we can see and feel the situation of the two lost lovers, though we do not yet understand the meaning which Dante gives it" (*SE* 245). Even after we connect Francesca's "That day we read no further" (*Inferno* 5.138) with Augustine's words in the conversion scene in the garden in Milan, even after we analyze her narcissism, we are unable to expel her

[3] Translations of quotations of Dante are as given by Eliot in his 1929 essay.

charm. Eliot gives other examples of images whose meaning is conveyed visually—Farinata's posture conveys his pride, Brunetto's running conveys his excellence. These images communicate before they are understood. They are meaningful both in themselves and as they survive in the "larger whole of experience" which is the poem (*SE* 251).

The *Purgatorio*, Eliot maintains, is "the most difficult" of the three (*SE* 264). Whereas the *Inferno* and the *Paradiso* refer to states of being (damnation and blessedness), the essence of which can be conveyed as a feeling, the *Purgatorio* refers to a process of purgation that can only be understood as a concept. The canticle does contain examples of immediacy—Sordello impetuously leaping out of the flame to embrace Virgil, Arnaut Daniel joyously diving into the refining fire. But although these images can be apprehended by the eye, the meaning Dante assigns to them cannot. Grasping the idea of purgation requires theological and psychological knowledge. Virgil's discourse in Canto 17 on love, for example, requires what Eliot in another context refers to as "fundamental brainwork" (Preface to *Anabasis* 10)

> *Neither Creator, nor creature, my son, was ever without love, either natural or rational...The natural is always without error; but the other may err through mistaking the object, or through excess or deficiency of force.... Love must be the seed in you both of every virtue and of every act that merits punishment.* (*Purgatorio* 17.91, 94-95; *SE* 260)

Virgil's words are actually counter-intuitive, and they contain no images apprehensible to the eye or ear. To fully appreciate them, one must understand theology and know something of Aristotle's *De Anima* and Augustine's *Confessions*.

In discussing the end of the *Purgatorio*, Eliot says that "we have left behind the stage of punishment [i.e., Hell] and the stage of dialectic [i.e., Purgatory]" (*SE* 261). In philosophical terms, we have left the stage of unmediated feeling, and we have left the stage of intellectual experience or dialectic. We have arrived at the stage of transcendent experience. Transcendent experience does not dissolve feeling and thought but carries them into a larger complex that gives them significance. An excellent example of the comprehensive nature of the higher experience is the appearance of Beatrice at the end of the *Purgatorio* in Canto 30.

> Olive-crowned over a white veil, a lady appeared to me, clad under a green mantle, in colour of living flame. And my spirit, after so many years since trembling in her presence...felt, through hidden power which went out from her, the great strength of the old love. As soon as that lofty power struck my sense, which already had transfixed me before my adolescence, I

> turned leftwards with the trust of the little child who runs to his mama when he is frightened or distressed, to say to Virgil: "Hardly a drop of blood in my body does not shudder: I know the tokens of the ancient flame." (*Purgatorio* 20.31-35, 38-48; *SE* 263).

These images are at once visual and ethereal. They infold Dante's immediate experience as a child, which we know from the *Vita Nuova*, and his intellectual experience as a politician and poet, into the present moment of shuddering sensation. The feeling of the nine-year-old boy is the foundation; it is not abandoned but enlarged; the ancient flame is rekindled in a "new emotion, in a new situation, which comprehends, enlarges, and gives a meaning to it" (*SE* 262).

In the *Paradiso* itself, the summit of his achievement, Dante creates the sensuous equivalent, the physical embodiment, of what could ordinarily be apprehended only as an abstraction. The unified whole he creates includes but is not dominated by powerful sensations and strenuous dialectic. A superb example of Dante's ability to both preserve and transcend subject and object in pure feeling occurs at the end and the pinnacle of the poem in Canto 33.

> *Within its depths I saw ingathered, bound by love in one mass, the scattered leaves of the universe: substance and accidents and their relations, as though together fused, so that what I speak of is one simple flame*. (*Paradiso* 33.85; *SE* 267)

In the *Paradiso,* Eliot says, Dante succeeded

> in making the spiritual visible...Nowhere in poetry has experience so remote from ordinary experience been expressed so concretely, by a masterly use of that imagery of *light* which is the form of certain types of mystical experience.... One can feel only awe at the power of the master who could thus...realize the inapprehensible in visual images. (*SE* 267-68)

Eliot appreciated Bradley's formulation of immediate experience because it confirmed something that rang true in his own life—that is, that a pre-analytical feeling is the foundation of consciousness, basic not only to how one knows but to what one is. Having devoted years to a patient study of philosophy, he discovered that one cannot start with philosophy and get to immediate experience; nor can one start with abstractions and achieve serenity. By immersing himself in Dante, he discovered that poetry enlarges immediate experience, making it possible to be intelligent without becoming mechanical, to privilege feeling without becoming sentimental. From Dante, he learned that the Word can be made Flesh.

Great poetry—that is, incarnational poetry—"clothes the abstract, for a moment, with all the painful delight of flesh" (*VMP* 54-55). No wonder that Eliot confessed in old age that Dante was the most profound, the most persistent influence on his own work.

CHAPTER TWO

ELIOT, DANTE AND THE POETICS OF A "UNIFIED SENSIBILITY"[1]

VIORICA PATEA

ELIOT TOOK DANTE MORE SERIOUSLY than he was to take any other poet: "Dante excelled every poet who has ever written" (*VMP* 58). Looking back on his career Eliot confessed: "I still, after forty years, regard his poetry as the most persistent and deepest influence upon my own verse" (*TCC* 125). For him Dante was "the one poet … who impressed me profoundly when I was twenty-two, ... [and] who remains the comfort and amazement of my age" (*TCC* 23). Unity and universality are two fundamental concepts of Eliot's thought as well as the hallmark of Dante's work. Throughout his career Eliot's main literary and philosophical concerns were to remain centered on the relationship between intellect and emotions. Loss of unity of feeling and thought accounts for the larger rupture of unity of being, which he believed to be the major cause of our divided culture. Eliot's poetic and philosophical program envisioned the retrieval of this lost unity, which constituted his main preoccupation from the beginning of his career to the end of his life, from the early poems such as "Preludes" to *The Four Quartets*.

Dante influenced Eliot in various ways. Eliot learned from Dante how to handle romantic love, reconciling desire with spiritual aspirations (Bush 85), and how to sublimate sexuality into Eros (Kearns 89-90). As Dominic Manganiello aptly argues in what remains a seminal study on the relationship between the two poets, Dante was also Eliot's guide in the pursuit of his "incarnational" poetics. He was an important factor in Eliot's Christian conception of life and eventual conversion. Eliot identified his own poetic yearning with Dante's poetic and spiritual achievement. For

[1] This study is part of a larger research Project funded by Consejería de Educación y Cultura de la Junta de Castilla León (Reference Number SA 082A07) and the Spanish Ministerio de Ciencia e Innovación (Ref. FFI2010-15063).

both, aestheticism translates into forms of spiritual quest. Furthermore, Dante's socio-political vision in *De monarchia* inspired Eliot's idea of a Christian society (Manganiello *Eliot* 4).

Dante taught Eliot various lessons "of craft, of speech and of explorations of sensibility" (*TCC* 135), which Eliot summed up in his 1950 essay "What Dante Means to Me." From Dante he took the idea that "the poet should be the servant of his language, rather than the master of it" (*TCC* 133), and that he should enlarge the frontiers of reality and experience, in order to enable "a much greater range of emotion and perception for other men" (*TCC* 134). In this sense, he considered *The Divine Comedy* a compendium of human emotions (*SW* 168). According to Eliot, the task of poetry was to enlarge sensibility, to extend the limits of human consciousness and "express the inexpressible" (*OPP* 169). In the Clark lectures Eliot argued that Dante enhanced human experience by "extending the frontiers of this world" and by taking us to "a new and wider and loftier world" (*VMP* 95). Dante's verse serves as this "constant reminder to the poet, of the obligation to explore, to find words for the inarticulate, to capture those feelings which people can hardly even feel, because they have no words for them" (*TCC* 134).

To Eliot the European civilization and the "mind of Europe" meant first and foremost the legacy of Dante. Time and again, Eliot proclaimed Dante to be the universal poet *par excellence*—"the most *universal* of poets in the modern languages" (*SE* 238)—and the icon of Western culture: "Dante is, beyond all other poets of our continent, the most *European*" (*TCC* 134). Eliot's high praise of Dante stemmed from his admiration for the unity and universality of his work. For Eliot, Dante was the standard by which to assess the achievements of other poets. He was a poet far greater than "Shakespeare, or Molière or Sophocles" (*SE* 240). When compared with him, not only Milton and Blake, but even Shakespeare, the Metaphysical poets and the French symbolists were found wanting.

Eliot's critique of English poetry was based on an absence of what had been brought to perfection in Dante: a common language that expressed universality. "Modern languages," Eliot observed, "*tend* to separate" (*SE* 239). But the Italian language of Dante's time "tended to concentrate on what men of various races and lands could think together" (*SE* 239). Dante's Italian derived from Medieval Latin, the European *lingua franca* of the period, which helped preserve the mental and cultural unity of the Middle Ages. His language overcomes "the modern division of nationality," cuts across "national or racial differences of thought" (*SE*

239) and possesses the capacity to unify disparate realities. Above all, Eliot's poetics of a "unified sensibility" lead directly back to Dante.

Eliot formulated his theory of the dissociation of modern sensibility in a series of essays beginning with "The Metaphysical Poets" (1921) and followed by "Dante" (1929), "Milton I" (1936) and "Milton II" (1947). He summoned modern poetry to strive towards a unified sensibility and retrieve the lost unity that he felt existed prior to the great divide of the seventeenth century, which for Eliot marked the dissociation between poetic imagination and positive thought. Chronologically, Eliot saw in the age of Shakespeare the first symptoms of this dissociation, aggravated later by the rise of Cartesian dualism and various historical events, including the Puritan revolution and the execution of Charles I, king and head of the Church.

Eliot's concept of a unified sensibility should be considered in the light of his philosophic outlook, concerned with ethical and religious values and wider socio-historical considerations. Eliot perceived the condition of contemporary culture as fragmented and divided. He held Descartes and Montaigne responsible for this fragmentation, from which Europe had never recovered. The present schism dates back to the development of scientific thought and its materialistic ethos. Scientific positivism divests reality of its transcendent dimension and dangerously undermines its spiritual values, which remain relegated to the limited sphere of the ego. Modern scientific thought conceives life not in terms of a moral struggle, but rather in terms of empirical categories. It erodes the magico-religious structures of the Medieval and Renaissance imagination and gives way to disillusionment and ontological insecurity.

Eliot situated his notion of a "unified sensibility" in a pre-Romantic and pre-Cartesian past, in the time of Dante, when visions were still a significant part of the prevailing mind-set and thought had not yet become abstract. Dante's age was capable of generating visions, and thought was expressed through unmediated, direct and symbolic images. In the age of reason, feelings and faith became subsidiary, reduced to mere social decorum. Scientific rationalism no longer conceived of life in spiritual terms and endowed existence with an abstract sense.

Eliot gauged the spirit of the age by the vitality of poetry. He diagnosed the crisis in the mind of Europe and tried to provide a cure to the ills of the isolated, fragmented and alienated contemporary self. His remedy was found in Dante's work. His models were those poets in whom the spirit of Dante survived: Shakespeare, the Jacobean dramatists, the Metaphysical poets and the French symbolists—Laforgue, Corbière and Baudelaire—who felt "their thought as immediately as the odour of a rose" (*SE* 287). After Dante, Shakespeare was the great master of an age in which "the intellect was immediately at the tips of the senses" (*SE* 209-210).

Early in his career, he envisioned a new poetic idiom that would express the emotional equivalent of thought and render the intellectual dimensions of emotions. Contemporary verse rejected the decorative, abstract and moralizing idiom. Instead, it aspired to condensation and direct presentation so as to recover the reality of commonplace objects and the accents of direct speech.

The requirements of the new poetry, as Moody aptly suggests, were "immediacy and ordered wholeness" (Moody *Poet* 75). The goal of modernist poetry was to remain free of rhetoric. Rhetoric implied inauthenticity and duplicity of language. It offered proof of the poet's inability to express his experiences and emotions directly. The cure for a poetics of rhetorical effects that misrepresents the processes of knowing and functions like a distorting and distancing filter of reality consisted in the poetics of "the objective correlative" and the theory of "impersonality" (*SE* 145-6; 13-22 passim). Eliot used Dante's visual imagination, his "astonishing economy and directness of language" (*TCC* 23) as the touchstone for modernity (Manganiello *Eliot* 3).

The modernist idiom is predicated on the convergence of intellectual speculations, feelings, sensations and emotions. The poetics of a "unified sensibility" consists in a "direct sensuous apprehension of thought, or a recreation of thought into feeling" (*SE* 286). This entails transmuting ideas into sensations and discovering intellectual formulations for emotions: "every precise emotion tends towards intellectual formulation" (*SE* 135). Dante's poetic practice translates into the modernist aesthetics Eliot envisaged.

The corollary to the notion of unity is universality. To Eliot, unity also meant the fusion of the universal with the concrete, which was another poetic goal of the modernist agenda. Dante had opened the terrain. From him Eliot learned how to write autobiography in "colossal cipher" (in Emerson's phrase) and how to "transmute his personal and private agonies into something ... universal and impersonal" (*SE* 137). Eliot's philosophy of the impersonality of art draws on the principle of universality.

Yet what did Eliot mean when he envisioned a poetic idiom that "transmute[s] ideas into sensations" (*SE* 290)? What are the larger cultural and philosophical implications of a poetic program that attempts "to find the verbal equivalent for states of mind and feeling" (*SE* 289)? How can a thought become an "experience" that modifies a "sensibility" (*SE* 287)?

Like all modernists, Eliot maintained that poetry was not the mere verse exposition of theories, and he expressed his hostility towards philosophical poetry. In "The Possibility of a Poetic Drama," Eliot went so far as to say that a work of art "should "*replace* the philosophy," not embody it (*SW* 66). In his opinion, Goethe was too much of a philosopher, and Tennyson and Browning indulged in versified arguments (*SE* 287). Eliot believed philosophy was concerned with the exposition of theoretical speculations, while poetry should express a vision. Yet he was aware that poetry needed a philosophical support in order to endure. "For a perfect art to arise," Eliot argued, "there must be a kind of co-operation between philosophy and poetry" (*VMP* 222).

In this respect, Dante was uniquely successful in expressing a philosophy that he directly and passionately experienced through concrete and palpable visions (*SE* 267). Dante's greatness consisted in his capacity to transmute philosophic thought into poetic vision, to present us with "the emotional sense equivalent for a definite philosophical system" (Eliot Introduction xiii). He let his readers experience the reality of hell "by the projection of sensory images," which for him was "not a place but a state" (*SE* 250). Conversely, he made us "apprehend sensuously the various states and stages of blessedness" (*SE* 265).

According to Eliot, during the twelfth and thirteenth centuries, there existed a perfect harmony between philosophy and art (*VMP* 99, 222). Eliot regarded the age of Dante as the Golden Age of Europe's "unified sensibility." As Eliot observed in the Clark lectures: "For the twelfth century, the divine vision or enjoyment of God could only be attained by a process in which the analytic intellect took part; it was through and by and beyond discursive thought that man could arrive at beatitude" (*VMP* 99). In his view, this unity of feelings, emotions and intellectual speculations accounts for the fact that "In the poetry of the thirteenth century the human spirit reached a greater sum of *range, intensity*, and *completeness* of emotion than it has ever attained before or since" (*VMP* 222). The happy symbiosis of Dante, Aquinas and Aristotle led to "the divine contemplation, and the development and subsumption of emotion and feeling through intellect into the vision of God" (*VMP* 103-104), which was also the method and goal of Eliot's own quest.

Dante, Eliot notes, benefited from "a mythology and theology, which had undergone a more complete absorption into life" (*SW* 163). He relied on "one coherent system of thought behind him" (*SE* 136) and enjoyed the privilege of living in an age in which "men still saw visions" (*SE* 243). Seeing visions was a "significant, interesting, and disciplined kind of dreaming" (*SE* 243). In the twentieth century visions have been relegated to children or the mentally deranged. At most the modern world seems capable of "*low dream*[*s*]" (*SE* 262), those that belong to the unconscious or the irrational. Yet in Dante's time, dreams were not a mere matter of the unconscious or the irrational, as they are today. They did not originate only from below; on the contrary, Medieval man also experienced ascensional dreams. The Medieval imagination is the result of this communication with the supernatural.

Visions are a cognitive function of imagination and a defining psychological trait of the Medieval sensibility. As a Medieval and Renaissance man, Dante perceived and created images that shaped his inner reality. His mental representations were concrete visible embodiments that he could manipulate as if they were palpable and real. Eliot remarked that Dante translated "the inapprehensible in visual images" (*SE* 267-68) and articulated a system of thought that conferred concreteness on the magic exuberance of his symbolic imagination. In his visions the real became fused with the ideal.

Medieval thought is predicated on ontological propositions.[2] The Medieval sensibility is convinced of the *a priori* ontological unity between language and reality. Its main assumption is our world's immediate proximity to the transcendent. Visions arise from this identification of the sensible with the numinous. The Medieval mind searches not for empirical evidence but for symbolic meaning. Within its framework, reality is derived from a set of symbolic and allegorical meanings.

As the Romanian philosopher H. R. Patapievici observes, the seventeenth century discriminates against images, and thought becomes abstract, almost "iconoclastic" (*Cerul* 360). Images lose their concreteness and dissolve into the mass of non-figurative representations. The development of a scientific-materialistic outlook divests thought of its mythic-religious values. The seventeenth century initiates the gradual replacement of figurative thinking based on images by thoughts based on words, and reduces the symbolic to mere literality, thus opening the way to the creation of arbitrary constructions and conventions.

In Eliot's view, this crisis of language was aggravated by the influence of "two of the greatest masters of diction in our language, Milton and Dryden," who achieved their "triumph with a dazzling disregard of the soul" (*SE* 290). Eliot finds Milton responsible for the rift between sound and meaning and the gradual decay of sensuous perception, a decay that leads to an abstract and rhetorical form of poetic expression. In Milton's

[2] Eliot argued, "The Aristotelian-Victorine-Dantesque mysticism is ontological" (*VMP* 104).

work, Eliot argues, the auditory imagination prevails "at the expense of the visual and the tactile" (*OPP* 143). Although in later years, Eliot was to revise his harsh judgment of Milton, he attributes to him "a peculiar kind of deterioration" in English poetry (*OPP* 138), which lasted into the twentieth century. "Milton," Eliot argues, "does not infuse new life into the word, as Shakespeare does" (*OPP* 140); he "writes English like a dead language" (*OPP* 141), producing verses with an abstract quality. Unlike Milton, the Metaphysical poets looked into "the cerebral cortex, the nervous system, and the digestive tracts" (*SE* 290) in order to give new life to poetic expression.

For Eliot, the sensual effect of Milton's verse is entirely auditory. Rhetoric is the consequence of "the hypertrophy of the auditive imagination" (*OPP* 143). Sounds and rhetorical effects are employed at the expense of meaning: "the syntax is determined by the musical significance, by the auditory imagination, rather than by the attempt to follow actual speech or thought" (*OPP* 142). Eliot insists that in Milton's poems, thought loses its sensual and emotional concreteness, leading to the "opacity" of words (*SE* 239). The artificiality of sonorous effects separates the internal meaning of words from the surface of sound and determines the complexities of syntax, whose intention, in Eliot's view, is not to express thought but to create sounds. Abstraction and "artificiality" (*SE* 290) render meaning superfluous: "inner meaning is separated from the surface, and tends to become something occult" (*OPP* 143), while words are arranged "for the sake of musical value, not for significance" (*OPP* 142). Eliot believes Milton's "tortuous style … is dictated by a demand of verbal music, instead of [… a] demand of sense" (*OPP* 141). In the labyrinthine tangle of surfaces of his complicated phrasing, meaning is lost in "the mazes of sound" (*OPP* 144).

Eliot counters Milton's abstract poetics with Dante's symbolic and allegorical imagination. Dante's thought is neither "abstract" nor "intellectual," like Milton's, but "visual" and "poetic." His words are not opaque, but "lucid, or rather translucent" (*SE* 239). Unlike Milton's, Dante's "clear visual images" are not arbitrary but endowed with "meaning," which accounts for their greater intensity (*SE* 242).

Modernity, in Eliot's view, is the result of the dissociation of sensibility, which harks back to the seventeenth century. The positivist explication of the world renders intellectual processes abstract. Once the intellective process loses its original unity, it expresses itself only by linguistic signs, that is, by arbitrary successions of forms and images. The acts of apprehension withdraw behind the boundaries of the material world and become quantitative. Figurative thought is replaced by non-figurative representations. The divorce from the supernatural causes an unprecedented degree of abstraction and accounts for the aridity of the self's inner experience. Eliot translates concretion and abstraction into parameters by which to gauge an existing ontological unity or rupture.

Unlike Milton, Dante possessed the Renaissance man's faculty for creating visions and structuring them into a comprehensive system of thought. Mystical visions were, for Dante, ontological manifestations.[3] His visionary imagination had access to a transcendent reality, the meeting ground between the human and the supersensible. Eliot acknowledges the dynamic faculty of Dante's imagination, its ability to create a complex system of images. Dante's allegorical method rejects a one-to-one correspondence between the word and its referent and instead engenders a welter of multiple meanings that ultimately lead to the unknown, the inexpressible. As a habit of mind, allegory draws on a belief in mystical correspondences (Manganiello *Eliot* 12). In Eliot's view Dante's symbolic-allegorical method is, first and foremost, a quest for meaning: "Allegory itself may be only a mode of expression of a mind passionately eager to find order and significance in the world" (*VMP* 98). As Manganiello aptly remarks, symbolism is Eliot's "modern counterpart to Dante's polysemy" (*Eliot* 123). In 1931, Eliot wrote:

> Symbolism is that to which the word tends both in religion and in poetry; the incarnation of meaning in fact; and in poetry it is the tendency of the word … to mean as many things as possible, to make it both exact and comprehensive, and really to *unite* the disparate and the remote, to give them a fusion and a pattern with the word. (Preface to *Transit of Venus* viii-ix; quoted in Manganiello *Eliot* 122)

Dante's fantasies give material form and presence to incorporeal ideas and essences. By "making the spiritual visible" (*SE* 267) and "realiz[ing] the inapprehensible in visual images" (*SE* 267-68), they acquire an *imaginal* quality. Patapievici was the first critic to point out the similarity between Eliot's analysis of Dante's thought and Henri Corbin's notions of the *imaginal and mundus imaginalis*, two concepts that play an important role in the formulation of mystical language and the construction of images (*Cerul* 356-62). He refers to a seminal 1964 essay, "Mundus Imaginalis; or the Imaginary and the Imaginal," by Corbin, a French scholar who studied Persian Zoroastrian and Shiite Muslim texts. In order to avoid the term

[3] In this respect see also H. R. Patapievici's extremely interesting analysis *Los ojos de Beatriz: Cómo era realmente el mundo de Dante*, trans. Natalia Izquierdo (Madrid: Siruela, 2007).

"imaginary," commonly used to designate visionary perceptions related to illusion and non-being, Corbin resorts to Latin terminology and coins the terms "imaginal" and "mundus imaginalis,"[4] thus eluding the kind of perception that produces utopian, fictitious and unreal things. Both terms refer to "a very precise order of reality which corresponds to a precise mode of perception" (1). Imaginative perception and consciousness have a cognitive function, the *imaginal*, which permits access to a realm Corbin calls the *mundus imaginalis:* the transcendent world seen in mystical revelations. This is a world of symbolic representations and visions in which time and space lose their Cartesian coordinates. Far from being unreal, the *mundus imaginalis* is a parallel world "as ontologically real as the world of the senses and the world of the intellect" (8). The *imaginal* is the cognitive function of imagination that "permits the transmutation of internal spiritual states into external states, into visionary events symbolizing those internal states" (13).

Analyzing Eliot's notion of the dissociation of sensibility, Patapievici explains the estrangement that intervened between the time of Dante and that of Shakespeare as a major shift in mental typology. He attributes this to what historian of religion Ioan P. Couliano terms "the great censorship of the imagination" (Couliano 193ff), perpetrated by the Protestant revolution against the Neo-Platonic, hermetic, occult and magic body of traditions of the Renaissance. Patapievici's thesis draws on *Eros and Magic in the Renaissance* (1984), a seminal book in which Couliano analyzes the joint attacks carried out by both the Reformation and the Counter-Reformation against the imagination of the Renaissance.[5] Couliano studies the writings of Pico della Mirandola, Marsilio Ficino and Giordano Bruno and analyzes the mnemonic techniques of the Middle Ages and the epistemology of magic (or "Eros") and "phantasms" (or

---

[4] *Mundus imaginalis* refers to a visualized reality that has no extension in space, that exists beyond common empirical perception, sensory knowledge or rational understanding. It is in consonance with Jung's archetypal realities of imagination. "The mundus imaginalis is precisely the realm where invisible realities become visible and corporeal things are spiritualized": Susanna Ruebsaat, "Taking the Inside View of Art-Making" <http://www.ierg.net/confs/2003/proceeds/Ruebsaat.pdf>. On the imaginal, see also Karen-Claire Voss (1996). For a brilliant survey of the research on the "imagination," the "imaginary," and the "imaginal," a field explored mainly by the French school and less known in the Anglo-American academic world, see Corin Braga, "'Imagination', 'imaginaire', 'imaginal'. Three Concepts for Defining Creative Fantasy," *Journal for the Study of Religions and Ideologies* 6.16 (2007): 59-68.

[5] Ioan P. Couliano, *Eros and Magic in the Renaissance* (Chicago: University of Chicago Press, 1987).

inner representations) in the Renaissance, which draw on the revival of pagan culture and Platonic beliefs. Renaissance sciences—astrology, alchemy, the art of memory, and magic—contributed in different ways to the enhancement of imagination and the communication with the unconscious. Couliano emphasizes the importance of imagery and "phantasy" in the doctrines of the *pneuma,* a *prima material*, generated by the heart or the mind that is analogous to the "soul" or "spirit" and forms a thin film around the body (Aristotle). Stoic medical theories claimed that images were formed in the *pneuma* and were then transmitted to the senses. Greek pneumatic doctrines became very popular in the Renaissance and left their imprint on the tradition of courtly love. Couliano considers the witch hunts the social consequence of the ongoing attack on "phantasy" and the deliberate eradication of its magico-religious imagery. Thus, with the suppression of magic in the sixteenth and seventeenth century, "qualitative" statements based on imagery become objectionable and are replaced by "quantitative" categories, which represent the only valid mode of knowledge. This religious censorship, which Patapievici reformulates as "the castration of the imagination," was to be perpetrated by the new philosophies of early modernity: rationalism, empiricism and positivism. Modern scientific practices represent not a continuation but a replacement of the epistemology laid down by the Greek Platonists, rediscovered and improved by the Italian Neo-Platonists. The sustained repression of the imaginary helped fashion our modern civilization, in which symbolic imagination is supplanted by a quantitative, abstract mode of thinking. The scientific mode of thinking is responsible for the psychological amputation of our modern worldview (Patapievici *Cerul* 359).

From the vantage point of the twenty-first century, Eliot's concepts of universality, unity, order and tradition contradict our most cherished postmodern convictions, which overtly undermine the notions of absolute value and universality. As J. Hillis Miller observes, postmodernism destroys the original unity of man, God, nature and language (*The Disappearance* 3). Intolerant of any doctrine that denies the mere materiality of the world, postmodernism embraces the ideas of heterogeneity, fragmentariness, difference and indeterminacy. Postmodern epistemology introduces a semantics of rupture. It denies the premise of Western logo-centric thought concerning the existence of a ground, an essence that guarantees its coherence. Foucauldian, Derridean and new historicist interpretations are exercises of de-sublimation of intrinsic values and *a priori* transcendent categories. They attempt to rid European culture of the impact of universality.

Postmodern thought inherits the deicidal and parricidal Nietzschean proposition "God is dead," and with it the disappearance of the criteria of objectivity and universality.[6] To the postmodern mind, all values are arbitrary. The whole world is a *récit*, an artifice, a solipsist game of appearances. Reality itself is made and invented, the result of human artifice. The text dissolves in its own referentiality, fictionality and rhetoric. Language loses its universal guarantee, the referent that warrants its cohesion, unity and meaning. In de Man's famous formulation: "Rhetoric radically suspends logic and opens up vertiginous possibilities of referential aberration" (*Allegories* 10), and these referential aberrations simultaneously affirm and deny the authority of their own rhetoric.

The larger implications of Eliot's theory of a unified sensibility also affect his philosophy of culture. Whereas the postmodern hermeneutic reduces culture to relativism, to fragmented narrations, confined in their own singularity and relevant only in a particular context, Eliot's defense of cultural diversity and pluralism draws on the very idea of unity and universality. As a philosopher of culture Eliot insisted on the value of alterity and cultural pluralism. He argued that interaction between various cultures ensures a culture's vitality (*UPUC* 152) in the same way that the preservation of its identity and idiosyncrasy guarantees its richness.

Eliot did not eschew judgments of value or ethical considerations and emphasized the necessity of discernment. He eloquently advocated an underlying unity and the deliberate, if controlled, cultivation of different points of view as means of preserving cultural identity and diversity in an ideal "constellation of cultures" (*C&C* 132). Eliot was one of the first to invoke the notion of an "ecology of cultures" (*C&C* 131), of small-scale societies, and to warn against the danger of the colonizing Eurocentric domination that destroys indigenous cultures and thereby unknowingly cuts Western culture off from the sources of its own regeneration.

While it is true that Eliot formulated an energetic apology of Western culture and believed that the adoption of a Christian model could present a cure for the prevailing materialistic values, expediency and spiritual bankruptcy, this did not prevent him from denouncing the arrogant self-confident superiority of Western imperialism. He strongly denounced the coercive imposition of enlightened cultural models and pleaded for a dialogue with other traditions (*C&C* 166).

Unity for him did not mean stagnation: he did not advocate "the unity of mere fixity" or "the unity attained by a man who never changes his

---

[6] For an extremely interesting analysis of modernity see H. R. Patapievici, *Omul recent* (Bucarest: Humanitas, 2001).

mind" (*SE* 453). Unity for him was a synonym for the coherence of different systems or points of view not exempt from the notion of transformation and growth. Similarly, order for Eliot connoted the aspirations of a private idiom towards a common, universal language validated by a core of ethical, philosophical values (*SE* 238-39, 252).

Eliot conceived of aesthetic creation as a transforming, unifying process between polarizing realities—feelings and thought, the concrete and the universal, the self and the other. The relationship between thought and feeling was a crucial element in his literary and philosophical considerations. Eliot readapted Bradley's theory of the unification of points of view and his notion of an absolute into a theory of a unified sensibility. Yet he opposed both Bradley and Bergson's speculations on the existence of a preexistent unity that is felt rather than conceived. In *Knowledge and Experience*, Eliot presents the limitations of Bradley's idealism. He dismisses Bradley's theory of "immediate experience" as a mere dogmatic assumption about reality, and he critiques the hypothesis of a stage of consciousness that implies rejection of thought, reflection and analysis. As Manju Jain has persuasively shown in a landmark study, *T. S. Eliot and American Philosophy* (1992), Eliot remained critical of all anthropological and psychological theories that emphasized the essentially irrational, anti-intellectual nature of religious experiences. He censured Bergson's notions of real duration and creative evolution premised on the dissociation of intellect and intuition, as well as Lévy-Bruhl's distinction between the pre-logical consciousness of primitive societies and the rational consciousness of developed cultures (Jain 207-210). Eliot believed that mystical experiences could not be fully known by being felt and experienced alone; they required subsequent interpretation and analysis in order to be understood and reported.

Eliot's thought oscillated between competing and countervailing beliefs, which he sought to bring to a synthesis. Dissatisfied with philosophical systems, which he found partial and insufficient, he finally found the ultimate answer in religious faith. Although he was prone to mystical illuminations, skepticism remained an important component of his thought: "the demon of doubt" was "inseparable from the spirit of belief" (*SE* 411). Skepticism was for Eliot, as for Charles Newman or Pascal, the "preface of his conversion":[7] "For every man who thinks and lives by thought must have his own skepticism, that which stops at the

[7] See T. S. Eliot, "Christianity and Communism," *Listener* 7.166 (16 March 1932): 382-83, (383).

question, that which ends in denial, or that which leads to faith and which is somehow integrated into the faith that transcends it" (*SE* 411).

CHAPTER THREE

"GERONTION" AND *THE WASTE LAND*: PRELUDE TO ALTERED CONSCIOUSNESS

NANCY K. GISH

IN A 1925 LETTER TO HERBERT READ, T. S. Eliot summarized his own purpose in writing the Clark lectures: taking Dante as his "*point de repère*," he intended to show in the twelfth and thirteenth centuries a standard of perfection from which "subsequent history" is "the history of the disintegration of that unity." For Eliot at that time, it was "the history of corruption" (*Letters* 2:797-98).[1] In "Gerontion," with its images of post-War fractures—personal and social—he anticipated, and perhaps illuminated, the world of *The Waste Land*. Representing in its most vivid form the "disintegration of the intellect," "Gerontion" defines the immediate post-War state of history's corruption. Dante is, thus, the background rather than the foreground of this essay. My purpose is not to show direct philosophic or aesthetic influence but to demonstrate Eliot's vision of history's decline; for his sense of "disintegration" assumes a time of perfected integration fully imagined only in Dante.

Lyndall Gordon, in her chronology dating *The Waste Land* fragments, claims that "the turning-point between a hoard of fragments and a unified poem comes about through 'Gerontion,' which was written in May-June 1919" (541). Whether or not a "unified poem" results, Eliot did see "Gerontion" as a prelude to *The Waste Land* but dropped it at the insistence of Pound. But a prelude in what sense? A prelude to what? In his recent careful dating of Eliot's early works, Lawrence Rainey places the original composition of "Gerontion" in February 1919, just after Eliot's fall series of lectures on Elizabethan literature (198). Eliot was then immediately involved in studying the images and rhythms of violence and

[1] In his "Author's Preface" to *The Varieties of Metaphysical Poetry*, Eliot states his intention to rewrite the Clark and Turnbull Lectures as a book, part of a trilogy entitled "The Disintegration of the Intellect."

tragedy that echo through his own poem. In Stephen Spender's words, Eliot "enters so thoroughly into the idea that the decadence, violence, intrigues, villainy, and deviousness of the Jacobean world of corridors and mirrors correspond to the post-1918 Europe, that the parallel of the post-Elizabethan disillusionment, with its haunting decayed poetry, takes over the rest of the poem" (Spender 63). In February 1919 the Great War had just recently ended; Eliot's marriage was a disaster; his poetry increasingly—as with Sweeney—filled with ominousness and violation; and his health, as well as Vivienne's, recurrently near collapse. In one sense, then, "Gerontion" preludes the sense of a world disintegrating. But in a more complex and revealing sense, it serves as a prelude to altered consciousness: Gerontion the character represents a re-appearance—now as central—of a figure hovering at the edges of poem after poem in Eliot's earliest work, the disturbed or mad, muttering, blind, and decayed old man as doppelgänger or alter self. In the persona of this mad old man, Eliot represents forms of consciousness central to modernist thought and to what he saw as a steady disintegration of consciousness since Dante. For as Spender also notes, Gerontion begins as an apparent character only to dissolve into fragments (61). He ends in the delirium and ennui characteristic of then-defined hysteria. Of all Eliot's voices and fluid "selves," the least noted and yet perhaps most constant is the old man double whose persistent evocation of self-loathing reveals the Hell of modern dis-ease.

In an earlier essay I traced Eliot's concept of "dissociation" or "disintegration," as represented in *Inventions of the March Hare*, to the terminology of Pierre Janet.[2] What appeared overtly in those poems as dissociated or disintegrated states returns throughout Eliot's work, increasingly coded or masked but extended to encompass the failure of history. A brief review, then, of the psychological background clarifies its significance for "Gerontion" as well. In the late nineteenth and twentieth centuries, a dominant medical concept was Pierre Janet's description of hysteria as always a form of dissociation or "*a form of mental depression characterized by the retraction of the field of personal consciousness and a tendency to the dissociation and emancipation of the systems of ideas and functions that constitute personality*" (Gish 111). It may take many forms, including amnesia; numbness; anaesthesia of all senses; aboulia or loss of will (which Eliot claimed as his own emotional problem); depersonalization—in which the subject experiences the self as unreal or

[2] See Gish, "Discarnate Desire: T. S. Eliot and the Poetics of Dissociation" for extended definition and commentary on these terms.

detached from experience or even dead; derealization, in which the external world seems "unreal"; or the extreme form of the double (or dédoublement) in which "a person may actually 'perceive' and even interact with an external double of him- or herself," including dual personality (Gish 109).

Eliot's poetry through *The Waste Land* (most explicitly in *Inventions of the March Hare*) represents all these states, and doubles appear repeatedly in *The Waste Land* as Stetson, the third man who seems a ghostly presence, and a host of allusions: "Unreal city" alludes to Baudelaire's "Les Sept vieillards,"[3] in which a loathsome old man multiplies seven times before the narrator's eyes until he turns, "enraged as a drunk man who sees double" (Baudelaire 35); the quotation from Hermann Hesse's *In Sight of Chaos* is from his discussion of Dostoevsky and the new Russian as hysteric—who may be saint or sinner; Madame Sosostris recalls Sesostris (whether directly borrowed or not) who is a man dressed as and performing as a woman fortune teller; Phlebas recalls the dirty, vile old waiter who appalls the narrator of "Dans le Restaurant" by having experiences like his—and who, like Gerontion, experiences delirium, a characteristic Janet describes in hysterics. Hieronymo is a special and significant example; his identification with another strange and desperate old man leads to his deadly plot. Whether characters, ghostly presences, hallucinations, or doubles, these figures all represent forms of what Janet considered extremes of dissociation.

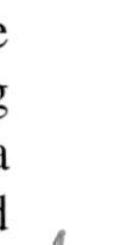

Read as prelude to *The Waste Land*, "Gerontion" is technically similar yet tonally discrete. It comprises vaguely related verse paragraphs without overt connections other than being in Gerontion's mind, but with images a reader can frame into a theme of loss or collapsing civilization or desire for the divine. Yet unlike earlier poems or *The Waste Land* itself, "Gerontion" has no moments of longing or desire for human love, fleeting idealism, or even sensuality: its passions and emotions are crass, depraved, and present in remembered echoes of Elizabethan drama in its most violent modes. Even the Maryland May is depraved, and any "passion" Gerontion recalls is sensation, introduced only as lost. Whoever "you" is, Gerontion gives no sign of ever having had closer contact. If the poem serves to introduce the despair, ennui, violation, and desensitization of *The*

---

[3] In his 1950 essay, "What Dante Means to Me," Eliot comments first on what other poets have meant to him. Baudelaire's significance for him, he said, was summed up in the opening two lines of this poem where the old man appears as "le spectre"; he knew, he said, what that meant "because I had lived it." However Eliot personally knew this expression of the double, he "turn[ed] it into verse" repeatedly.

Waste Land, it works as a partial thematic prelude. But its boundaries of desire within the echoes of textual lust and murder and the desecration of all Europe after World War I exclude the rediscovered moments of early yearning in *The Waste Land*—the Hyacinth girl, St. Magnus Martyr, the sailor's song, sweet Thames, Phlebas who was once handsome and tall as you. It is thus but one side of the coin, the horror without the glory. This is the only poem in which Eliot's vile, blind, mad old man is the "I" of the poem, not the observed, reported, or quoted voice of the doppelgänger. Here the double speaks for and as himself in his own state of aboulia, depersonalization, and anaesthesia.

Neither for Eliot nor for literature is this loss of a unified Romantic "self" new. And many critics have noted Eliot's multiple voices and doubled selves. In recent psychological texts, moreover, there have been studies of these as a response to the "modern" world that parallel many of Eliot's own accounts of modernism. In *The Protean Self* Robert J. Lifton argues for the emergence of a new form of self as "fluid and many-sided." This multiplicity of self and consciousness—if not first recognized in the early twentieth century—was nonetheless a key characteristic of modernism: indeed, *Strange Case of Dr. Jekyll and Mr. Hyde* is as originary to modernism as *Heart of Darkness*, and for similar reasons of finding in "one" person opposing "selves" of good and evil or civilized and primitive. Roger Vittoz, Eliot's psychiatrist at Lauzanne, wrote that there were actually two brains—the higher or civilized and the lower or primitive, and that neurasthenia (nearly indistinguishable from hysteria but mainly used to describe men) occurred when the lower or primitive brain wandered and had to be brought back under the control of the higher. His exercises and laying on of hands—Eliot's treatment—was aimed at restoring that control (Gish 115-16). This division parallels the "dissociation" of hysteria in Janet and the "dissociation of sensibility" Eliot discussed, not in one esssay, but over many years. In *The Waste Land* dissociative images of doubling are coded and allusive versions of earlier and more explicit representations of divided consciousness like the muttering, mad old man of "Prufrock's Pervigilium" whom Prufrock calls "my Madness," or the "blind old man who coughs and spits sputters / Stumbling among the alleys and the gutters" in "First Debate between the Body and Soul," or the drunken old man in "The Death of St. Narcissus" by whom a young girl is caught in a forest and with both of whom Narcissus identifies. For Robert Lifton multiplicity and fluidity occur across a range from healthy to pathological—a continuum of possible responses to seeming chaos. For Eliot, as for Janet and other psychologists of the time, it was defined as a kind of mental weakness, disturbed and disturbing.

While Eliot clearly creates characters who identify across gender, such as St. Sebastion, St. Narcissus, Tiresias, perhaps the Hyacinth girl, the most frequent and terrifying double is the old man, for whom all sense is lost, no love possible, and the absolute—the pure idea—is never present. He lives only in the physical world of decayed sense, poking and prodding "with senile patience / The withered leaves of our sensations" (*IMH* 64) or "stained in many gutters" singing and muttering on the streets at dawn (*IMH* 43) or, "drunken and old," tasting the whiteness of a young girl caught in the woods (*Waste Land Facsimile* 97) or remembering long-ago delirium at finding a little girl in a meadow (*Collected Poems* 43) or stiffening in a rented house, recalling lost sensation and mentally disintegrating into chilled delirium.

Gerontion, then, is one of a long line of blind, dirty, drunken, or mad alter selves; they are identified as such in other poems by terrified narrators, but here the obsessive thoughts and voice, like those of Kurtz, are all that is left. These old men are linked by both linguistic contexts and forms of identity. They are repeatedly found in windy, arid spaces; they are repeatedly drunken and dirty; they are set off in contrast to flowers, gardens, or meadows; they are withered, disgraced, degraded; and they induce deep revulsion in the narrators of poems other than "Gerontion," who nonetheless feels his own sense of disgust and impotence. When they appear in other poems, they carry sensations disavowed as disgusting, and sensual desire bearable only as idealized and unconsummated childhood longing. Yet they appear in contrast to or repudiated by narrators up to and through *The Waste Land*; the "familiar compound ghost"of "Little Gidding," overtly named as a double, has transformed this voice of a doubled self into philosophical reflection, though he too appears in windy streets and speaks of soul and body fallen apart.

In "Gerontion," they are already apart, and body is left in an intolerable void, characterized by major symptoms of hysteria in Janet's terms: anaesthesia, aboulia, hallucinations, and delirium. In his analysis of *The Waste Land* as an hysterical text, Wayne Koestenbaum opened up our reading to the ruptures, sexual anxieties, and language dysfunction in what had increasingly been read as a unified mythic vision of the modern world. But Eliot's own language, personal experience, and representations of dissociation suggest that the text's hysteria is more fully understood through Janet than Freud. It is useful, I think, to note that Eliot went to Roger Vittoz after consulting several friends, that Vittoz's analysis of neurasthenia uses a model comparable to Janet's, and that Eliot specifically claimed in a letter to Sydney Waterlow that Vittoz was not a psychoanalyst "but more useful for my purpose." (*Letters* 1:495) At this point, December 1921, he was in Lauzanne, "feeling much better," and "trying to finish a poem." *The Waste Land's* fascination and "glamour," what Lawrence Rainey calls its "lacerating wildness and stubborn refusal to accomodate our expectations" (128) appear in its move beyond "Gerontion," a move that nonetheless incorporates the twisted, cynical, shuddering quality "Gerontion" reveals as the direct voice of the "other" within.

In the published version of *The Waste Land*, the old man appears directly in the very center as Tiresias and at the end as Hieronymo. Had the original opening remained, it would have opened with "old Tom, boiled to the eyes, blind," and the younger narrator "down at Tom's place" in a scene of drunken singing and a girl who squeals. Or had "Gerontion" been used as a prelude, the old man would have introduced dissociation and themes of lust, violation, and death. In the Pound-edited poem, these are all present as allusion but coded beyond immediate recognition: the red rock is taken from "The Death of St. Narcissus"; "unreal city" transforms Baudelaire's "teeming city" to a form of derealization while evoking an image of multiplying old men and dédoublement. The last line of the first section has nearly always been read as addressing the reader, as it is in Baudelaire's "Au Lecteur." But it remains in the quotation marks that identify speech directed to Stetson, who thus also becomes the double—one like Tiresias who is both modern and ancient, having been at Mylae but having planted a corpse last year. While the source in Baudelaire may well evoke us as readers also, in the poem the line is said *to* Stetson and thus *to* an immediately present dissociated self.

My point is that, in his role as recurrently present yet loathsome double, the "little old man" as prelude represents a form of consciousness always divided, at odds, aware of inevitable deradation in the material world yet resisted and even transformed or partially redefined in Tiresias as later in "Little Gidding." Three figures—Gerontion, Tiresias, and Hieronymo—frame the scenes of *The Waste Land*. What they have in common is dissociation, doubling, exhaustion and despair at civilization's collapse. But while Eliot represents a fragmentation of consciousness so extensive as to be disintegration, it is at the same time, paradoxically, claimed as a form of cohesion: if Gerontion dissolves into thoughts of a dry brain, Tiresias "unites" disparate figures and provides a vision of the whole, however broken. Hieronymo, ironically, turns his madness into vengeance in a strangely hideous form of desperate justice. He is mad but not simply mad; he forms a deliberate plan for which the disparate languages and their failure of meaning have a purpose.

The first draft of "Gerontion" had two epigraphs: the lines from *Measure for Measure* in which the Duke urges Claudio to be "absolute for death" (3.1.5) because life is continual struggle for riches, and in age "Thou hast neither heat, affection, limb, nor beauty / To make thy riches pleasant" (3.1.37-38) and "in this life / Lie hid moe thousand deaths" (3.1.39-40). The second, removed from the published version, is from Dante's *Inferno*, Canto XXXIII, in which Friar Alberigo is in Hell for betraying and killing a guest. Alberigo's soul is in Hell, but he does not even know if his body is dead: "Come 'l mio corpo stea / nel mondo su, nulla scïenza porto" ["How my body fares in the world above I have no knowledge"] (410-11). What these epigraphs share is not only a sense of life as death but the dissolution of body and soul, in the Dante passage, literally. The Duke's portrait of an old age without emotion, sensation, or desire introduces Gerontion's own dissociation of sense and thought, and Friar Alberigo's total separation of body and soul define his horror. Gerontion's thoughts are, in one sense, filled with passion, the lusts and betrayals and murders of Elizabethan and Jacobean drama and Dante, but they are not his own: he speaks almost nothing of his own life after the opening lines except his present, with empty, sterile and obsessive ideas swirling in his brain. He is, moreover, aware that this is delirium. His images of Christ as tiger devouring us or sinister cosmopolitan figures enacting empty rituals are hallucinatory. Little is left as a personality or self except multiplying personae in a kind of mental frenzy.

"Gerontion" exposes the little old man as a fluid and multiple but terrifying consciousness detached from any physical experience or sensation, as Friar Alberigo is or Claudio is urged to be. His dissociation, like the line from *Heart of Darkness* Eliot dropped, is "somewhat elucidative" in its introduction of extremes of modern dis-ease.

Tiresias, "the most important personage in the poem" according to the notes, shares characteristics with Eliot's other old men: he is blind, degraded, and strangely identified with other characters whom he "sees." Eliot's notes send us to Ovid, but this is not Ovid's Tiresias, who became a woman and was changed back into a man. In Ovid, when Tiresias strikes the serpents the second time, "his former state was restored and he became as he had been born" (Ovid 46). Eliot's Tiresias is male and female at once, his body as well as his mind retaining his past: "old man with wrinkled female breasts" who "foresuffered all." He retains his duality, both watcher and watched, victim and victimizer, like the old man in "The Death of St. Narcissus." One could read this, ironically, as a primary identification with the typist, since he too awaits the guest, but he has "foresuffered all / Enacted on this same divan or bed," as if he too has taken both parts, as his body contains both anatomical sexes. If he unites "all the rest," his fluid and multiple consciousness goes beyond the vision of the Greek prophet to the accumulated experience of human existence, here narrowed to sensation without soul. Tiresias sees his double as doubled. Yet because it encompasses opposites, his multiplicity is coded as uniting all.

Hieronymo appears in only one line of *The Waste Land*, but as a culmination of these representations, that line reverberates throughout. "Hieronymo's mad again" is generally read as pointing to the breakdown of language into meaninglessness like that of Hieronymo's "show" in *The Spanish Tragedy*, a kind of early snuff drama in which the ostensibly dramatized murder is literally carried out while the actors speak many languages to obscure any understanding. But Hieronymo's return into madness, in a scene where he initially contemplates cautious, strategic action, is induced by the sight and words of Bazulto, an "old man" who appears in only this scene weeping and begging justice for his murdered son. In him Hieronymo sees himself, as Baudelaire's narrator sees the multiplying old men and is "enraged as a drunk man who sees double," and Tiresias who sees both his selves in the typist and young man carbuncular. Having tried to control himself, Hieronymo is shamed by the absoluteness of the old man's cry for justice. "Ay, now I know thee," he says, "Thou art the lively image of my grief." Bazulto, too, heaves windy sighs and mutters sad words abruptly broken off. Hieronymo directly identifies with him and takes him in to his wife, "three parts in one." The old man, who appears neither before nor after this one scene and functions as both double and mirror, reveals to Hieronymo his own violence; it is after this that he says "Why then Ile fit you" and deliberately constructs a drama in "unknown languages"—Latin, Greek, Italian, and French. When told this will be mere confusion, he says "it must be so." His madness is thus, at least in part, cunning strategy, and his conciousness the desires and rage evoked by his double. The broken language at the end of "What the Thunder Said" is, similarly, both dissolution and meaning—recollections of horrors mentioned earlier.

Throughout his early prose, Eliot uses Janet's term, "désagrégation" (translated as both "dissociation" and "disintegration") not only in the essay on the Metaphysical poets but in uncollected work and in the central arguments of *The Varieties of Metaphysical Poetry*. By the time Eliot composed *The Waste Land* in its published version, his prose comments on "désagrégation" had shifted from primarily using "dissociation" to primarily using "disintegration," a more total dissolution of self, like that of Gerontion's "thousand small deliberations" and "fractured atoms." In

The Waste Land, while retaining images of depersonalization, derealization, and doubling, Eliot represents a fragmentation of consciousness so extensive as to be disintegration and at the same time, paradoxically, to define an attempt at cohesion. In Robert Lifton's words, rather than collapse in the face of confusion and loss of "psychological moorings," "the self turns out to be surprisingly resilient" (1).

But Lifton is describing a post-modern response of "tactical flexibility" to the "threats and pulls" in a world of contradiction; the modern response was far less affirmative. *The Waste Land* confronted this breakdown of unified consciousness, immediately during and after WWI, at a time when "a heap of broken images" left Western culture without apparent ways to reconstruct a cohesive "self." While the many fragments, drafts, and unused poems of *The Waste Land Facsimile* sustain an unassimilated dissociative consciousness, one function of "Gerontion" and Tiresias is to regain a kind of aesthetic "unity" through forms of multiple or fluid consciousness. Their juxtaposition reveals ambiguity and ambivalence at the center of the poem; the desire for unity dissolves over and over and ends with Hieronymo who, like Eliot's other old men, defines his own "madness" in the presence of his double. Read as a "prelude," "Gerontion" articulates the collapse of self characteristic of the modern in a peculiarly perverse way as the voice of that persistent "other" self who haunts so many of Eliot's narrators. Yet the most dispersed of all "personages" is said to contain all. *The Waste Land*, thus, stands as a defining reaction to "désagrégation." Read as a "prelude," "Gerontion" overtly reveals forms of dissociation that define *The Waste Land's* "hysteria" and unease with any coherent "self."

CHAPTER FOUR

THE DANTEAN ROSE AND THE HINDU-BUDDHIST LOTUS IN THE POETRY OF T. S. ELIOT

P. S. SRI

> From the unreal lead me to the real,
> From darkness lead me to light,
> From death lead me to immortality.
> —*Brihad-aranyaka Upanishad*

IN HIS LIFE-LONG QUEST for the "still point of the turning world" ("Burnt Norton," *CPP* 119), Eliot often attempts an East-West ideo-synthesis. For example, he brings St. Augustine and the Buddha together in the section called "The Fire Sermon," at the very core of *The Waste Land*, noting that "the collocation of these two representatives of eastern and western mysticism, as the culmination of the poem, is not an accident" (*CPP* 53). Eliot was well-acquainted with the Upanishads, which form the philosophical portion of the Vedas, the Hindu scriptures which are the most ancient religious writings now known to the world. His personal library had a copy of *The Twenty-eight Upanishads* for ready reference. He makes a direct and incontrovertible appeal to the *Brihad-aranyaka Upanishad* in the fifth section of *The Waste Land*, entitled "What the Thunder Said."

Eliot's admiration for Dante coalesces with his fascination with Hindu-Buddhist thought in *Four Quartets*, but it was incubating for a very long time before that masterwork was inaugurated with "Burnt Norton." Eliot had already said that the Buddha's Fire Sermon "corresponds in importance to the Sermon on the Mount" (*CPP* 53). He also later declared that "what we learn from Dante or *Bhagavad Gita* or any other religious poetry, is what it feels like to believe that religion" (*UPUC* 95), and he described *The Bhagavad Gita* as "the next greatest philosophical poem to *The Divine Comedy* in my experience" (*SE* 258).[1]

In the *Divine Comedy*, Dante describes the individual's journey through Hell (*Inferno*), Purgatory (*Purgatorio*), and Paradise (*Paradiso*), guided first by the Roman epic poet Virgil and then by Beatrice, the subject of his love and another of his works, *La Vita Nuova*. While the *Inferno,* is filled with vivid descriptions of Hell, and *Purgatorio,* the most lyrical and human of the three, has the most poets in it, *Paradiso,* the most heavily theological, has the most beautiful and ecstatic mystic passages in which Dante tries to describe what he confesses he is unable to convey — his ecstasy on having a vision of God.

> Potent as it is, in tantric art the lotus is a symbol of the unfolding of the self and expanding consciousness, which cuts through psychic opacity and ultimately raises the aspirant from the dark depths of ignorance to the radiant heights of inner awakening. Just as lotus plants grown in the "darkness of mud" and gradually blossom out on the surface of the water, unsullied by the mud and water which nourished them, so the inner self transcends and transforms itself beyond its corporeal limits uncorrupted and untarnished by illusion and ignorance. (Mookerjee and Khanna 68)

> Since early times the lotus flower has been the symbol of creativity producing the world of things from its fertile seeds and of purity, because the water does not cling to its leaves. This symbol is used...in describing the peak experience of Being in *this world*, but not just this world...a blue or white lotus flower or jasmine flower can enthrall a person with its lovely colour, its softness and fragrance. That it can do so lies in the fact that it grows in the unclean ponds of villages and hamlets, but is not affected by their uncleanliness. The same holds good for the yogi. Even if he thinks of the objects of the outer and inner world, by knowing the real, he is not affected by the mire of the objects and taking the lotus flower without its (surrounding) mire, he understands the absolutely real without its (deflecting) ideas. (Guenther 82-83)

Eliot can often be observed combining Dante's symbolism with that of Hindu-Buddhist thought in articulating his experience of the "still point." "The deeper design," Eliot writes in his "Introduction" to Djuna Barnes' *Nightwood*, "may be that of human misery and bondage which is universal" (5) But the sensitive and discriminating individual can still penetrate "the bold imposing façade" ("East Coker," *CPP* 126) of *maya*

---

[1] For a thorough investigation of Eliot's *explicit* as well as *implicit* use of the perceptions of Hindu-Buddhist philosophy, please see my book, *T. S. Eliot, Vedanta and Buddhism* (Vancouver, B.C.: U of British Columbia P, 1985).

(the deceptive appearances of the phenomenal world), liberate himself from the terrible wheel of *samsara* (of birth, death and rebirth), be free of craving, compulsive action and suffering, and find *shanti* or peace that passes understanding. That such a state exists in the midst of universal suffering and that this resting place in the midst of flux can be attained by the individual is the overwhelming paradox of the great religions of the world. Thus, the Hindu avatar or Incarnation of the Supreme Reality, Krishna asserts that "the man of pure vision without pride or delusion, in liberty from the chain of attachment, with his soul ever in his Inner Spirit, all selfish desires gone, and free from the two contraries of pleasure and pain, goes to the abode of eternity" (*Bhagavad Gita* 106). And the Buddha speaks to his disciples of nirvana or freedom tout court from the universal bondage in uncompromising terms.[2] Christ too affirms that the individual can find refuge from the woes of the world in the eternal being of God.

The poems published before *The Waste Land* focus on the cyclic purposelessness of existence in the phenomenal world and there seems to be little or no hope of escape from the wheel of action and suffering, suffering and action, birth, death and rebirth. These earlier poems focus on particular situations which illustrate the general human predicament. Our attention is usually captured by one person — Prufrock, Sweeney, Grishkin, or Gerontion — who reflects facets of our own personalities. *The Waste Land*, on the other hand, multiplies "variety / In a wilderness of mirrors" ("Gerontion," *CPP* 23). Our interest is claimed by a host of incidents which take place simultaneously in the ancient and the modern world. Historical fact and literary fiction reside cheek by jowl. Characters coalesce and fuse, disintegrate and vanish, in a dreamlike manner with the nonchalance and unpredictability of the multitudinous gods of the Hindu pantheon; they are no one and everyone at once. *The Waste Land,* in fact, has no specific location in space and time; it harbours all beings of all worlds in all ages, who labour under the "universal bondage" and long, even though only for a moment, to be free.

Tiresias experiences such a moment of freedom which he cannot find words to describe, in the hyacinth garden:

> I could not
> Speak, and my eyes failed, I was neither
> Living nor dead, and I knew nothing,
> Looking into the heart of light, the silence. (*CPP* 38)

---

[2] "Udana 8," *The Minor Anthologies of the Pali Canon*, Part II, tr. F.L.Woodward (London: Oxford UP, 1935), 97.

He has a momentary glimpse of the supreme truth, at once in and out of time. The hyacinth girl is a catalyst stimulating a harmonious reaction between the narrator and his environment, so that he gains a sudden insight into the centrality of being, where the spokes of the turning world converge. When he tries to recapture the experience in words, however, he is quite unequal to the task; he can only indicate it negatively; he could *not* speak or see, he was *neither* living *nor* dead and he knew *nothing*; yet, he apprehends "the heart of light, the silence." The negative and paradoxical mode of expressing the nature of *nirvana* is quite common to both Vedanta and Buddhism. Eliot was well aware of the "subtleties" of the Indian philosophers, directly from his reading of Sanskrit philosophy and indirectly through Western authors such as Kipling, Edwin Arnold and Schopenhauer. Not surprisingly, therefore, he adapted the oriental attitude in his own poetic evocation of enlightenment.

The momentary experience of enlightenment is pondered and cherished, amplified and enriched, to be savoured again and again in Eliot's poetry. Towards the end of *The Waste Land*, it is recalled vividly by Tiresias as a surrender of the individual self or ego to the overwhelming reality of the noumenon: "The awful daring of a moment's surrender/ Which an age of prudence can never retract/ By this, and this only, we have existed" (*CPP* 49). It cannot be found in "obituaries" or "memories," or "under seals" because it is not limited by space, time, and causation; the experience is indefinable, known only by its fruits in our daily lives.

The central paradox of *The Waste Land*, then, is that man, who is enchained to the wheel in the domain of *maya*, can still emancipate himself from constant becoming and be one with the eternal being. Man is intimately related, in other words, to both time and eternity. Not surprisingly, *The Waste Land* is full of references to both temporal and eternal values: we see the London crowds flowing down King William Street to "where Saint Mary Woolnoth kept the hours/ With a dead sound on the final stroke of nine" (*CPP* 39); we hear the gossipy Cockney women being asked by the pub owner to "HURRY UP PLEASE IT'S TIME" (*CPP* 41,42) — time for what? to leave the pub? or to prepare for eternity by working out their salvation with diligence? — and we listen to Tiresias' ghastly parody of Marvell, "But at my back from time to time I hear/ The sound of horns and motors which shall bring/ Sweeney to Mrs. Porter in the spring" (*CPP* 43). But man's relationship to time and eternity is not understood by most of us. Like the apostles on the way to Emmaus, we may not even be conscious of the nearness of Christ. Consequently, we lead a harrowing, anxiety-filled existence most of our lives:

What shall I do now? What shall I do?
I shall rush out as I am, and walk the street
With my hair down, so. What shall we do tomorrow?
What shall we ever do? (*CPP* 41)

This bleak, horrifying, time-conditioned existence, however, is not quite hopeless; for it is possible for us to refine our consciousness like Tiresias and grasp how our time on earth may not just be endured or diverted but actively embodied and possessed, so that, however alone and unbelonging our 'I' may be, it can still break through, break in, and find the Kingdom of Heaven waiting there.

The apprehension of the moment of peace occurs suddenly in the hyacinth garden; later, it is spoken of as self-surrender. It is, therefore, a gift; in Christian-Dantean terms, it is grace. Yet, individual effort is necessary to draw near to the moment; the entire action of the poem is *seen* and pondered by the blind Tiresias, so that his consciousness is gradually purified. He comes to understand that it is craving (*tanha*) for evanescent things that binds him to the phenomenal world and makes him suffer.

The practical means of rooting out craving and eliminating suffering are drawn from the *Brihad-aranyaka Upanishad: datta, dayadhvam* and *damyata* (*CPP* 49, 50). Literally translated, these words counsel us to give, sympathize and control; they also imply that we should practice self-surrender, compassion and self-control. Only by giving up the ego may we hope to attain *nirvana* and fruitfully serve our fellow beings. Only by broadening our sympathy into a universal compassion for our fellow creatures imprisoned again and again in their earthly lives can we grow in awareness. Only by controlling our present lives, like an expert sailor at sea, can we "at least set [our] lands in order" (*CPP* 50). These lessons imparted by the crashing chords of thunder, lend an optimistic note to the "fragments" which Tiresias, seeker of reality, shores up against the ruins of former lives. The poem concludes, therefore, by reiterating the instructions received from the thunder and intoning the formal ending of the Upanishads: Shanti Shanti Shanti (*CPP* 50) — a fitting reminder that, ultimately, the peace that passes understanding will prevail.

Taken as a whole, *The Waste Land* — very much like *The Divine Comedy* — traces the journey of the human soul across the desert of ignorance, full of thirst (*tanha*) and suffering (*dukkha*) to a vantage point from where the freedom of *nirvana* is tantalizingly glimpsed, if not fully realized. Thus, the pervasive Dantesque images of sterility and futility serve to stress the dark night of the soul in its emptiness caused by separation from God, while the positive moments point to detachment from craving as a means to emancipation. All opposites and contraries are reconciled in the exquisite moment in the hyacinth garden, the memory of which enables the seeker to survive. There are oblique references to the blissful experience of freedom from the universal bondage in the poems Eliot wrote between *The Waste Land* and *Four Quartets*.

The empty effigies in *The Hollow Men* are immobilized by despair; subject to selfish desires and deluded by appearances, they not only do not apprehend reality but also avoid working towards it. Their evasiveness is underscored by the image of the "eyes" they "dare not meet in dreams" (*CPP* 57). It is not clear whose eyes these are, but they challenge the human spirit; hence, the refusal of the hollow men to meet them indicates their spiritual bankruptcy. The fact that the hollow men shrink from "that final meeting/ In the twilight kingdom" (*CPP* 57) suggests that the eyes may be those of a saviour like Christ. Ironically, these eyes are the hollow men's only hope of release from suffering. Unless the eyes reappear "As the perpetual star/Multifoliate rose/Of death's twilight kingdom" (*CPP* 58), the hollow men are doomed to remain "sightless," bereft of any hope of salvation. "The perpetual star" seems to be associated with the Star of Bethlehem, which led the Magi to the infant Christ, while the "Multifoliate rose" seems to be linked with Dante's image of the saints in Paradise, clustered together like the petals of a white rose. When Dante steeps his eyes in the river of light and looks at the celestial rose, he sees the eyes of the myriad Christian saints reflecting the glory of God, so that the rose appears to be a vast shining circle. This is the image Eliot evokes when he equates the eyes, the star, and the rose. Together they symbolize the reality of God, whose absence is keenly felt by the hollow men in their cactus land. Sunk in inertia, however, they decline to strive towards this reality.

The single rose is essentially "a symbol of completion, of consummate achievement and perfection,"[3] and figures prominently in Western mystical literature as an image of unity. To Dante, the "white rose" represents the end of his long journey, the fulfilment of his quest for the eternal Being of God. The "multifoliate rose" as a symbol of the reality beyond appearances is the Western equivalent to "the thousand-petalled lotus" (*sahasrara*) of Eastern mysticism.[4] Tantrism, an esoteric branch of yoga in Hindu-Buddhist mysticism, symbolizes the spiritual current in man as a serpent coiled up at the base of the spinal cord.

When the yogi (one who seeks, like Tiresias, Dante, Eliot or Everyman, to unite himself with the divine essence) advances spiritually,

---

[3] J. E. Circlot, *A Dictionary of Symbols* (London: Routledge and Kegan Paul, 1967), 205.

[4] *Dictionary of Symbols and Imagery* (London: North Holland, 1974), 305.

the current gradually uncoils and rises upwards, enfranchising a series of lotuses or spiritual centres in the body. The powers and perceptions of the yogi increase as the current travels from centre to centre. When the current culminates in the (*sahasrara*) or the thousand-petalled lotus in the brain or the crown of the head, the yogi attains enlightenment; he is one with the reality behind all appearances.

Has Eliot then attempted an East-West ideo-synthesis of symbols? Has he fused Dante's "white rose" (*candida rosa*) and Tantrism's "thousand-petalled lotus" (*sahasrara*) to create a particularly arresting symbol in the "multifoliate rose"? Quite probably, especially since he uses the oriental and occidental symbols of the ultimate reality simultaneously in "Burnt Norton" to indicate a momentary experience of enlightenment: *the lotus blooms in the rose garden.*

The protagonist of "Ash-Wednesday" is caught in "the time of tension between dying and birth," struggling to detach himself from the temptations of the phenomenal world and to unite himself with the changeless reality of the noumenon. Intuitively, he apprehends the apparent contradiction between the phenomenal world and the noumenon, between appearance and reality:

> Still is the unspoken word, the Word unheard,
> The Word without a word, the Word within
> The world and for the world;
> And the light shone in darkness and
> Against the World the unstilled world still whirled
> About the centre of the silent Word. (*CPP* 65)

The movement of the world seems to oppose the Word; the world does not heed the Word and crucifies the Word made flesh in the person of Christ. Paradoxically, the world cannot exist apart from the Word, for the Word is within "the world and for the world." In other words, the Word is central to all existence, a perception precisely expressed by the image of the "unstilled world" revolving around the "still" and "silent Word." Significantly, the protagonist of "Ash-Wednesday" resembles Tiresias when he tries to convey his insight into the nature of reality. He too perceives that the Word shines as light amidst darkness. He too has recourse to a negative and paradoxical mode of expression: the Word is "*un*spoken" and "*un*heard," "still" and "silent"; yet, it is the hub of all activity.

Taken as a whole, passionate concern with man's spiritual destiny characterizes *Four Quartets.* They are, perhaps, the most intensely religious of Eliot's poems since they assert "the primacy of the supernatural over the natural life" (*SE* 398). They trace the journey of the human soul, akin to *The Divine Comedy*, from the darkness of ignorance to the dawn of wisdom, when the still point is at least perceived, if not fully grasped. Thus, "Burnt Norton" and "East Coker" stress the dark night of the soul caused by separation from God, while "The Dry Salvages" advocates right action as a means to emancipation. All opposites and contraries are reconciled through the prayerful accents of "Little Gidding" where all the "contrived corridors" ("Gerontion," *CPP* 22) of history are seen as a pattern of timeless moments, and all our explorations as a way back to our starting point.

Indeed man's intimate association with both time and eternity, properly understood, constitutes the core of religion. But to most of us, the understanding has not dawned; we are so caught up in our regrets about the past or in our worries about the future that we are never quite conscious of the innocence and promise of the present: "What might have been and what has been/ Point to one end, which is always present" (*CPP* 117). We look before and after and pine for what is not, as Shelley points out, quite unaware of the eternal presence of the blissful reality of God. Consequently, we drag out a maimed half-existence all our lives:

> Neither plenitude nor vacancy. Only a flicker
> Over the strained time-ridden faces
> Distracted from distraction by distraction
> Filled with fancies and empty of meaning
> Tumid apathy with no concentration
> Men and bits of paper, whirled by the cold wind
> That blows before and after time,
> Wind in and out of unwholesome lungs
> Time before and time after. (*CPP* 120)

This bleak, horrifying, time-conditioned existence is, however, not quite without hope. There *are* intense, isolated moments when we glimpse the eternal:

> For most of us, there is only the unattended
> Moment, the moment in and out of time,
> The distraction fit, lost in a shaft of sunlight,
> The wild thyme unseen, or the winter lightning
> Or the waterfall, or music heard so deeply
> That it is not heard at all, but you are the music
> While the music lasts. (*CPP* 136)

At such deeply perceptive moments, music is heard with such intensity that there is no longer a separation between the person listening and the music listened to; there is no "I" opposed to "music," for subject and object have coalesced and there is simply music: "you are the music." Such intense moments of aesthetic rapture, when the egotistical self is so completely submerged in the object of contemplation that it no longer seems to exist, are the closest most of us ever get to liberation from the flux of time-conditioned existence.

Three such moments seem to be experienced by the poet himself and are eloquently described: in the rose garden, in the arbour where the rain beats and in the draughty church at smokefall. Of the three, the moment in the rose garden seems to be most vividly remembered and is movingly evoked at the beginning of "Burnt Norton." Speculating on the nature of time, like Dante in *The Divine Comedy,* the poet is arrested by the memory of an earlier moment in his life which he had not fully explored:

> Footfalls echo in the memory
> Down the passage we did not take
> Towards the door we never opened
> Into the rose garden. (*CPP* 117)

The sharpening recollection of what might have been urges him to investigate the possibilities of the present moment:

> Other echoes
> Inhabit the garden. Shall we follow?
> Quick, said the bird, find them, find them.
> Round the corner. Through the first gate,
> Into our first world. (*CPP* 117-18)

Suddenly, he recalls the earlier experience with such intensity that it seems to unfold before his mind's eye; the present and the past moments fuse into each other, time stands still and he experiences a momentary rapture:

> And the bird called, in response to
> The unheard music hidden in the shrubbery
> And the unseen eyebeam crossed, for the roses
> Had the look of flowers that are looked at. (*CPP* 118)

In this blessed mood, the poet and the companion of his memory move "in formal pattern" and make their way to the dry concrete pool in the garden, now mysteriously filled with "water out of sunlight," and witness the miraculous flowering of ecstasy in the midst of sterility: "And the lotos rose, quietly, quietly,/ The surface glittered out of heart of light" (*CPP* 118). The lotus is a peculiarly oriental symbol, associated with ultimate reality in Hindu-Buddhist thought. *The Tantric Way*, an examination of esoteric yogic practices, throws further light on the significance of this symbol in plain language. In *The Tantric View of Life*, an account of the tantric practices extant in Tibetan Buddhism, we read this interesting interpretation of the lotus symbolism: Eliot was probably aware of the profound significance of the lotus. Certainly he was conscious of its mystical implications since he uses the lotus in conjunction with the rose, a symbol of the ecstatic union of the human soul with God, not only in Western mysticism, but also in Dante's poetry.

It is also quite likely that Eliot knew something of Tantra. He speaks of entering the rose garden through "the first gate" (presumably there are other gates), of moving into the "box circle," and of looking down into the drained pool; the pool is mysteriously filled with "water out of sunlight," and the "lotos" blooms in the pool. Diagrammatically represented, this seems to be the plan of the rose garden:

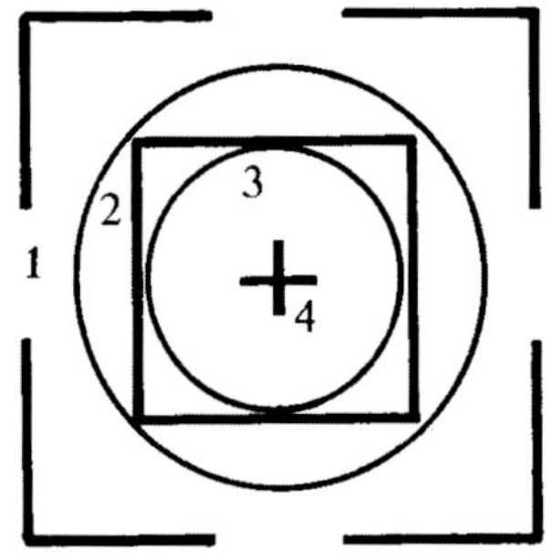

1. "the first gate"
2. "box-circle"
3. "pool"
4. "lotos"

In Tantrism, the *mandala*, "a composition of complex patterns and diverse iconographic images," is often used as an aid to meditation. *The Tantric Way* gives a vivid description of the structure of the *mandala*:

Obviously, there are remarkable correspondences between Eliot's rose garden and a *mandala*. The *mandala*, moreover, is not a mere geometric pattern; it is full of psychic significance:

Is Eliot disciplining the artist in himself by evoking "the psychic complex" of the rose garden? His poetic self does move "in a formal pattern" (*CPP* 118) along with other unseen presences, enacting a "march towards the centre." This process of interiorization does lead to a momentary apprehension of reality, if not to a total emancipation from a time-bound existence, and enables the poet to reflect deeply on the nature of man's relationship to time and eternity, on birth and death, on suffering and action. In short, by an extension of the symbolism of the rose garden, *Four Quartets* as a whole may be seen to be a *mandala*, leading the poet and his readers towards a progressively greater awareness of unity in diversity.

> At the still point of the turning world. Neither flesh nor fleshless;
> Neither from nor towards; at the still point, there the dance is,
> But neither arrest nor movement. And do not call it fixity,
> Where past and future are gathered. Neither movement from nor towards,
> Neither ascent nor decline. Except for the point, the still point,
> There would be no dance, and there is only the dance. (*CPP* 119)

Eliot's negative and paradoxical mode of expressing the nature of timeless reality finds here its fullest flowering. This attitude is common to both Hindu and Buddhist thought and Eliot probably adapted to suit his own poetic needs. He has not added essentially to the Hindu or Buddhistic description of the ultimate enlightenment. But he *does* articulate in moving words the psychological aspects of an experience which the individual may attain through Patanjali's yoga or the Noble Eight-fold Path of the Buddha or the Adoration of the Madonna or the contemplation of Dante's white rose — the experience of the still point:

> I can only say, there we have been, but I cannot say where.
> And I cannot say, how long, for that is to place it in time.
> The inner freedom from the practical desire,
> The release from action and suffering, release from the inner
> And outer compulsion, yet surrounded
> By a grace of sense, a white light still and moving,
> *Erhebung* without motion, concentration
> Without elimination, both a new world
> And the old made explicit, understood
> In the completion of its partial ecstasy,
> The resolution of its partial horror. (*CPP* 119)

This evocation illuminates at least three aspects of the experiential reality: the "still point" is a state of enlightenment to be attained in this life itself and not in some world beyond death — the Kingdom of Heaven or Paradise is within and at hand; it is a condition that transcends the senses, spells freedom from desire, action, and suffering, and bestows peace that passes understanding; it is both momentary and unforgettable, temporal and eternal, in time and out of time — a present where past and future are gathered and opposites are reconciled. These three interconnected *motifs* are heard again and again in *Four Quartets*. That Eliot explores their oriental "subtleties" in such rich detail, without ever sacrificing his fundamental Christian-Dantean framework, speaks volumes for his poetic power of reconciliation and amalgamation.

The appearance of the lotus, then, at the climax of the experience in the rose garden marks the transformation of earthly desire into divine love. The moment of ecstasy, however, is shortlived, and the poet is once again caught up in time, "the form of limitation / Between unbeing and being" (*CPP* 122). Like Dante, he is left with thoughts of childhood and innocence; they are tokens of his brief visit to the lost Eden of the race.

Such intense and isolated moments, with no before or after, are not quite the still point of the turning world; they are but "hints and guesses/ Hints followed by guesses; and the rest / Is prayer, observance, discipline, thought and action" (DS, p. 190). This fivefold path probably reflects the Noble Eightfold Path of the Buddha and is no guarantee to emancipation. Eliot is quick to point out that total emancipation from the wheel of *samsara*, the phenomenal world of appearances, is at best rare and infrequent:

to apprehend

> The point of intersection of the timeless
> With time, is an occupation for the saint —
> No occupation either, but something given
> And taken, in a lifetime's death in love,
> Ardour and selflessness and self-surrender. (*CPP* 136)

Eliot does not elaborate on the nature of the still point, symbolized by the Dantean rose and the Hindu-Buddhist lotus. Instead, he leaves us the task of piecing together the hints scattered throughout his poetry and drama, particularly *Four Quartets*, and of forming a coherent picture: the still point is thus "a liberation/From the future as well as the past" (*CPP* 142); it does not, however, negate time, for, when we are liberated, we consider "the future/And the past with an equal mind" (*CPP* 134); in other words, past and future are reconciled in an eternal now. The still point spells "inner freedom from the practical desire" (*CPP* 119), but freedom from desire is not desirelessness, for there is still the "unattached devotion which might pass for devotionless" (*CPP* 132) and "the expanding of love beyond desire" (*CPP* 142). The still point is "release from the inner and outer compulsion" (*CPP* 119), but it is not inaction, for "right action is freedom/From past and future also" (*CPP* 136), and we act freely when we have surrendered our will to the Source of all our strength, the noumenal reality within us.

The still point is thus not freedom from time and space, but freedom from the feeling of being confined by time and space; not freedom from desire, but freedom from the slavery to shifting desires; not freedom from suffering, but freedom from the crushing power of suffering, through understanding and compassion; not freedom from death — for "the time of death is every moment" (*CPP* 134) — but freedom from the fear of death.

When we reach the still point, then, we apprehend the rose and the lotus completely and attain *mukti* or freedom *tout court*, a condition of "complete simplicity" (*CPP* 145). And as *jivan-muktas*, those who have attained freedom in this life itself, we live unattached and cling to nothing in the world, transcending, not denying, impermanence and suffering. Or, as Iqbal Singh expresses it eloquently in his book, *Gautama Buddha*:

It is clear that Eliot's philosophical and spiritual orientation is essentially in accordance with the basic tenets of Christianity as well as those of Hindu-Buddhist thought and that he has fused together in his poetry and drama the truths embodied in the Dantean rose as well as the Hindu-Buddhist lotus.

The basic concern that animates Eliot's poetic "raid[s] on the inarticulate" (*CPP* 128) — the awareness of the fact of human bondage in time and the possibility of human freedom in eternity — is absolutely universal and may well be called the *philosophia perennis* that surfaces variously time and again in the religious and philosophical traditions of the East and the West.

Ultimately, what gives Eliot's poetry and drama an enduring beauty and a penetrating power is the fact that he has perceived the perennial and most ancient truth of humanity and invoked THAT which is universal and eternal, common to both the East and the West.

> The predominant shape is the circle, or concentric circles, enclosing a square, which is sometimes divided into four triangles; this basic composition itself is contained within a square of four gates. Painted in fine brush-strokes between the spaces in hot reds, evanescent emeralds, soft terra-cottas and pearly whites, are labyrinthine designs, serene and static images of deities in meditative postures or terrific deities spewing out aureoles of smoke and flame...all with symbolic meaning. The centre of the mandala projects the cosmic zone; it may be represented by a ring of lotus as the seat of Vajrasattva, the embodiment of the supreme wisdom, immersed in union with his Sakti in a fathomless ocean of joy. (Mookerjee and Khanna 62)

> The mandala indicates a focalization of wholeness and is analogous to the cosmos. As a synergic form it reflects the cosmogenic process, the cycles of elements, and harmoniously integrates within itself the opposites, the earthly and the ethereal, the kinetic and the static. *The circle also functions as the nuclear motif of the self, a vehicle for centering awareness, disciplining concentration and arousing a state conducive to mystic exaltation*...The mandala is a psychic complex which conditions the return of the psyche to its potent core. Hence *the initiation process is often referred to as a "march towards the centre" so that the adept can interiorize the mandala in its totality*, counterbalance the opposing dimensions projected in its symbolism and finally be reabsorbed in the cosmic space represented symbolically in the inner circle. The process of interiorization is a matter of orderly progression, wherein each inner circuit marks a phase in spiritual ascent...To evoke the universe of the mandala with its wide-ranging symbology accurately, the artist has to practice visual formulation...*The image, like a mirror, reflects the inner self which ultimately leads to enlightenment and deliverance...* the actualization of this awareness is known as "liberation through sight." The act of seeing, which is analogous to contemplation, is in itself a liberating experience. (Mookerjee and Khanna 64-66—my emphasis)

The experience of a supra-temporal reality, negatively implied in the reverie of *The Waste Land* and tersely indicated in the penitential soul-searching of "Ash-Wednesday", becomes central, therefore, to *Four Quartets*. The intimations of time and eternity, which have so far been churning in a rather vague and uncertain manner in the poetic consciousness, now become crystal clear. The dynamic contrast that prevails between the temporal world of constant becoming and the eternal world of being is illustrated through striking imagery:

Here we are in a universe which is devoid of tension — not because contraries and conflicts have ceased to operate, but because they have somehow become intelligible. Here, in the very contemplation of transience, we receive a measure of eternity...Here the wheel turns and does not turn. Here the paradox is no longer a paradox, but rather a luminous certitude. Here we are in the very heart of peace.[5]

[5] Quoted by Christmas Humphreys in *Buddhism* (Harmondsworth: Penguin, 1951), 215.

CHAPTER FIVE

SQUARING THE CIRCLE: DANTESQUE ASPECTS OF "THE POINT OF INTERSECTION OF THE TIMELESS WITH TIME"

TEMUR KOBAKHIDZE

His was the true Dantescan voice...
—Ezra Pound (*Selected Prose* 464)

T. S. ELIOT'S POETRY IS RIFE with crucial recurring imagery in the manner of Wagnerian *Leitmotive*, which explains the frequent comparison of his poetic structures to music. That critical commonplace was formulated as early as 1949 by Dame Helen Gardner in her famous essay on the music of *Four Quartets*. Gardner's observation was made from the viewpoint of poetic syntax, not *morphology*, to borrow the term from linguistics. The musical patterning—the recurrence of images—in Eliot's poetry is realized not only syntactically, as Gardner emphasized, or through the "music of ideas" as I. A. Richards puts it (234), but also through the recurrence of their latent and often complex intellectual meanings, which take different imaginative, symbolic, and poetical forms in different works. Recognizing the poetic morphology of some of Eliot's central images reveals not merely the structure of their literal and symbolic meaning, but also their indebtedness to Dante. This often manifests itself in the language of paradox, which is perhaps common to Christian theology as well as to the religiously-oriented poetry of all time but in this particular case should be viewed as Dante's direct influence. What I mean here is not simply borrowing of phrases like "figlia del tuo figlio" in *Four Quartets* but also the putting images together, creating a paradox, as in this passage from *Burnt Norton*: "Except for the point, the still point, / There would be no dance, and there is only the dance" (*CPP* 173).

From the very beginning of his literary career Eliot seems obsessed with the poetical depiction of the moment of Incarnation, the moment "in and out of time." All things and events "which have been and might have been... point to one end, which is always present," and the present is not time, but the essence of the perceiving consciousness which expands into eternity. In his poetic vision this moment is sometimes depicted as the revelation of the holy trinity in Baptism ("Mr. Eliot's Sunday Morning Service"), or the parodic apotheosis of the Lamb ("The Hippopotamus"), or in the quite different context of the epiphany of Dionysus ("Sweeney Erect" and "Sweeney Among the Nightingales"). In his earlier poetry, Eliot generally adopts the idea of Incarnation for parody purposes, for witty artistic analysis of the eternal truths of the Christian faith. This reflects young Eliot's deep interest in Christian mysticism, and his aspiration to find a contemporary poetic medium for conveying these truths, rather than mere mockery or caricature. Although parodic devices, including the grotesque, are widely put to use in *Poems* (1920), beneath the superficial layer of ironic imagery, the young Eliot's wish to apprehend reality in terms of basic Christian values is easily perceived. As Cleanth Brooks observes, commenting on *The Waste Land*, the poem makes a "statement of surface similarities" which are then "ironically revealed to be dissimilarities, which culminates in a later realization that the dissimilarities are only superficial—that the chains of likeness are in reality fundamental. In this way the statement of beliefs emerges *through* confusion and cynicism—not in spite of them" (172). Although at a first glance Eliot is estranged from Christian values, which he appears to parody—exhibiting cynicism—they nonetheless serve as the point of departure toward the formation of his own morals and ethics. Eliot exhibits what Cleanth Brooks (in an Arnoldian chapter title) dubbed "wit and high seriousness" (18-38), reminiscent in this case of the seventeenth century Metaphysicals and their conceits.

The image of "the point of intersection of the timeless with time," or "the still point of the turning world," represents a whole complex of erudite and intellectual aspects, and is, in a sense, akin to the famous "familiar compound ghost" of *Little Gidding*, for it also reconciles seemingly contradictory ideas in one image. In his illuminating study of *Four Quartets* Northrop Frye suggests that we imagine Eliot's intersection-point by the following physical exercise:

> Draw a horizontal line, then a vertical line of the same length cutting it in two and forming a cross, then a circle of which these lines are diameters.... The horizontal line is clock time, the Heracleitan flux, the river into which no one stepped twice. The vertical line is the presence of God descending

> into time, and crossing it at the Incarnation, forming the "still point of the turning world." (*T. S. Eliot* 77)

The still point, Frye argues, becomes also "the moment in and out of time," and the circle, we should presume, represents the world. The circle rotates, the world turns, but the movement slows down closer to the centre, and at the very centre, at the mathematical still point, which is real and actual, and ideal and transcendental at the same time, there is complete stillness, or "only the dance," both stillness and dance being parts of the paradox, just like "the moment" itself, which implies the timelessness of the seemingly temporal.

Eliot's image of the still point of the turning world, with all its symbolic, geometrical, and numerical complexities, is certainly not solely a Dantesque borrowing. He could have been referring to Aristotle's idea of the "Unmoved Mover," or to the Platonic concept of time revealed in *Timaeus*, where definitely a similar concept of time and the universe is described. As Plato states, "we say that he 'was,' he 'is,' he 'will be,' … These are the forms of time, which imitates eternity and revolves according to a law of number" (84). As is well known, the number four, or quaternity, is the numerical designation of a circle: it is not a coincidence that Eliot's quartets are so named, and that they are four in number. These ideas may be as old as philosophical thought itself, but Eliot could have borrowed them from the works of early Christian thinkers, like Boethius's *Consolation of Philosophy,* or the Pseudo-Dionysius's *Mystic Theology,* widely recognized as among Dante's minor sources. And Eliot could have borrowed his extremely complex image from countless other sources, starting with the popular depiction of "the wheel of Goddess Fortune" or even the trivial metaphor "the whirlpool of life," not to mention the non-European religious traditions he really adopts, like Hinduism and Buddhism (I mean not only Tibetan graphic symbols of meditation, but also the wheel of Samsara, or the Great Wheel of Death and Rebirth).

The pattern of a rotating circle with a fixed center implies the essential canonical features of the magic circle, or *mandala,* which is often referred to and described by Carl Gustav Jung as one of the central archetypes of collective unconscious (15:96). This aspect of the image demonstrates its psychological and mythical depth which is combined with extensive associative richness. Myth, as described by Frye in his *Anatomy of Criticism*, is the structural organizing principle of a work of art (341), and in this sense the abstract patterns that model the world in terms of time, space, and number, are essentially mythical in quality. In *Four Quartets* these are the patterns of quaternity—a point, a circle, a square, and straight lines forming a cross, as well as the generalized ideas of the process of action or state (rotation, recurrence, rhythm, stillness, etc.).

The whole poetical world of *Four Quartets* is based not only on the pattern of a rotating circle and a still point, but also on the corresponding numerical designation of the process of circulation and of the circle itself—the all-important four. The cyclical time of *Four Quartets* suggests not only the "rotation" of the entire poetic structure of the poem, as of "a single cycle that begins and ends at the same point" (Frye, *Eliot* 77); it also determines the poetic realization of the effect of stillness in the centre, the very *nunc stans,* or the *everlasting Now*, that was defined (by Eliot in poetry and by Thomas Mann in fiction) as the essence of perception of a work of art as an aesthetic whole. This reminds us of Claude Lévi-Strauss' statement in *The Raw and the Cooked* about "music which turns the time-span needed to listen to it into a synchronic and self-contained whole" (43). Thus, listening to music we may be approaching a kind of timelessness or immortality. Music constitutes both the formal subject-matter and the poetical structure of *Four Quartets*, for it is

> music heard so deeply
> That it is not heard at all, but you are the music
> While the music lasts. (*CPP* 136)

But I would like to return to the mythical quality of the still point and the circle, with a cross (a quaternity symbol) contained in it. In analytical psychology mandala is man's inner experience, an unconscious symbol of a universal mythical quality, "Das Selbst," which expresses the unity of man with the universe. As early as his essay "The Function of Criticism" (1923), Eliot shed light on the creative techniques he employed in some of his most complex and erudite poetic experiments. He argued that "as our instincts of tidiness imperatively command us not to leave to the haphazard of unconsciousness what we can attempt to do consciously, we are forced to conclude that what happens unconsciously, we can bring about, and form into a purpose, if we make a conscious attempt" (*SE* 24). What Eliot suggests here is the need for a poet to use acquired bookish knowledge in the field of psychology instead of putting himself in the hands of his unconscious creative instincts. That's why the mythical patterns in Eliot's poetry, however complicated and sometimes even overburdened with intellectual imagery, always constitute part of his conscious creative activity. There are many examples of such imagery that cannot be adequately described as Jungian archetypes, like "the still point of the turning world," or "the point of intersection of the timeless with time," or "the evening circle in the winter gaslight," or "the circulation of the lymph," which is "figured in the drift of stars," or peasants dancing "round and round the fire / Leaping through the flames, or joined in circles," or phrases like "in my beginning is my end," and "in my end is my beginning." These are not simply unconscious Jungian archetypes, since they are created in the full light of consciousness and form part of Eliot's conscious creative design. Their main source and decisive influence here is Dante.

As early as *Vita Nuova*, Dante is visited in his dream by the God of Love in human guise, who tells him: "Ego tamquam centrum circuli, cui simili modo se habent circumferentie partes, tu autem non sic" ("I am similar to the centre of the circle, equidistant from all parts, but you are not"—12). If we take the scene literally, or in a "myth-criticism" manner, it will appear that being bitterly in love with Beatrice, young Dante dreamt of Jungian mandalas. But "centrum circuli"—for the Point most powerfully appears in his much later visions, as the symbol of God or divine presence. In *Paradiso* 17 Dante addresses his ancestor Cacciaguida: "you gazing upon the point to which all times are present"—a phrase identical to Eliot's own concept of time in *Four Quartets*, i.e., of the eternal moment "to which all times are present":

> What might have been is an abstraction
> Remaining a perpetual possibility
> Only in a world of speculation.
>
> What might have been and what has been
> Point to one end, which is always present. (*CPP* 117)

The blazing Point (*un punto)*, or God as Primum Mobile, recurs in *Paradiso* 28, where it is surrounded by glittering circles of multitudes of angels singing Hosanna:

> I saw a point that flashed a beam of light
> So sharp the eye on which it burns
> must close against its piercing brightness.
> ... and there whirled about that point a ring of fire.

Beatrice tells Dante that:

> From that point are strung the heavens and all nature.
> Observe that circle nearest it,
> And understand its motion is so swift...

Dante sees the truth of this, and the nine concentric angelic circles glitter with sparks. Beatrice explains that there is a spiritual rather than a spatial correspondence between the point and the circle, and God is both centre and circumference.

Beyond doubt, Eliot's central image of the Still Point and the turning world is greatly influenced by the last cantos of *Paradiso*. Of course the pattern is changed and the symbolic meaning is modified a great deal too, as Eliot adopts it to his own poetic design and his own poetic vision, but Dante's fundamental influence is not in question.

In the last cantos, Dante is clearly puzzled by the impossibility to perceive the divine essence—he is definitely unable to grasp his own vision. In Canto 33, within the depths of divine light he perceives a geometric image of the Holy Trinity; he "sees" three circles of the same circumference. No man can see God face to face in this world, as stated in John, but Dante manages to in his afterworld vision, and he is greatly perplexed by what he sees, when he is faced with the paradox of the Incarnation. His sight is "all absorbed," as he says, in detecting "our (i.e., human) likeness" in one of the three circles (the Son). To put it otherwise, he is completely at a loss, encountering the double nature of Christ as Man and God at the same time. He "tried to see how the image fit the circle / And how it found its where in it. / But my wings had not sufficed for that" (33.137-139). This leads him to adopt again (as in the beginning of Canto 33 and elsewhere), the language of paradox ("Vergine Madre, figlia del tuo figlio").

The paradox Dante uses to demonstrate the impossibility of grasping God is that of quadrature, or squaring the circle, which is an ancient mathematical riddle, unsolvable since the times of Anaxagoras, who first attempted it. Dante's poetics of Euclidian geometry is extremely interesting, as he recurs to geometry as a metaphor here. He wishes to illustrate the impossibility of achieving the Beatific Vision by human efforts alone—God's saving grace is required, a gift of love. This metaphor for that which is unattainable (except as a gift from God) occurs in the final lines of the *Commedia*:

> Like the geometer who fully applies himself
> to square the circle and, for all his thought,
> cannot discover the principle he lacks,
> such was I at that strange new sight.
> (*Paradiso* 33.133-136)

In the literal sense, not in imagery, this very closely resembles Eliot's meditation on the same subject:

Men's curiosity searches past and future
And clings to that dimension. But to apprehend
The point of intersection of the timeless
With time, is an occupation for the saint—
No occupation either, but something given
And taken, in a lifetime's death in love,
Ardour and selflessness and self-surrender. (*CPP* 136)

But for most of us sinners, who are by far not saints,

... there is only the unattended
Moment, the moment in and out of time,
The distraction fit, lost in a shaft of sunlight,
The wild thyme unseen, or the winter lightning
Or the waterfall, or music... (*CPP* 136)

What is implied in Dante's image is that the circle can be squared only approximately, never exactly or fully. This is how Dante designates the infinite nature of God and the impossibility for the human mind to perceive the nature of God. Implied here is the irrationality of the most important mathematical constant used to square the circle, namely π (*pi*), which is defined as the ratio of a circle's circumference to its diameter: 3.14159... The numerical value of *pi*, even truncated to fifty decimal places has been explored many times, but in fact the fractions are infinite and the combinations of digits in these fractions never repeat. So *pi* was described as an irrational and transcendent number. Dante never mentions *pi* but it is evident that he is aware of its existence and uses it as an extended metaphor.

It is the very association of quaternity that matters here in the first place, as it echoes Dante's final vision in Eliot's image. Eliot does not square the circle; the connection between Dante's squaring the circle and "the still point" of *Four Quartets* is by no means direct or literal, although there still are strong resemblances that point to Dante's profound influence. These resemblances are for the most part associative. In the first place the subject-matter of both images is the same—apprehension of God as the Primal Cause of the universe and its movement.

It should be remembered that Eliot's poetry is essentially associative and referential, and associations and references are much more important in it than is direct logic. Constantly recurrent "circular" imagery in *Four Quartets* is masterly intertwined with images implying quaternity and generalized quaternaries of many kinds, sometimes vivid and certain (like the title of the poem and the actual number of quartets, and the quartets themselves). Sometimes generalized quaternity is just hinted at, like an occasional mention of a violin (one of the instruments of the string quartet), or of a lotos flower, which also denotes the Four Elements in the Eastern tradition, as its roots grow in the earth, and it's stem goes through the water, while the flower comes to air and bursts into blossom in the sunshine (fire). Besides, the lotos if often depicted in the centre of the Eastern mandalas, which also have a quaternary structure. There are also four corners of the world, symbolized by the titles of each separate quartet, four seasons, four elements, four cardinal directions, four gospels, four stages of human life, etc. The succession of symbolic associations is practically endless.

Thus, to borrow an expression from the Russian structuralist Yuri Lotman, the poem, which demonstrates utmost generality of semantic, associative and symbolic connotations, turns into "a poetic model of the universe" (254-66). And this does not happen intuitively, in the sense that any literary form, whether novel, play, or poem, objectively represents a model of the world. Quite to the contrary, with Eliot it is asserted "subjectively," on the level of the author's conscious intention, as he sets himself the task of creating a miniature model of the universe using to this end a most comprehensive and generalized means of expression. Therefore, myth should be considered as a modelling and form-creating principle that confers universality to the whole emotional content of the poem; it brings the imagery to the utmost generality and re-creates aesthetic order from the chaos of the surrounding world.

Symbolically, Eliot places a square within his rotating circle, or rather a multitude of squares which fit the diameter. Eliot is not squaring the circle, although the very image of quaternity and square refers to Dante's poetics of geometry. Eliot chooses a reverse path: for him the aspiration to grasp the inconceivable is movement towards the centre, which distantly resembles Zeno's paradox of Achilles and the Tortoise. No matter how and to what extent you square the world or the circle, you will never be able to grasp the divine essence, or perceive God. The way of Salvation is movement towards the centre until complete stillness is reached, but you can never attain it, and this is also a paradox. Thus, Dante fails to square the circle, but for Eliot the square and the circle are one.

PART II:

DANTE'S GHOST AND ELIOT'S MODERNISM

CHAPTER SIX

DANTESQUE PERSPECTIVES IN T. S. ELIOT'S *INVENTIONS OF THE MARCH HARE*

ARIANNA ANTONIELLI

IN THE SUMMER OF 1910, spent as always with his parents in Gloucester, Massachusetts, T. S. Eliot started transcribing his poems in a book. As Lyndall Gordon has described it, "He bought a marbled notebook from the Old Corner Bookstore, inscribed his title—INVENTIONS OF THE MARCH HARE—and copied in the more experimental poems he had been writing since November 1909. […] He continued to use the notebook during the following year in Paris, on his return to Harvard and, finally, on arrival in London in 1914" (Gordon 33). Eliot actually used this *Notebook* until 1917, the year of *Prufrock and Other Observations*. As is well-known, when Eliot subsequently gave the manuscript of *The Waste Land* to his American patron, John Quinn, he also sold him the *Notebook* including fifty poems for the sum of 140 dollars, on condition that it should remain unpublished. The *Notebook* and *The Waste Land* both disappeared, and it was only in 1968, three years after Eliot's death, that the Berg Collection of the New York Public Library announced the rediscovery of both manuscripts.[1] Eliot's early lines, both from the *Notebook* and the so-called "loose leaves,"[2] were published for the first time on April 9, 1996, by Christopher Ricks, as part of a volume made up

---

[1] The New York Public Library announced its rediscovery on October 25, 1968. In November, Donald Gallup wrote a detailed review of Eliot's first poems, entitled "The 'Lost' Manuscripts of T. S. Eliot." *Times Literary Supplement*, (November 1968).

[2] These pages, including a small number of obscene poems written by Eliot in this same period, were removed from the Notebook probably by Eliot himself, before they were bought by Quinn. Subsequently, they were discovered among Ezra Pound's papers at Yale.

of several unpublished poems and the first versions of other prominent compositions which had later entered the early printed collections.[3]

These poems delineate Eliot's artistic and personal *Bildung* by means of a dense map of symbols, images and metaphors modulated by visionary, obscene and ironic tones, developed through dirty "blind alleys" and "vacant lots" after an "overwhelming question" never to be pronounced. They were written by Eliot during a period in which he was seeking to shape his poetic voice. His was a continuous search influenced by literary-philosophical interests, which extended from the *Bhagavad-Gita* to Bradley's idealism, and also his wide readings, which included Milton and Shakespeare, metaphysical and symbolist poetry and, last but not least, Dante. The *Notebook* poems clearly highlight the fact that Eliot was already quite involved in Dantesque visions and poetry, and deeply fascinated by his symbols, images, and metaphors. These compositions, developed through an interesting series of hallucinatory or dreamlike states of consciousness, often appear to be borrowed from Dante's *Inferno*. Along this "fragile, tattered web of language, stretched over a void" (Jenkins 3), madness, griminess and isolation are the chosen perspectives from which Eliot's characters watch or approach the world around them. Frequently, Dante's imagery, stylistic features, vocabulary and diction emerge in the manuscript poems in the form of faint echoes which were to reverberate rather powerfully in his later compositions. For Eliot, Dante's poetry was also a model in opposition to the Romantic abstractions. Dante's allegories, similes and metaphors served him as an instrument for effecting an "escape from emotion" (SW 58) and contextualising them, as Stuart McDougal has argued.[4] Eliot's formal debt to Dante—a kind of debt he himself was to describe in the essay "What Dante Means to Me" as "the most persistent and deepest influence" (*TCC* 125) on his own verse—is actually a visible thread passing through his entire poetic output.

---

[3] The *Notebook* contains the first versions of the poems included in the volume *Prufrock and Other Observations* (1917): "Humoresque (After J. Laforgue)," "The Love Song of J. Alfred Prufrock," "Portrait of a Lady," "Preludes," "Rhapsody on a Windy Night," "Morning at the Window," "Mr. Apollinax" and "Conversation Galante;" and the early versions of the poems found in the "loose leaves" and later published in *Poems* (1919), *Ara Vos Prec* (1920) and *Poems* (1920): "Gerontion," "Burbank with a Baedeker: Bleistein with a Cigar," "Sweeney Erect," "A Cooking Egg," "Mélange Adultère de Tout," "Lune de Miel," "Dans le Restaurant," "Whispers of Immortality," "Mr. Eliot's Sunday Morning Service," "Sweeney Among the Nightingales" and "Ode."

[4] See Stuart Y. McDougal's "T. S. Eliot's Metaphysical Dante," in his *Dante Among the Moderns*, 57-81.

In his *Notes* to the volume, Ricks himself does not fail to show a conspicuous number of Dantesque intimations, emphasizing that the kind of debt Eliot owed to his master during this phase of his poetic *Bildung* was mainly on two levels. Besides a first thematic or visionary level, determined by a sort of re-adaptation of Dante's images in his own poetic situations, a linguistic one can also be identified, produced by a rather imitative use of Dante's very words and lines. Actually, in focusing attention on *Inventions of the March Hare* and keeping in mind Rick's two levels, we can immediately assert that Dante's *Divine Comedy* is iconically manifest in these early poems, almost in the form of its *infernal* scenery, which appears to be very clear in Eliot's imagination as a frightening place inhabited by his still present hollow men. Thus, the figure of 'Gerousia [Gerontion]' (July 1919), represented as a living corpse ("Here I am, an old man in a dry month…waiting for rain," ll. 1-2; "I an old man,/ A dull head among windy spaces.," ll. 15-16; "An old man in a draughty house/ Under a windy knob.," ll. 31-32; with his "Thoughts of a dry brain in a dry season," l. 72); the personification of the Londoners depicted as a group of "living dead" in the first section of *The Waste Land*, "The Burial of the Dead" (ll. 64-65, "Sighs, short and infrequent, were exhaled, / And each man fixed his eyes before his feet"), as well as *The Hollow Men* of the 1925 poem represent, all of them, the most accomplished form of the coarse archetypes we find in the *Notebook* poems, which still evoke the protagonists of Dante's *Divine Comedy*. As observed by Paul Murphy:

> These early poems lead us into the themes which dominate Eliot's later work, even the vocabulary, rhyme and diction echoes the style of his later work, or rather of the more successful poems of the same period. They may be seen, in fact, as adumbrations, in miniature, of the Collected Poems.[5]

Yet, at this stage, Eliot is far from being "a strenuous emulator and intrepid pirate" as Allen Mandelbaum described Dante, at least so far as his *fictio* is concerned (Mandelbaum x). Accordingly, Eliot's inheritance from Dante proves to be not well re-elaborated and readapted, above all with regard not so much to the thematic or visionary level, as to the linguistic and rhythmical one, the former lacking in directness and clarity, and the latter in musical climax. Eliot's style, characterized in these poems by frequent repetitions, ambiguous semantic relations and empty

---

[5] "A Childe's Alphabet," 3, Dec. 2003.
http://homepage.ntlworld.com/david.bircumshaw/ChideThree/PaulM.htm

ornamental rhymes, mostly appears to be employed so as to ease the rhythm and gratify the reader's ear, rather than conciliating with the poem's very content and sharpening its semantic value, as he would perfectly fulfill in, for instance, *The Portrait of a Lady* or *The Waste Land*, where form and content are perfectly integrated.

"Technically," Murphy points out, "the poems range over a variety of forms, none of which are classical literary forms, such as the sonnet or the ode, which Eliot tended to avoid in any case, but lyrical pieces, satires, urban pastoral and the prose poem. In this last category," he continues, "Eliot tends to analyse particularly atomised states of mind in a surrealistic manner reminiscent of various psychoanalytical methods which he may or may not have been aware of at the time" (*ibid.*). This is the case of "Introspection,"[6] for instance, where, in its fantastic setting and mysterious symbolism, it is immediately possible to recognize Dante's infernal *milieu* and atmosphere.

> The mind was six feet deep in a
> cistern and a brown snake with a tri-
> angular head having swallowed his
> tail was struggling like two fists
> interlocked. His head slipped along
> the brick wall, scraping at the
> cracks. (*IMH* 60)

Eliot's hallucinatory image and dreamlike situation of a mind plunged in a cistern, even though we are not to understand whether the latter is full of water, or of any other substance, together with the symbolic presence of the snake taking on the shape of a circle by its frenetic activity of swallowing its tail, recalls, to some extent, certain Dantesque categories of sinners who are eternally suffering in the different circles and ditches of the Inferno. As is widely known, in his Comedy, Dante represents the 'Inferno' as the third realm of the human condition after death. It properly corresponds to death itself, since in hell men are deprived of the celestial vision of heaven and cannot change their present state and ascend the great ladder. In Dante's hell, sinners undergo a 'contrapasso,' or a punishment

---

[6] A brief chronology of the poems in *Inventions of the March Hare* is given by Ricks in his *Introduction* (xxxviii-xlii). It appears that most of the poems were written between November 1909 and 1915, but Ricks is unable to date some of them: "The Little Passion: from 'An Agony in the Garret, "Introspection," "While you were absent in the lavatory," "Inside the Gloom," "Do I know how I feel? Do I know what I think?," "O Lord, have Patience," "Hidden under the Heron's Wing," "The Engine I-II," "In Silent Corridors of Death."

appropriate to their worldly human misbehaviour. In Canto 19, for example, we recall that the Eighth Circle, Third Ditch, is inhabited by the Simonists. These sinners, in Dante's portrait, appear to be pushed and held upside down in subterranean barrels (evoking the baptismal fonts to him) or "holes in the rock," in Mandelbaum's words (169), while their feet are the only part of their bodies still visible. Evidently, while Eliot's hallucinatory perspective is able to cross the border separating air from water, thus proving to reject any human-like vision, Dante's view remains much more real and thus constrained inside his aerial perspective.

Here Eliot looks inside the cistern and gives us a detailed description of his vision. On the other hand, Dante can see the sinners' feet burnt by flames, but he is not able or keen either to see or imagine their suffering faces.

Io vidi per le coste e per lo fondo
piena la pietra livida di fóri,
d'un largo tutti e ciascun era tondo.
Non mi parean men ampi né maggiori
Che que' che son nel mio bel San Giovanni,
fatti per loco d'i battezzatori;
l'un de li quali, ancor non è molt'anni,
rupp'io per un che dentro v'annegava:
e questo sia suggel ch'ogn' omo sganni.
Fuor de la bocca a ciascun scoperchiava
d'un peccator li piedi e de le gambe
infino al grosso, e l'altro dentro stava.
Le piante erano a tutti accese intrambe;
per che sì forte guizzavan le giunte,
che spezzate averien titorte e strambe.

Along the sides and down along the bottom,
I saw that livid rock was perforated:
the openings were all one width and round.
They do not seem to me less broad or more
than those that in my handsome San Giovanni
were made to serve as basins for baptizing;
and one of these, not many years ago,
I broke for someone who was drowning in it:
and let this be my seal to set men straight.
Out from the mouth of each hole that emerged
a sinner's feet and so much of his legs
up to the thigh; the rest remained within.
Both soles of every sinner were on fire;
their joints were writhing with such violence
they would have severed withes and ropes of grass.
(ll. 13-27; Mandelbaum 169)

However, despite the two different perspectives adopted for representing the objects of their vision, the relation between both scenes and atmospheres is extremely close. Similarly, in Cantos 21-22 (Ditch 5), Dante meets the sinners of the Malebolge, that is of the fifth Pouch of the eighth Circle; these sinners, called the Barrators, are submerged in boiling tar and guarded by a group of demons known as the "Malebranche."

As well, Eliot's image of the snake in "Introspection" might be borrowed from Dante's *Inferno*, where there are Serpents that wind themselves around the damned. It is worth noticing that in Dante's *Comedy*, snakes often stand for or recall a very hellish pattern of spiritual depravation. In particular, it is worth noting that in Canto 24, Thieves are bitten and punished by hideous snakes assaulting them, as well as in Canto 25 snakes are called to attack Vanno Fucci, the thief who stole the treasury of Saint James from the Cathedral of Pistoia, after his speech and obscene gestures against God. Still in Canto 25, the centaur Cacus, who was killed by Hercules, is described as covered by snakes, while the noble Florentine thief, Agnello de' Brunelleschi, is grasped by a serpent with six feet, melting with it like wax. However, if Eliot's snake, after swallowing its very tail, appears to fight against itself in order to get free and break the circle it has created, indirectly negating the symbol of eternity that the circle itself represents and suggesting a Buddhist ying and yang symbol, Dante's serpents, as in Canto 24, twist around the naked sinners, biting and wrapping them till they explode into fire and arise once again from their ashes, like the phoenix, thus suffering the same punishment in eternity. Actually, this poem, like many others from the *Notebook*, appears to be simply evocative of Dante's scene through strong, visionary imagery, rather than of his retaliatory and revelatory goal and thus of his very vision.

Furthermore, far from Dante's plain style with his aba, bcb, cdc, etc. tercet rhymes, hendecasyllabic meter based on number three and internal alliterative associations, Eliot chooses a prose poem, where he avoids any rhyme pattern, where a syncopated rhythm is mostly given by the way he abruptly cuts each sentence so as to give the effect of bringing the action of the poem forward, and musicality is maintained by the alliteration of the "s" sound, openly relating to the snake, to its qualities and movement. It is interesting to note that Eliot often turns to prose when he wants to portray visionary states of mind and, in general, to escape from reality.

In Eliot's undated poem "In silent corridors of death," Dante's *Inferno*, with its decadent setting and gloomy atmosphere, probably emerges even with stronger intensity through a series of well detailed pictures:

In silent corridors of death
Short sighs and stifled breath,
Short breath and stifled sighing;
Somewhere the soul crying.
And I wander alone
Without haste, without hope, without fear
Without pressure or touch
There is no moan
Of souls dying
Nothing here
But the warm
Dry airless sweet scent
Of the alleys of death
Of the corridors of death. (*IMH* 93)

Eliot's "corridors of death" clearly evoke Dante's journey through the hellish alleys, possibly representing their very metaphors. Also, the emotional condition the author claims to perceive while walking along these passages recalls the very opening words of Dante's *Comedy*, when he is still alone, without his mentor Virgil (Canto 1.1-63). Immediately before starting his journey and passing through the gloomy portal of the *Inferno*, Dante reads above its entrance the following inscription: "LASCIATE OGNI SPERANZA, VOI CH'INTRATE" ("ABANDON EVERY HOPE, WHO ENTER HERE" —Canto 3.9; Mandelbaum 20-21)—a hope that Dante the wanderer or quester actually claims to be on the point of losing several times along his journey through the after-life, and that he confesses he would definitely have lost without the presence of Virgil, his mentor and master, along "the alleys of death." In Eliot's composition, the first-person narrator, explicitly walking along the deadly corridors without a mentor ("And I wander alone," l. 5), is not able to see the goal of his journey; no clear light is visible at the end of these passages by which they might be even faintly illuminated. He appears to proceed aimlessly, without the "pressure or touch" (l. 7) Dante probably received from his guide; a pressure that enables him to persevere through this terrible landscape, even during the most difficult moments and visions, constituting the real agent of his quest. Eliot's 'I' has neither a guide, nor a precise aim and, as a consequence, he appears to move on hopelessly. He is not accomplishing any particular quest. He is simply wandering, staggering along this dreadful landscape in the most terrible physical and psychological condition: he is alone and moves on "Without haste, without hope, without fear" (l. 6)—an emotional crescendo rendered by the reiteration of the preposition "without" followed by three nouns, "haste," "hope," and "fear," which are meant to highlight his state of depression.

The rhyme pattern is quite irregular. The poem starts with two plain couplets rhyming "aabb" and closes with the same couplet rhyming "aa," while of the remaining eight lines only ll. 5 ("alone") and 8 ("moan") perfectly rhyme together, as well as l. 6 ("fear") and l. 9 ("here"). The alliteration of the sound "s" in the first four lines and of the "n," "m," and "w" in the remaining lines, are effecting, perfectly joining the musicality given by the "aabb" rhymes. The last lines are repetitive and quite banal and do not give the poem any additional meaning, recalling the opening vision without adding anything new or different.

This poem clearly evokes and brings to mind the already mentioned first part of *The Waste Land*, "The Burial of the Dead," which as is well-known refers to the inhabitants of modern London, i.e., the opportunists who failed to take sides while alive, flowing like dead men towards their numbing jobs while listening to the dead sound of bells.

> I had not thought death had undone so many.
> Sighs, short and infrequent, were exhaled,
> And each man fixed his eyes before his feet.
> Flowed up the hill and down King William Street,
> To where Saint Mary Woolnoth kept the hours
> With a dead sound on the final stroke of nine. (*CPP* 39)

Here the poet represents a fallen wasted urban society, inhabited by schizophrenic, alienated people who act like marionettes, and who are immolated by Eliot on the altar of his first poems. It is a society plunged into squalor and ruin, where the everyday landscape disturbs the beholder's eye, and the familiar becomes *Unheimlich*. The short infrequent sighs emitted by Eliot's figures convey the rhythm of their steps and, more remarkably, their gait suggests a resemblance to marionettes. These very lines, where Eliot's imagination focuses on a brief but explicit description of the Londoners, unmistakably suggests Dante's third Canto of *Inferno*:

e dietro le venìa si lunga tratta	Behind that banner trailed so long a file
di gente, ch'i' non averei creduto	Of people—I should never have believed
che morte tanta n'avesse disfatta.	That death could have unmade so many souls.
	(ll. 55-57; Mandelbaum 22-23)

It is also worth remembering that in the fourth Canto of the *Inferno* Dante enters, together with his mentor, the First Circle or Limbo, the Mineral Realm, where they meet the great poets of antiquity. And he observes that

Quivi, secondo che per ascoltare, *non avea pianto mai che di sospiri* *che l'aura etterna facevan* *tremare;*	Here, for as much as hearing could discover, there was no outcry louder than the sighs that caused the everlasting air to tremble. (ll. 25-27; Mandelbaum 30-31)

On this occasion, Dante immediately remarks that his senses could perceive no weeping or "moaning" (to adopt Eliot's own word), but only sighing, which comes from the sinless, the unbaptized, including children. Actually, the Mineral Realm is not characterized by weeping, but only by the damned souls' groans, since it is inhabited by those who lived before Christianity or were not baptized. Thus, the air itself flickers with their laments and sighs—an agonizing landscape that probably left its mark on the young Eliot's imagination

In his 1950 essay on Dante, Eliot wrote "the kind of debt I owe to Dante is the kind which goes on accumulating." Undoubtedly, in the aforementioned lines taken from *The Waste Land*, we can immediately realize this sort of 'accumulation' in his very description of the Londoners; an accumulation that also represents a sort of hiatus between the *Notebook* poems and his later compositions. Actually, if a sterile imitation of Dante's landscapes and atmospheres might be imputed to Eliot's *Inventions of the March Hare* compositions, his later poems, from *The Waste Land* on, are no longer subject to this fault, since we cannot speak of imitation "which can only sterilize," but rather of an influence or inheritance "which can fecundate" (1961). In *The Waste Land* Dante's infernal scenery is completely transposed into a new and typically Eliotian landscape. Here the American poet evokes his master's visions and atmosphere by decontextualising them and readapting them to his particular geographical and temporal coordinates.

As I have already mentioned, a significant trait of the *Notebook* verses is Eliot's wide use of citation from other poets, incorporated into his own compositions in their original languages. One such case occurs for example in the poem entitled "The Burnt Dancer" (1914). This poem, written in the years immediately following the composition of "Prufrock" (1911), inaugurates, together with "The Love Song of St. Sebastian" (1914), "Oh little voices of the throats of men" (1914) and "The Little Passion: from 'An Agony in a Garret'" (undated), the topic of martyrdom that so deeply fascinated the young Eliot. These three poems deserve close attention since, even though they were not to be included in *The Waste Land* manuscript as fragments, they still appear to anticipate, with their focus on religion, the most important vision emerging from *The Waste Land*. In "The Burnt Dancer," Eliot's concept of martyrdom is expressed by the tongues of fire with which the protagonist expiates his lust, just as Dante's characters do. The poem begins with a quotation from Dante's *Inferno* 16.6: "sotto la pioggia dell'aspro martiro" ("beneath the rain of bitter punishment," p. 143), the rain of sharp torment where Eliot's protagonist, a moth, ends its life (ll. 1-4):

Within the yellow ring of flame
A black moth through the night
Caught in the circle of desire
Expiates his heedless flight

Except for this quotation, the poem is characterized by a simplicity of diction and situation which is unquestionably atypical of Eliot[7] and very far from his more elaborate and erudite intricacies discoverable in other poems of this period. There is in "The Burnt Dancer" just one other case of an untranslated quotation, namely Corbière's line "O danse mon papillon noir," a sort of refrain echoing at the end of each stanza and conferring the whole poem a songlike rhythm. This evident absence of other allusions to classic literature is what principally differentiates this composition from the other *Notebook* poems.

At a thematic level, it narrates the story of a moth which falls victim to its irresistible desire to immolate itself in the "golden values of the [candle] flame." As far as Dante's punishments are properly accomplished with the damned souls' metamorphosis since, as we have already seen, at the crucial moment of their suffering they undergo a rather physical transformation representing the passage from a spiritual disorder to a spiritual order, Eliot's moth would appear to be the object of this same Ovidian metamorphosis with a main difference. In Eliot's poem, metamorphosis is once again neither the consequence of punishment nor the symbol of a spiritual *Bildung*. The moth's "twisted dance" (l. 31) towards martyrdom starts at the very moment it is "caught in the circle of desire" (l. 3), explicated by "the yellow ring of flame" (l. 1). It appears to be bent on accomplishing its impossible flight, to "expiate[s] his heedless flight" (l. 4) with "wings that do not tire" (l. 5) since the "golden values of the flame" (l. 7) are the only thing that really matters to the moth. In the second stanza the poet foregrounds the fact that the moth's desire is a primitive one "from Mozambique or Nicobar" (l. 16). This association

[7] At the age of fifteen, Eliot had already learned the first rudiments of French, Greek, Latin, and even some German (*Letters* 7).

with the tropics recalls Eliot's typical struggle between the civilized and the savage worlds; a theme also emerging from other poems such as *Circe's Palace* and obviously *The Waste Land.* In the last stanza, where the moth returns as a figment of the protagonist's consciousness ("Within the circle of my brain / The twisted dance continues," ll. 30-31), its death by fire is an unquestionable evocation of Dante's hellish victims, who can no longer turn away from their very lustful desires (ll. 38-41):

> O strayed from whiter flames that burn not
> O vagrant from a distant star
> O broken guest that may return not
> O danse danse mon papillon noir!

Here Eliot adopts a metaphor that possibly refers to Satan in a metonymical way. He claims that his moth is "caught on those horns that toss and toss" (l. 35), implying that these horns might be related to the devil's horns. The moth becomes a "Broken guest that may return not" (l. 40), pertaining to the very state of death. In his own comment to this poem, Christopher Ricks maintains that "This Dantesque poem of TSE's *The Burnt Dancer*, points towards the Dantesque section of *Little Gidding*," including the lines

> unless restored by that refining fire
> Where you must move in measure, like a dancer. (*CPP* 142)

These lines evoke Arnault Daniel's Provencal speech in *Purgatorio* 26: "s'ascose nel foco che gli affina" (26.148). Yet, unlike Arnault Daniel in the *Purgatorio*, the *personae* we meet throughout the *Notebook* poems are never passive in a positive sense, their passivity having nothing to share with Dante's purgatorial passivity, which is not feared but chosen. Dante's Purgatory protagonists choose a passivity that does not paralyse them in the manner of Eliot's characters. The paralyzed hero or patient—in "The Burnt Dancer" the speaker imagines himself to be a "patient acolyte of pain" (l. 32)—figuratively reproduces Eliot's feeling of helplessness, also considering that the word 'patient' both relates to the word 'patience' in its modern sense and also, etymologically, to passivity.

"The Burnt Dancer" appears to anticipate, in its interpenetration of the external world with the internal one of the protagonist, *The Portrait of a Lady.* Actually, the moth belongs both to the inner world of the protagonist and the concrete reality where it is an autonomous being. What is really worth noticing in this poem is Eliot's capability to harmonise form and content, where style and diction converge towards the semantic and imaginative conclusion of the poem, suggesting the moth's death reached by its dancing in the flames.

The *Inventions of the March Hare* poems, despite their fragmentariness, and the coarseness and triteness of some of their rhymes and situations, are a fertile field for analysing Eliot's stylistic varieties and poetic visions, their origins and development in Eliot's later work. From these *juvenilia* to his greatest poems, we are directly plunged into Eliot's most recurrent themes, symbols and images, at once aware of how deeply they were inspired by Dante's "clear visual images," by "the lucidity" of his style and "his extraordinary force of compression." In his 1929 essay on Dante Eliot stated that "more can be learned about how to write poetry from Dante than from any English poet,"[8] and during one of his lectures he added:

> *The Divine Comedy* expressed everything in the way of emotion, between depravity's despair and the beatific vision, that man is capable of experiencing. It is therefore a constant reminder to the poet, of the obligation to explore, to find words for the inarticulate, to capture those feelings which people can hardly even feel, because they have no words for them; and at the same time, a reminder that the explorer beyond the frontier of ordinary consciousness will only be able to return and report to his fellow-citizens, if he has all the time a firm grasp upon the realities with which they are already acquainted. (*TCC* 134)

---

[8] Even if Dante's influence was to remain the most important and unaltered along Eliot's poetic *Bildung*, it is worth noting that the *Inventions of the March Hare* poems are also evocative of other important influences, such as those of Jules Laforgue, Tristan Corbière and Charles Baudelaire.

CHAPTER SEVEN

PARADISE DEFERRED: ELIOT'S TRUNCATED DANTEAN PILGRIMAGE

DAVID SUMMERS

IN HIS EARLY ESSAY ON DANTE (1920) Eliot wrote, "It is one of the greatest merits of Dante's poem that the vision is so nearly complete; it is evidence of this greatness that the significance of any single passage, of any of the passages that are selected as "poetry," is incomplete unless we ourselves apprehend the whole" (170). Much the same could be said of Eliot's own canon of poetry, if for "vision" one substituted "poetic progression" or "modernist pilgrimage." The trajectory of Eliot's major poems follows a Dantean arc, from the early "Prufrock" to the more mature *Waste Land* with their allusions and overtones connected to *Inferno*, then on though the purgatorial motifs of the Ariel poems, "Ash-Wednesday", and much of the *Four Quartets*. This trajectory implies a promise of some modernist version of *Paradiso* While *Four Quartets* aims in that direction, the concluding lines of "Little Gidding" evoke only a hint of a Dantean beatific vision, and instead defer that vision in favor of an ongoing, perhaps ceaseless, ouroboric wandering. What looked to be a linear pilgrimage—following of course the Dantean model of apophatic descent rather than direct spiritual ascent—gives way to endless exploration and revisitation of beginnings. How shall we account for this?

The main arena for exploring this question must the *Four Quartets*, but as those poems are the culmination of a trajectory, and understanding of the *Quartets* depends on "apprehending the whole," first we should turn to the early stages of the Pilgrimage. Clearly the great divide in Eliot's canon comes after *The Waste Land* and before "Ash-Wednesday". As Helen Gardner pointed out many years ago: "The change in Mr. Eliot's poetry cannot be discussed without reference to the fact that the author of "Ash-Wednesday" is a Christian while the author of the *Waste Land* was not. Nobody can underrate the momentousness for an mature person for acceptance of all that membership of the Christian Church entails"

(Gardner 103). That was probably never more true, before or since, than it was in the middle decades of the twentieth-century. The major poems prior to Eliot's conversion beginning with "The Love Song of J. Alfred Prufrock," through "Gerontion," and *The Waste Land* (and including in my view, "Preludes," "Rhapsody on a Windy Night" and "Portrait of a Lady") are all in what could be called a modernist infernal mode. Not only does Eliot invite us into his poetry with a quotation from Dante's *Inferno*, citing Guido de Montefeltro's reticence about speaking his infamy to anyone still among the living (*CPP* 3), but his preoccupation in these poems is the conversation between the dead and the living. Indeed, between the damned and the dying, as it were. If Sartre believed that Hell was "other people," Eliot anticipates that insight, but adds that Hell can also be simply oneself—like Milton's Satan who laments "Me miserable! Which way shall I fly / Infinite wrath, and infinite despair? / Which way I fly is Hell, myself am Hell" (*Paradise Lost* 4.73-75). Prufrock finds his greatest agony in his own companionship. *Gerontion* seems to me to be a meditation on introspection as merely a refined and modern version of damnation, and Tiresias is not hard to image as a kind of Vergilian tour-guide showing us not just Fear, but Hell itself in a handful of dust through a series of postcards from the Infernal City of Dis, posing as London.

Craig Raine has recently suggested, in the context of the *Four Quartets*, that much of that poem is about conversing with ghosts. No pastime could be more Dantesque, and that pastime saturates Eliot's entire *oeuvre*—the difference is that the conversations with the dead in the poems prior to 1926 are uniformly infernal, while after 1927 they become purgatorial. As early as the 1950's we have seen criticism exploring the purgatorial aspects of "Ash-Wednesday" and the Ariel poems. One could say that these poems are simply about spiritual anxiety and desire, but the clearly Dantean elements of "Ash-Wednesday" seem to insist on a more specifically Purgatorial approach to those poems. Sister M. Cleophas, for example, not only provided a Dantean and Purgatorial reading of "Ash-Wednesday", but also suggested considering the *Four Quartets* as a version of the *Paradiso* in a modernist mode.

While finally unconvincing, the move is understandable given that *Four Quartets* contain several poetic rifts that point toward the *Paradiso*—and of course, it would be so elegant if it were so. Certainly there is something edenic about both the Rose-garden at the beginning of "Burnt Norton," and in the utopian dream represented by Nicholas Ferrar's utopian community at Little Gidding. The Rose Garden is an encounter with the dead who are neither damned nor in any appreciable way in purgatorial torment. They are moving in a harmonious and transcendent concord, which comes as close to Paradise as anything Eliot will offer us, and which *suggest* the harmony of the end of the *Paradiso*. Later in "Little Gidding" we are even given a glimpse of the Multifoliate Rose—Dante's beatific vision. But Ferrer's Little Gidding was a failed experiment, and in *Four Quartets* that longed-for beatific vision always pulls back into the blending of Rose and the purgatorial Fire. These remain only among the "hints and guesses" of paradise, granted fleetingly to those on a purgatorial pilgrimage, more like Red Crosse's vision of the New Jerusalem from the Mount of Contemplation than Dante's multifoliate rose.

Nevertheless, the Dantean debt in Eliot's pilgrimage is found explicitly and pervasively in the details of the poems. Consider the line "In the middle way, not only the middle of the way / But all the way, in a dark wood" of "East Coker" II, so clearly an invocation of Dante's "In the middle of the journey of our life, I came to myself in a dark wood, for the straight way was lost" (*Inferno*1.1-3). Eliot locates this invocation of Dante tellingly at the close of a passage lamenting the "intolerable wrestle with words and meanings," echoing Dante's recurring lament over the inadequacy of language convey his visionary imagination of ineffable and transcendent things. "East Coker" is largely concerned with ancestry, so for Eliot the problem of articulating the transcendent is compounded by the challenges of writing poetry in the shadow of powerful and suspect ancestral voices.

Take for instance what is the most Dantean episode in *Four Quartets*, the *terza rima* encounter between Eliot and his "familiar compound ghost" as the poet walks his dawn patrol of a burning and shell-shocked London. Yes, it is a conversation with one of the dead, and assuming this poetic mentor is largely Dante, one of the redeemed dead at that. But the conversation they share as they walk together is entirely about refining and *becoming*, rather than pure and essential *being*: it addresses the process of "purifying the dialect of the tribe" rather than the anticipation of some paradisiacal language where meaning and utterance are so closely attuned that purification becomes unnecessary. As Little Gidding is a place where prayer has been valid, this conversation turns into a prayer that both poems and poetic theories might be eventually "forgiven" in some sense—suggesting that redemption is still on-going. By the time we reach the end of this section, it becomes clear that what is at stake is the need to dissociate from a preoccupation with the self, "as soul and body fall asunder." Eliot is presented with a moment of coming to terms "all that you have done, and been; the shame of motives late revealed and the awareness of things done ill, or to other's harm ..." and the chastisement goes on. The entire episode has effortlessly slipped from a reflection on poetic diction to an inspection of the state of the poet's moral standing, the state of his soul. This encounter is a far cry from "Hale fellow, well met" Dante writes for himself as the greeting he receives from the virtuous pagan poets in the *Inferno*. Eliot was far less at ease with his poetic ancestors than was Dante, but more importantly this chastisement reminds us that, even late the aging poet of "Little Gidding" was interested in, as Aeschylus put it, "suffering into wisdom" more than merely being wise.

Souls already admitted to Paradise do not need to change, but purgatorial pilgrims desire change, and they believe change comes about through experience rather than the anchorite cell. Eliot locates changes in the self, or the soul, in a peregrination that is, paradoxically, of enduring presence: the meandering around to the garden pool at Burnt Norton, the journey down an English country lane to East Coker, the voyages of the fishermen in "Dry Salvages," and of course in both the sad trek of Charles I to Little Gidding—as well as the 'dawn patrol' walked by Eliot himself. The pilgrim is motivated by, perhaps rewarded with, occasional transcendent moments rather like what Jean-Luc Marion calls "saturated phenomena," because the intuition received goes far beyond the significance of the grounding object. Wild thyme, winter lightning, a cracked pool in a neglected rose garden—all become intimations of eternity and transcendence itself. But these are, in the *Four Quartets*, always momentary revelations of elsewhere, not the representation of an unmediated Dantean *Paradiso*. Of course it must be noted that Dante was drawn to these saturated moments as much as Eliot was, as can be seen in the fourth Canto of *Purgatorio*:

> When any of our faculties retain
> a strong impression of delight or pain,
> the soul will wholly concentrate on that,
> neglecting any other power it has
> (and this refutes the error that maintains
> that—one above the other—several souls
> can flame in us); and thus, when something seen
> or heard secures the soul in stringent grip,
> time moves and yet we do not notice it (*Purgatorio* 4.1-9).

This is Dante's version of "music heard so deeply that / That it is not heard at all, but you are the music / while the music lasts" (*CPP* 136), and its proper place is in the *Purgatorio*. In the *Paradiso*, the problem of ineffability, of "too much reality," is given very different treatment.

The presence of Charles I in "Little Gidding" evokes a political connection to Dante's *Purgatorio*. In Canto 7 Dante and Virgil arrive at the Valley of Princes, where to Dante's surprise great kings and princes from all parties in the disputes that wracked Christendom of his day are preparing to begin their ascent through purgatory by coming to terms with each other. Their peculiar sin has been too much care for earthly matters, in particular their own fame, power, and the advancement of their party. Yet here they sing together the "Salve, Regina," and of peculiar poignancy is the image of Ottakar comforting his former rival Rudolph over the lives they both squandered in pointless competition for earthly power. The distress Eliot comes to feel about poetic competition expands to encompass broader cultural and political conflict in the third movement of "Little Gidding," where, if we felt he was establishing Charles as an alter-ego in the first movement, he disclaims all parties and allegiances of an earthly sort, so that Charles and Milton can finally be "united in the strife which divided them" (*CCP* 143). The detachment advanced as wisdom in the opening of that movement becomes a complete renunciation of factions and policies, in favor of accepting a "constitution of silence" and "a single party." Only by means of such a renunciation, while also reclaiming authentic history, can one hope to attain the edenic epiphany found at the end of "Little Gidding." The final section of *Four Quartets* mirrors the last few books of *Purgatorio*, an earth-bound prospect from which the potential, always future, aim of the pilgrimage can be tentatively glimpsed. There is confidence in the glimpse, but that confidence is predicated by a conditional: that "we shall not cease from exploration" (*CCP* 145). Such a line would have been absurd at the end of Canto 100 of the *Commedia* where the mimesis of Paradise has been full, encyclopedic and ultimately satisfying.

What *Four Quartets* represents, then is a complex pilgrimage—vacillating between moments of *angst* and ecstasy, between an apophatic negation of self and attempts at a meaningful reconstitution of identity through commitment, belief, love and even doubt. In the final analysis it is the record of a "progress of the soul" (Moody, *Four Quartets* 146.) In that aspect, as in so many things, Eliot's poem of pilgrimage and transcendence is a modernist response to Dante. Like the *Divine Comedy*, it presents to us encounters with the dead, with the many ghosts around which Craig Raine shaped his recent discussion of the poem. Not all of Eliot's transcendent "moments in and out of time" are explicit encounters with the dead, but many are, and the experience in the rose garden at Burnt Norton is, and this experience serves as a template for all such experiences of "too much reality" alluded to later in the poem. The transcendent moment in the Rose Garden is a double experience. Part of it is perception of form, a version of the sublime in which the fragmentary—the broken and empty pool, the burnt house—is supplemented to a point of overwhelming excess. Part of it is temporal, in which the subject is allowed a glimpse of what the simultaneity of Time—the topic of the opening lines—might look like. The effect is that of a brief communion with the eternal, and with the dead, whose ghosts moved "as our guests, accepted and accepting," drawing Eliot's pilgrim-persona into a fleeting pavane of past and present.

As Dante uses his encounters with the dead to find those truths that will serve to redeem his own spiritual defects, so to does Eliot's pilgrim. The diseases of the soul addressed are different in *Four Quartets* than they are in *Purgatorio*, since the religious paradigms of the respective centuries bear little resemblance to each other. Dante has a relatively easy go of it, having only to deal with Seven Deadly Sins for a readership still comfortable with such language and concepts, while Eliot has to deal with all the soul-shriveling conditions of the modernist moment. What both of these elements, formal and temporal, share is an Idealist set of metaphysical assumptions: the broken pool is less real than the pool filled with water out of sunlight; the moment in time, isolated as "present only," is less real than the moment of past, present and future together, the moment in which "we move, and they." Indeed, it is more reality than human kind can bear. The end that these moments serve, however, is the remembering *in time* that constitutes the function of what Paul Ricoeur refers to as *idem*-identity—that part of us that, while the self evolves through time, remains durable and makes memory and identity coherent concepts. Remembrance and self-knowledge are only available to the durable self; ghosts are the quintessence of that durability. While "moment in the rose garden" is both in and out of time, "only in time can the moment ...be remembered: involved in past and future. / Only through time is time conquered" (*CCP* 119-20). The narrative nature of the pilgrimage concept is remarkably useful for exploring these matters: it is both experience, and because of its sustained nature, it is also opportunity for reflection upon experience. Awareness of the pilgrim narrative, replicated in the "pilgrimage" of reading a poem of some length and complexity, represents our only hope to both have the experience and not miss the meaning. Reconstituting meaning through temporal reflection demands that readers see themselves as pilgrim "others," just as in the enigmatic passage in the Dawn Patrol episode where the speaker claims to be at once the same and to know himself, and yet is "someone other" (*CCP* 141).

If the *Four Quartets* are pervasively purgatorial in mode, and if Eliot so thoroughly admired the coherent unity of vision he found in Dante, the question remains: Why does Eliot defer from giving us the modernist

Paradiso? The most immediate and perhaps inviting answer is to argue for the impossibility of a real beatific spiritual vision in the philosophical context allowed by secular modernism. His readers would simply not have stood for it, perhaps. Eliot himself, writing his second "Dante" essay recognizes the problem of contemporary taste in this regard. Referring to the *Paradiso* he writes:

> It belongs to the world of what I call the High Dream, and the modern world seems capable of only the Low Dream. I arrived at accepting myself only with some difficulty. There were at least two prejudices, one against pre-Raphaelite imagery, which was natural to one of my generation, and perhaps affect generations younger than mine. The other prejudice—which affects this end of the *Purgatorio* and the whole of the *Paradiso*—is the prejudice that poetry must not only be found through suffering but can find its material only in suffering. Everything else was cheerfulness, optimism and hopefulness; and these words stood for a great deal of what one hated in the nineteenth century. (*SE* 262)

What we are up against here is not the reticence of a timid Christian poet—a person of self-proclaimed medieval intellectual bent is hardly going to be worried about what anyone else thinks of him—but an arbiter of poet movements paying attention to what the current state of play can endure. Like humankind, perhaps not very much "reality." Eliot goes on to say that "It took me many years to recognize that the state of improvement and beatitude which Dante describes are still further from what the modern world can conceive as cheerfulness, as are his states of damnation" (ibid.).

That Eliot is able to get past his own prejudices against rendering poetic mimesis of "states of improvement" in his purgatorial poems, is therefore a notable accomplishment. What separates "states of improvement" from "states of beatitude," I assume, is change itself. Souls in paradise *are*, while souls in purgatory *are becoming*. That is why, perhaps, Eliot can sustain his interest in the purgatorial pilgrim soul, and convince himself that such a pilgrimage is suitable material for poetry even in an age that has largely dismissed the soul *per se*. They still believed in selfhood, especially suffering selves. Perhaps it is the concrete experience of these evolving selves that interests Eliot, not the philosophical and theological abstractions of Dante's *Paradiso*. Mark Musa has argued in his introduction that the *Paradiso* takes a sharp turn from the *Purgatorio*, with regard to its reliance on Ideals, Ideas and Abstractions rather than figurative language and imagery—hardly the stuff to stir a poet informed by the Imagist and Symbolist (Musa xiv). In his essay "Shakespeare and the Stoicism of Seneca" (1927), Eliot objects to thinking about Dante as a philosopher-poet—the organic unity and depth of theo-philosophical thought of Dante's *Commedia* results not from Dante's own quality as a philosophical thinker, but because "it happened that at Dante's time thought was orderly, strong and beautiful...the thought behind it is the thought of a man as great and lovely as Dante himself: St. Thomas" (*SE* 136). Perhaps then it is Eliot's own reticence about philosopher- poets that prevents Eliot from writing a "Little Gidding" that represents a more Dantean vision of paradise.

And yet, the Clark Lectures on metaphysical poetry make very clear that Eliot—while not wanting to cast himself as a working philosopher or granting that title to Dante either— is interested in defining the variety of ways philosophy and poetry intersect: metaphysical poems can include philosophical epigrams (as found so often in Shakespeare), expound on philosophical systems (Lucretius, Pope and Dante), or—and this is the consummation devotedly to be wished—manage to represent thought in such a way that it can be experienced as feeling, and cast the experience of feelings in such a way that they can be recognized as ideas (Dante, and to a lesser degree, Donne), (*VMP* 53-54). To admire Dante and Donne would be, for Eliot, to assume a degree of their philosophical shaping of his own poetic practice, and *Four Quartets* are undoubtedly "philosophical poems," as defined in the Clark lectures. Eliot's assessment of Dante as a non-philosophical poetic is therefore undermined by Eliot's own poetic practice, and his attempt for separate Dante from Aquinas, assigning to one thought and to the other poetry, is belied by his own uniting of culture criticism, philosophy, and poetry in the Dantean trajectory and spirit of his own late poetry. In the third of the Clark Lectures Eliot gives to Dante preeminence as a philosopher—poet, if one understands the highest metaphysical poetry as being a sublime coming together of thought, sensibility, and language:

> There are...essentially two ways in which poetry can add to the human experience. One is by perceiving and recording accurately the world—of both sense and feeling—as given at any moment; the other by extending the frontiers of this world. The first is the first in order of generation—you find it in Homer; and I do not say that it is necessarily second in order of value. A new and wider and loftier world, such as that into which Dante will introduce you, must be built upon a solid foundation of the old tangible world...Among those poets who have thus extended reality—and I will admit that they are those who interest me the most—I place Dante first absolutely (*VMP* 95).

The best way, perhaps, to describe that change in Eliot's poetics following his conversion is to say that he moved from a Homeric recording of the world to a Dantean expansion of our experience of the world. Erich

Auerbach's thesis that when philosophy reaches its limits, it naturally translates itself into poetry represents a more nuanced analysis of the connection between Aquinas and Dante than Eliot's own; and Eliot's own late poetry is evidence that Auerbach's view has considerable merit (Auerbach 15).

If it is not a sincere reservation about the enterprise of metaphysical poetry as such, we might look to other quarters to account for the absence of paradise in Eliot. Perhaps there is a sense in which the only paradise Eliot is interested in as a poet is a paradise of language. The description of the "sentence that is right: where every word is at home, taking its place to support the others...the complete consort dancing together" is, Gardner tells is, one of the ways the conclusion of *Little Gidding* brings us back to the edenic beginning of *Burnt Norton*, and the vision of the people by the pool (Gardner 183). But that argument only offers a slender and semantic tie to a moment that, for Eliot, represented a transitory and earth-bound glimpse of edenic innocence and reality—the Rose Garden should never be confused for heaven itself.

Another account might suggest that writing paradise is simply not the English "thing to do." A long line of first-rate English poets have either opted out of dealing with Heaven, or failed to do it well. Spenser, in Book One of the *Faerie Queene,* shows Red Crosse a fleeting glimpse of the New Jerusalem, but while he wants to go straight there, Spenser has more dragons for St. George to fight. By most readers' account, Milton botches Book Three of *Paradise Lost* rather badly (if his representation of God the Father and the courts of Heaven were meant to be attractive), and Blake will only deal with Heaven by turning it into Hell. C. S. Lewis, who would never I think stake a place himself among the poets mentioned here, wrote a very compelling version of "heaven" in his little book *The Great Divorce* (1946), but he made it look a good deal like Blenheim Park (just as his Hell was reminiscent of mid-century Birmingham), and even then he took it back in a way by saying that the place was only really the narthex of Heaven, and that only if one decided to stay—otherwise the same landscape was merely a deceptive antechamber to Hell. Among the first order of English poets, perhaps only the author of *Pearl* comes close to getting right, in a Dantean sense.

Perhaps writing a modernist *Paradiso* simply never occurred to Eliot. At the end of the day, Eliot simply was not as rigorously and pervasively intentional in his Dantean path as we, in retrospect, might be inclined to see him. Surely he did not write "Prufrock" and the *Waste Land* as "infernal" with a prescience that told him he would one day become a serious convert to Anglo-Catholicism, and start writing poems shaped around purgatorial pilgrimage motifs. That we now, and have since Gardner's time, read the *Four Quartets* as one grand schematic poem, makes it hard to credit that poems seemly so much of a piece were originally, to Eliot, piecemeal. "Burnt Norton" was initially published as a self-contained poem, made up of the bits left over from *Murder in the Cathedral*. Undoubtedly, having "Burnt Norton" in hand, and the structure and themes of *The Waste Land* in the back of his mind, shaped Eliot's plan for the other three "Quartets." But perhaps Eliot never thought of his late poems as in any way anticipating a modernist *Paradiso*, or that they would reposition his early poems (à la "Tradition and the Individual Talent") into appearing as the early stages of a Dantean narrative trajectory. Once Dante had enjoined in the *Divine Comedy* project he had to write a *Paradiso*, and given his orderly, fourteenth-century mind, his theological situation, and his poetic hubris, no doubt took delight in the fearful symmetry of it all. Eliot, however, may not have ever sensed the Dantean pattern in his own carpet, or perhaps he simply lost interest and never got around to finish the weaving.

Dante's unity of vision, so admired by Eliot, is cosmological, with the mimesis of soul's pilgrimage being essential, but also subordinate to the articulation of cosmic theological order. Eliot's world view, on the other hand, is in flux from beginning to end, and the pilgrimage function of the early poems can only be seen in retrospect from the vista of the *Four Quartets*. For Eliot, representing experience, spiritual and temporal, is more important than figuring forth the order behind and beyond the experience. Eliot's poetry resides in the creases between experience and meaning, and in many ways, Dante's does as well. In Eliot's view, Dante's *Commedia* remains a poem that we experience prior to understanding (*SE* 237). Most readers, on first approach, "have the experience" while they "miss the meaning," even—if not especially—while reading *Paradiso*, where we should most hope to have experience, meaning and language come together. Redeemed souls experience transcendence without mediation of any sort: experience and meaning become one in *Paradiso* for its denizens, but never completely for the Pilgrim-Dante. Dante's *Inferno*, on the contrary, is pure and essential mimesis of experience, as Auerbach would say, without any redemptive meaning possible, not even a moment of existential comprehension or genuine tragic insight on the part of the damned. For them, no change is possible, just as none is needed for Dante's souls in paradise. Therefore both poets, Dante as well as Eliot, write for the living reader, in this purgatorial world, like Lazarus come from the dead to tell us all. In this, Eliot and Dante are mere shades apart in emphasis.

That much is certain, and it may have to be enough of an account. Other elements already mentioned may have also played in part in deferring paradise in Eliot's poems, bringing us up against a principle of literary criticism Eliot advances in first Clark Lecture:

> When a subject matter is in its nature vague, clarity should consist, not in making it so clear as to be unrecognizable, but in recognizing the vagueness, where it begins and ends, and the causes of its necessity, and in checking analysis and division at the prudent point. In literature, one can distinguish but one cannot dissect (*VMP* 60)

On that prudent point, and with enough ambiguity in play to maintain a pretence toward getting it right, we shall have to leave T. S. Eliot's modernist take on Dante's *Paradiso* among the many what-might-have-beens of literature, "remaining a perpetual possibility only in a world of speculation."

CHAPTER EIGHT

T. S. ELIOT, DANTE AND IRONY

ANDRIJA MATIC

THE INTERTEXTUAL RELATION between T. S. Eliot and Dante has been thoroughly analyzed in a large number of books. Eliot himself wrote several essays in which he described his debt to Dante. Few have recognized, however, the character of such a relation. Its analysis shall reveal — regardless of the critical method one chooses to follow — that Eliot employed his borrowings from Dante mostly for ironic purposes. But, more importantly, such an interpretation will show us the complexity of the poet's irony, a wide range of ironic elements which make the meanings of his poems deeper and more fluid than they seem to be. Likewise, it will give a clear picture of the development of Eliot's irony and its eventual recession, which will help us understand the fundamental change of tone in his poetry that occurred after *The Hollow Men*.

That ironic relation first appears in some early poems collected in *Inventions of the March Hare*. In the third part of "Mandarins," Eliot uses the image of cranes flying across the screen to make ironic contrast with an obese, "intellectually" double-chinned mandarin. That image probably comes from Dante's *Inferno* (5.46-48), that is, from the lines preceding the famous Paolo and Francesca episode—a passage Eliot quoted in his main essay on Dante (*SE* 245). In "Prufrock's Pervigilium" the protagonist hears his "Madness singing" which, apart from the allusion to John Donne's mermaids, evokes the lines from *Purgatorio* (26.142-43) in which Arnaut Daniel, who weeps and sings, mentions his past folly—or madness, as it read in the translation that Eliot used when young (*IMH* 186)—before entering the refining flame. We know that the bedrock streak in Prufrock's personality is the inclination to compare himself to famous characters from history and literature (like Lazarus, Hamlet or the bold lover from Marvell's "To His Coy Mistress"), so Arnaut Daniel would be in good company. The introduction of this soul striving for purgation ironically depicts the futility of Prufrock's living, since his urge for redemption comes down only to verbal comparisons. The epigraph to the poem beginning "O lord, have patience" is taken from the inscription at the Hell Gate in the third canto of *Inferno*. Here Dante's verse ironically contrasts the supreme artistic consciousnesses of the past and the shallow convictions of the present. And finally, in the poem beginning "In silent corridors of death" Eliot makes the well-known allusion to the souls in the first circle of *Inferno* (4.25-27), which prefigures the city clerks trooping over London Bridge in "The Burial of the Dead." The ironic effect is in the atmosphere of cruel indifference which puts the persona and his companions in the position of "metaphysical" or "general" irony. This emerges, according to D. C. Muecke, when "self-valued and subjectively free but temporally finite egos" are found "in a universe that seems to be utterly alien, utterly purposeless, completely deterministic, and incomprehensibly vast" (69). This type of irony will acquire more complex dimensions in later poems, especially *The Waste Land*.

In "The Love Song of J. Alfred Prufrock" Eliot continues to create irony by means of Dante's verses. The epigraph, referring to the words of Guido de Montefeltro uttered immediately before he decides to explain to Dante the main reasons for his punishment, can be interpreted in many ways, but some of its meanings are undoubtedly ironic. If we understand Guido's words in the epigraph as Prufrock's thoughts, irony has at least two possible components. First, by evoking Guido's words, Prufrock obviously equates his trivial love problems and acute self-consciousness with the tortures in hell, wishing to provide his life with greater significance. Unfortunately, the outcome is opposite—that comparison only emphasizes the meaninglessness of his life. Second, as Dominic Manganiello argues, Guido reveals his double nature, fearing to be exposed but also wanting to tell his story (19). Therefore, quoting this part of *Inferno*, and endeavouring to compare his and Guido's tortures, Prufrock inadvertently expresses the doubleness of his personality. That doubleness is confirmed in the line immediately following the epigraph ("Let us go then, you and I").

In "La Figlia Che Piange," written several months after "The Love Song of J. Alfred Prufrock," Eliot again uses Dante's imagery for ironic effect. In some way, the lady whose portrait the persona wants to sketch resembles Dante's Beatrice, especially because he wants to place her "on the highest pavement of the stair" (*CPP 20*), which may be an allusion to Beatrice's position in *Paradiso*. The sunlight of her hair resembles the light of Beatrice's aura that dazzles Dante during his ascent to the highest sphere of paradise. It is the upshot of the persona's attempt to create one such character that is ironic, for despite his arrogant belief that he has gained control over the girl's existence, he turns out to be controlled. The girl does not have the expected appearance and, instead, she compels his imagination for many days and many hours. This implies that one can create such a symbol only through unfeigned inner transformation—which is the core of Dante's poetic achievement—and not through the simulation of that process.

The Dantesque imagery in "A Cooking Egg" also creates irony. Piccarda de Donati, from the third canto of *Paradiso*, is a part of the powerful historical and artistic heritage, an element in a dynamic structure of the world's experience, which stands in ironic contrast to "weeping multitudes" that "droop in a hundred A. B. C.'s" (*CPP* 27).

The first version of "Gerontion" had two epigraphs, one of which was taken from *Inferno* (38.121-22). Eliot later discarded that epigraph, though it added a strong ironic dimension to Gerontion's life, much more than the retained epigraph from Shakespeare's *Measure for Measure*. The lines taken from Dante are the beginning of Friar Alberigo's monologue. His soul appears in Tolomea—the third zone of the ninth circle of hell, reserved for traitors to their friends—because he had his two cousins killed during a banquet at his home. The position of fra' Alberigo is extremely ironic since his soul is in hell, whereas his body is still on earth. Eliot uses Dante's irony to portray the ironic character of Gerontion, who is not dead yet, though his senses are cooled and the soul seems to have already faded away.

"Mr Eliot's Sunday Morning Service" brings another ironic contrast based on Dante's imagery. Eliot compares "red" and "pustular" youngsters who clutch "piaculative pence" to the souls of the devout burning "invisible and dim" (*CPP 34*). The irony in this image can be clearer if we bear in mind a paragraph from Eliot's "Dante":

> The souls in purgatory suffer because they *wish to suffer*, for purgation. And observe that they suffer more actively and keenly, being souls preparing for blessedness, than Virgil suffers in eternal limbo. In their suffering is hope, in the anaesthesia of Virgil is hopelessness; that is the difference. (*SE* 256)

The "active" and "keen" suffering of the souls in *Purgatorio* defines by contrast the cheap redemptive attempt of the unfortunate youngsters. But this is not the only ironic element of the image; or more precisely, the image anticipates the irony of the motif of fire in Eliot's poetry, particularly in *The Waste Land* and *Four Quartets*.

The Waste Land is the poem which most prominently highlights the basic elements of Eliot's irony. The poet uses Dantesque imagery to create, or at least to support, all of those elements. For example, the passage introducing Madame Sosostris in "The Burial of the Dead" does not allude to any particular verse of Dante's, but seems like an ironic reversal of Dante's concept of imagination. Eliot himself elucidated such a phenomenon in the essay on Dante:

> Dante's is a *visual* imagination...it is visual in the sense that he lived in an age in which men still saw visions. It was a psychological habit, the trick of which we have forgotten, but as good as any of our own. We have nothing but dreams, and we have forgotten that seeing visions—a practice now relegated to the aberrant and uneducated—was once a more significant, interesting, and disciplined kind of dreaming. (*SE* 243)

Dante's "visual imagination" is an ironic contrast to the not very imaginative practice of "the wisest woman in Europe."

In the famous passage from *The Waste Land* depicting city workers flowing over London Bridge, Eliot does not use Dante's lines (*Inferno*, 3.55-57; 4.25-27) to create ironic meaning. Those lines are used, as he mentions in the essay "What Dante Means to Me," to make a reader aware of the relationship, or parallel, between medieval hell and modern life (*TCC* 128). However, together with Baudelaire's lines from "Les Sept Vieillards" portraying the city population unaware of the horror dwelling among them, Dante's imagery becomes a part of an interesting ironic scene which implies that the city clerks, routinely trooping from the railway station to their offices, are unaware of the horror, or spiritual hell, in which their souls roam. That is, Dante's lines take part in making the city clerks victims of metaphysical irony.

The original version of "Death by Water" was partly based on the Ulysses episode from *Inferno* (26.124-42). In the context of *The Waste Land*, the shipwreck of Ulysses reinforces several ironic meanings of "Death by Water." First, it is included in the motif of sacrifice of the preordained, which, ironically, does not result in salvation of the waste land. Second, it invokes the image of mermaids whose song puts the enchanted sailors into an ironic condition since they are lead to death listening to pleasant melodies. If we interlock this image with the shipwreck of Titanic—which Graham Nelson has shown to be implied in "Death by Water" (356-358)—and its cosmopolitan character, we have a picture of modern Europe, enchanted by the "pleasant melodies" of the most influential ideologies of the time, heading towards its own disaster. But, if one takes into consideration the allusions to *The Tempest* or "Dans la Restaurant," other ironic interpretations of the shipwreck of Ulysses are possible. For instance, it can be an ironic reversal of Ferdinand's shipwreck, for it brings to the protagonist neither love, nor more comprehensive knowledge of the world he inhabits. Likewise, the shipwreck of Ulysses in "Death by Water" may be interpreted as a metaphor of the "spiritual death" of the protagonist—or an illustration of his striving for spiritual rebirth—which, ironically, does not lead to salvation of his soul. So the role of Dante's verses in "Death by Water" can best be defined by Wayne C. Booth's metaphor of the building (36), in which the Ulysses episode could be one part of the roof under which lies a whole collection of ironic meanings.

"What the Thunder Said" contains two well-known allusions to the *Commedia* which can also be interpreted as ironic. The first refers to the story of Count Ugolino, who was immured in a tower with his children and grandsons, where they starved to death. Along with this allusion, Eliot refers to a passage from Bradley's *Appearance and Reality* in order to point out that the waste land is not something external, but the inner prison of every human being. Several lines later, he refers to "broken Coriolanus," who died because of his pathological vanity. In such a synthesis of poetic images, the Ugolino episode serves as an element in a complex ironic depiction of a vain man proud of living within the walls of his own prison. The second ironic allusion comes at the end of "What the Thunder Said." In the famous multilingual passage there is a line from Canto 26 of *Purgatorio*, to which Eliot also alluded in "The Love Song of J. Alfred Prufrock." It comes, as noted above, from the episode of Arnaut Daniel. But this time Daniel's story is used to create an ironic symbol of fire, for now it is a refining fire, in purgatory, as opposed to the fire of hell. In "Dante," Eliot provides the following explanation of the meaning of flame in *The Divine Comedy*:

> In this canto [26] the Lustful are purged in flame, and we see clearly how the flame of purgatory differs from that of hell. In hell, the torment issues from the very nature of the damned themselves, expresses their essence...In purgatory the torment of flame is deliberately and consciously accepted by the penitent. (*SE* 255)

So the fire in Eliot, as in Dante, is composed of two contradictory features, making a man's life extremely ironic since he has to redeem himself by the basic substance of his sin. This could be an illustrative example of "differential" aspect of irony, to use Linda Hutcheon's term (64), because the general meaning of fire in Eliot's poetry unites two different, contradictory meanings, none of which can be neglected; that is to say, the meaning of fire cannot exist without equal contribution of those contradictory meanings.

We can find the ironic relation between Dante's works and "The Hollow Men" in the second part of that poem—or, more precisely, in the image of eyes. This seems to be a reference to the eyes of Beatrice, which are the essential element of her divine beauty and which Dante cannot look at until the final sphere of Paradise. In "The Hollow Men" those eyes are only "a sunlight on a broken column" (*CPP 57*). The irony of this verse implies that a spark of divine beauty is always present within mankind, but can never prevail. In other poems there are further examples of this ironic mechanism, though it seems to be best represented in "What the Thunder Said," in the lines based on Shackleton's expedition which conjure up Christ appearing among his followers on their way to Emmaus.

After "The Hollow Men," irony becomes a less frequent means of expressing Eliot's poetic ideas. Likewise, the meanings are less impregnated with quotations and allusions. The intertextual collage is rarer, and its function is mainly to support the meaning, not to create it. This corresponds with Eliot's conversion, which occurred two years after the publication of "The Hollow Men," and fits the general change in his poetry. Still, there are some allusions to Dante that add ironic flavour to the poems of Eliot's later period.

"Animula," for example, develops the ideas of free will and pre-existence of the soul elaborated by Marco Lombardo in *Purgatorio* (16.85-96). According to Marco, the human soul is pure when it issues from the hands of God, but confronted with the everyday world its purity gradually spoils, unless it has a higher law to obey. In Eliot's poem this ironic feature of a human being, whose pure soul is doomed to strive for impurity, gets another component since, in an attempt to uncover the secret of its own existence, the soul ends its journey in a window seat behind the *Encyclopaedia Britannica*.

Being one of the greatest religious poems of the twentieth century, and also one of the most beautiful love poems, "Ash-Wednesday" does not contain so many ironic elements. However, some of the lines referring to Dante's works express ironic meanings. In the second part, initially titled "Salutation"—which may allude to Beatrice's salutation to Dante in *Vita Nuova*—we find a "Lady of silences" who seems to have something of Beatrice's divine features. She becomes a Rose first and then a garden "where all loves end" (*CPP 62*). The garden introduces an ironic stance common to all Christian faiths, whereby the love of God terminates the torment of unsatisfied loves, but, at the same time, it brings "the greater torment of love satisfied." For in such a state man finds relief of all unsatisfied loves, or ordinary "human affections," as Eliot explained in a well-known letter to Bonamy Dobrée (Tate 81), but he also suffers greater torment because the love of God can never be requited. "Ash-Wednesday" contains yet another ironic passage referring to Beatrice. In Part IV we encounter a figure who walks "between the violet and violet" and "goes in white and blue." She is also "in ignorance and knowledge of eternal dolour" (*CPP 64*). This line makes her character ironic because her mind is both free from the eternal pain of mankind and, in a way, affected with it, for she, as a human being, has the awareness of the pain that mankind has been condemned to experience ever since the primordial sin.

Irony in *Four Quartets* mainly takes the form of conventional "Christian irony." Thus, illness is a precondition for health, and the love of God can be reached only without hope, love and thought. Even faith should be passive, so that "the darkness could be the light, and the stillness the dancing" (*CPP 127*). Quotations and allusions expressing Christian irony are mainly from the works of St. John of the Cross and Julian of Norwich. However, *Little Gidding* contains two ironic passages based on Dante.

The first passage appears in the famous compound-ghost part, which Eliot himself characterized as "a passage...intended to be the nearest equivalent to a canto of the Inferno or the Purgatorio, in style as well as content" (*TCC* 128). The persona treads the pavement with a manifold master from the past and is told of the three gifts which will "set a crown" upon his "lifetime's effort." But before this, the master tells him that "last year's words belong to last year's language," and also that "next year's words await another voice" (*CPP 141*). It is in that seeming discrepancy that irony can be discovered. For a *new* poetic language is formed by means of the *old* one. That is, the poet does not base new poetic ideas on the present issues or on the anticipation of some future issues, but extracts them from the substratum of past poetic achievements.

The second ironic passage of *Little Gidding* may be found in the fourth section. It juxtaposes two types of fire—one of a bomber in action, the other of refining flame—an ambivalence anticipated in "Mr. Eliot's Sunday Morning Service" and more thoroughly developed in *The Waste Land*. This Dantesque concept of fire as, on the one hand, the symbol of sin, and, on the other, the symbol of purgation, shows the ironic fate of human beings, since they carry inside both the urge for self-destruction and the urge for redemption.

Dante's imagery in Eliot's poetry has complex ironic resonance, especially in the early poems. It is primarily used for contrast to unimaginative, cruelly simplified scenes from the modern world or as a highly imaginative means of depicting man's ironic position in all ages. Certainly the ironic function of Dante's imagery has other aspects as well.

For instance, it contributes to ironic characterization, it brings various examples of tragic and metaphysical irony and, quite frequently, it helps in producing powerful satire. Sometimes allusions to Dante do not create ironic meanings, but reinforce them. That seems to happen when they evoke significant religious and philosophical themes, such as man's attitude to the love of God or his perpetual struggle with time. But even in such cases these allusions are not less important, since they provide other ironic elements, or those "general" ironic meanings, with yet another dimension in relation to which those meanings are deepened and artistically enriched. Ultimately, the use of Dantesque imagery shows the development of Eliot's irony and its eventual recession. In the early period, comprising the poems up to "The Hollow Men," almost all of Eliot's borrowings from Dante are used to create or support ironic meanings. In the later period, after his conversion, Eliot alludes to Dante more extensively, but only a few of the allusions can be interpreted as ironic, in keeping with his general turn away from strong, overt ironical juxtapositions.

CHAPTER NINE

"... *RESTORING / WITH A NEW VERSE THE ANCIENT RHYME*": T. S. ELIOT'S AND EZRA POUND'S POETIC HOMAGES TO DANTE

STEFANO MARIA CASELLA

DANTE'S INFLUENCE ON, and presence in, T. S. Eliot's and Ezra Pound's works is everywhere: in their critical essays, in the development of their personal poetics, and in their poetry (through direct inspiration, quotations and allusions, titles, and epigraphs). As regards their critical works, the earliest contribution appears in Pound's *The Spirit of Romance* (1910), whose seventh chapter is dedicated to (and indeed titled) Dante, and gives a detailed analysis, primarily from the poetical point of view, but without omitting biographical aspects of the Florentine. Pound's following studies, *How to Read* (1931), *ABC of Reading* (1934), and *Guide to Kulchur* (1938), offer other remarkable critical evaluations of Dante. Eliot also wrote substantial essays: the early paper "Dante" (1920), then the longer and more famous *Dante* (1929), and finally "What Dante Means to Me" (1950); but he had dealt at length with the subject also in the Clark Lectures (Trinity College, Cambridge, 1926), and the Turnbull Lectures (John Hopkins University, 1933). The focus of this essay is, however, the two poets' artistic effort in the Dantean vein, particularly Eliot's "Little Gidding" II and Pound's Canto 72, which are the most significant efforts to recreate the "Dantescan voice" for the modern(ist) era.

Much of the general design of Eliot's and Pound's poetry is shaped after Dante, including most prominently Pound's masterpiece, *The Cantos* (though this nonetheless provides "By no means an orderly Dantescan rising"—Canto 74), and the overall architecture of, and interrelationships among, Eliot's three major works: *The Waste Land*, "Ash-Wednesday", and *Four Quartets*—even though the Dantescan filigree reveals itself only "a posteriori" (Tamplin, 82; Manganiello 16; Kenner, *Invisible Poet* 219).

Dante's influence on Eliot and Pound begins remarkably early. In the young Pound's second notebook one encounters a very short but telling handwritten note: "*Dante and Browning / as best models if one / has anything to say*" (Pound 1899-1907: 107). Like Eliot, Pound began reading Dante as a student in the first decade of the twentieth century, first at the University of Pennsylvania and then at Hamilton College (Kenner 1998, 36-38; Litz 39-41). Almost in the same years Eliot was introduced to the Florentine by his masters at Harvard (1906-1910), whose school of Dante studies was one of the most famous at the time (Kenner 1998, 35-36; Litz 41-44).

Pound's first volume of verse, Dantesquely titled *A Lume Spento* bears the ambitious and prophetic imprint "In the City of Aldus MCMVIII." (The "City of Aldus" Manutius is Venice.) The title indicates that the pupil follows the master—and in the very same path he will end "that great forty-year epic" ("Scriptor Ignotus," *A Lume Spento* 24), when, more than half a century later, the circle of his *Cantos* (another unmistakably Dantescan title) will be concluded by two memorable fragments on the theme of Paradise. Dante was therefore, Virgil-like, Pound's poetic and moral guide from the beginning of his artistic journey.

In an almost identical way, both the beginning and the end of Eliot's poetry stand in, and under, the sign of Dante, from "The Love Song of J. Alfred Prufrock" with its epigraph deriving from the speech of Guido de Montefeltro to the concluding ineffable vision of the "crowned knot of fire" and of "the fire and the rose" in "Little Gidding" V, which is shaped after Dante's beatific vision of the "candida rosa," through the images of the knot (*Paradiso* 30.91), the crown (*Paradiso* 30.134, 31.71), and the "coronata fiamma" (*Paradiso* 30.119). Not to mention the Dantesque echoes, quotations, and allusions in *The Waste Land*, the epigraph for *Prufrock and Other Observations* from *Purgatorio* 31, the Dantescan sub-titles in the early draft of "Ash-Wednesday",[1] and the theme and source of "Animula" (the third *Ariel Poem*) in *Purgatorio* 16.

As regards the development of personal poetics, both Pound and Eliot focused on Dante's lexical precision, from his exact verbal representation of spiritual experiences, defined by Eliot as "clear visual images" (*SE* 242), and described by Pound as "the thing which he [Dante] had clearly seen" (*SR* 126): note that in both cases the stress is laid on the visual faculty. The two American poets also responded to Dante's emotions,

[1] The second and third sections of "Ash-Wednesday" in draft included brief bits of Arnaut Daniel's speech in Provençal: "jausen lo jorn" and "som de l'escalina" (*Purgatorio* 26.144, 146); the third section transcribes "vestita di color di fiamma" (*Purgatorio* 30.33); and the fourth includes "la sua voluntade" (*Paradiso* 3.85).

feelings, and thoughts. Perhaps most importantly, they embraced the concept of the poem's four levels of meaning, as expressed in Dante's treatise *Convivio* (second book, 1st paragraph) in a passage occurring after Canzone I, "Voi che 'ntendendo il terzo ciel movete." Both Pound and Eliot stress not merely the literal and the moral meaning—in a sense they take these two semantic levels for granted—but above all they insist on the "allegorical" (mainly Eliot) and on the "anagogical" (mainly Pound). In general, their parallel essays on Dante note and applaud those very characteristics which became peculiar to their own poetry: as poet Eugenio Montale remarked: "the two Americans were two barbarians (the word is not to be understood in a negative sense), who assimilated European culture through a most inventive but also superficial revision of that part of the classic heritage which could be employed for their personal development."[2]

Having paid long and passionate attention to Dante's work, Eliot and Pound each took on the hardest task for a poet, that of deliberately vying with his master, by writing *à la manière de* Dante, offering two of the longest and loftiest instances of such a creative challenge, from the lexical, rhythmic, stylistic, thematic, imaginative, ritual and mythical points of view. Theirs is not only a challenge to measure up to Dante, but also an act of deep human, artistic, "poietic" (i.e., creative) homage, perhaps the highest tribute a poet can pay another poet. When they set about this task, they had already written their well-informed and detailed critical essays: but how arduous and hazardous to consciously compose verses similar to another poet's and, at the same time, original; verses echoing the style, rhythm, cadence, music, imagery, and spirit of the model, yet keeping one's personal and unmistakable voice. Without attempting a thorough Bloomian reading of their individual attempts, the second section of "Little Gidding" could be inscribed in the categories of "kenosis" and "askesis," while Canto 72 sums up and concentrates aspects of "tessera," "clinamen" and "demonization" (cf. Bloom 14-15 and passim).

For Pound and Eliot to take on the emulation of Dante meant to re-embody, in their own voices, the literary Tradition represented by Dante's own unequalled "individual talent": their poems therefore become part of an uninterrupted chain of relationships, influences, and re-inscriptions—a reshaping of classical "topoi" originating from the archetypes themselves. Dante relies on Virgil as master and as guide (in his words: "tu se' lo mio maestro e 'l mio autore" = "you are my master and my author" (*Inferno*

---

[2] Eugenio Montale, "Esule volontario in Italia," *Corriere della Sera*, 3 Nov. 1972, rpt. In *Sulla Poesia*, Milan: Mondadori, 1976, 529. Trans. Stefano Maria Casella.

1.85)); Virgil, in turn, honours another precursor *par excellence,* Homer, by beginning his own epic (the *Aeneid*) where Homer concludes his *Iliad*. At the same time the Latin poet also writes, in a sense, a different kind of "nòstos" (or "homecoming"—in this case the model being the *Odyssey*), a palingenetic and founding "nòstos": Aeneas's voyage from the burning walls of Troy to the coasts of Latium, where he will give origin to a new glorious civilization. At each stage of this chain of poetic re-creations, the hero undergoes the ritual "katabasis," the descent into the Underworld, and the "nèkuia," the evocation of the spirits of the dead. Different as they are—Eliot's effort in English, Pound's, quite exceptionally, in Italian—they each center on Dante, Virgil, and Homer as regards the ritual, mythical, archetypal, and initiatory aspects, giving evidence of their belief in Dante's unceasing modernity.

In the "Little Gidding" encounter with a "familiar compound ghost," and in Canto 72, described by Pound as "a meeting with spirits,"[3] the very "topos" of the meeting is characteristically Dantesque. How many spirits does pilgrim Dante meet in his journey through the three kingdoms? How often does he question his guide Virgil about the identity of an unknown ghost, and asks his permission or encouragement to directly address the souls? How many times does Dante speak, enquire, reply, scorn, sympathize, marvel, learn, weep, and then—when the conversation is finished or interrupted—take his leave of his shadowy interlocutor? As far as the Florentine is concerned, it is the poet himself who literally (and allegorically, morally and anagogically) descends into Hell, to climb then the mountain of Purgatory, and to finally reach Paradise. About such an extraordinary experience, Pound writes: "Dante's precision… in the *Commedia* comes from the attempt to reproduce exactly the thing which he has *clearly seen*" [my emphasis] (*SR* 126); and Eliot explicitly states that "Dante *visited…*" [my emphasis] the three other-worldly kingdoms (*TCC* 128): thus both modern poets stress the real experience undergone by their precursor and master, and his innumerable meetings with damned and blessed souls.

As regards the other necessary step of the "katabasis/nèkuia" process, that is the revelation of the hero's destiny, in Dante's case it is explained to him by his ancestor Cacciaguida, who prophesies the hardships,

---

[3] See Ezra Pound, *I Cantos*, ed. Mary de Rachewiltz (Milan: Mondadori, 1985), 1566.

sufferings and pains of his exile, but also the glory and recognition to come (*Paradiso* 17).[4]

Some six centuries later, the time did come also for his two modern disciples to undergo their own "katabasis" and "nèkuia," and their meeting with the spirits of the dead, according to the mythical, ritual, and literary models and patterns mentioned above. The infernal and apocalyptic (i.e., revelatory) moment occurred during "the enormous tragedy" of the second world war: near its beginnings for Eliot (1941/42), and almost at the end for Pound (1944/45). The former was serving as fire-warden in London, an "unreal city" and a "waste land" under the Blitz. The latter was scanning the horizon from the Ligurian hills overlooking Rapallo and its bay, getting news of the allied air raids against Italian cities ("Rimini is burned down, Forlì is destroyed"— "Annotated Translation" 12),[5] and bitterly and disappointedly realizing that his political and historical utopia was miserably failing: he thus went on to composed a hymn and an elegy to the "enormous tragedy of [*his*] dream."

Dramatic and traumatic experiences of this kind are generally the turning point of one's life, as Dante teaches in his most famous ìncipit: "Nel mezzo del cammin di nostra vita" (*Inferno* 1.1)—where the plural possessive "nostra" (our) means everybody's life. Furthermore, such crucial events are always beyond any reasonable human expectation and hope of recovery or salvation: as regards Dante, in fact, it is only thanks to an act of divine mercy decided *ab aeterno* that he can undertake his journey through the three otherworldly kingdoms guided respectively by Virgil, Statius, Beatrice and St. Bernard.

And what about the two modern poets? The poetic persona Eliot devised and shaped for himself in "Little Gidding" II meets the "familiar compound ghost" that plays the role both of classic/mythic soothsayer, and of Dantescan guide—at least for the time (if we can still speak of "time")

---

[4] "You will abandon all things most loved / this being the arrow that the bow of your exile first darts. You will experience how bitter is the taste / of other's bread; how hard it is to go / down and up on other's flights of stairs. / But what shall weigh your shoulders more will be / the wicked and foolish company / you'll have to share in this very valley" (*Paradiso* 17.55-63)

[5] Here and elsewhere I cite from the translation provided by Massimo Bacigalupo, "Ezra Pound's Cantos 72 and 73: An Annotated Translation," subsequently referred to as "Annotated Translation." Another English translation of the Italian Cantos, by Richard Reid, appeared in William Cookson, *A Guide to the Cantos of Ezra Pound* (London: Anvil Press Poetry, 2001), 113-26. Both translations are satisfactory, but both overlook some hidden references and allusions in the original.

of their dialogue, when he dispenses to the modern disciple his moral teachings. Pound encounters the spirits of three deceased people: Filippo Tommaso Marinetti (who died Dec. 2, 1944); the Lord of the Tarvisian lands, Ezzelino da Romano (who died in 1259); and Galla Placidia, daughter to Emperor Theodosius (who died in 450). The two men, Marinetti and Ezzelino, not unlike various souls in the *Commedia*, animatedly discuss with the poet current topics: the course of the war, the fall of the Italian regime, and the hopes for recovery at hand (Marinetti); the lies and slanders of the Guelfs of the past and of the present (Ezzelino); and the influence and interference of the Roman church in State affairs (both of them). Galla Placidia, on the other hand, resembles more a heavenly soul and utters only a few dreamy words: "Placidia fui, sotto l'oro dormivo": "I was Placidia, I slept under the gold" ("Annotated Translation" 15).

The similarities with the *Commedia* are immediately evident: many souls talk with Dante about the contemporary (that is Trecento) situation of Italian politics, about Florentine civil life and strife, about corruption and errors, about the Papacy and the Empire (as in Pound's *Canto*); others reveal to him the future course of events and provide moral teachings (as in Eliot's encounter).

As regards the frame of the meeting, whereas Pound is abruptly thrown *in medias res*, Eliot's introductory lines in "Little Gidding" II carefully prepare the scene trough the focalization of precise details in the sequence of time-and-place prepositions and adverbs: "In the uncertain hour before the morning / Near the end of the interminable night" (*CPP* 193). followed by other prepositions (at, after, while, below, while, over, etc.) leading the protagonist progressively closer to the goal of his quest, in the time suspended between the very dead of night and the early faint antelucan glimmers; through the succession of metallic rustles and unreal silence: "While the dead leaves still rattled on like tin / Over the asphalt where no sound was," up to the destined meeting point "between three districts" immersed in smoke. (Note that the crossroads among three streets, in ancient times called *trivium*, is a magical and initiatory place par excellence.) Out of this very smoke (infernal? Dantesque? undoubtedly other-worldly) the ghost materializes: it is an unforgettable apparition.

Unmistakably Dantesque and infernal—as well as symbolic—are the images of "wind," "blowing," and "leaves," which should be compared to *Inferno* 10.112 for the simile between autumn leaves and damned souls, and to *Inferno* 5.31-33 and 5.73-75 for the reference to the "infernal storm that never rests," and for the memorable episode of the two unfortunate lovers, Francesca and Paolo, "so lightly carried by the wind."

By comparison, Pound's scene is much more immediate, marked as it is by Marinetti's abrupt speech expressing his will to fight again:

> After his death Filippo Tomaso came to me, saying:
> "All right, I'm dead,
> But I don't want to go to Paradise, I want to continue to fight.
> I want your body, with which I could still make war."
> ("Annotated Translation" 9)

Pound's poetic persona, which may to a large extent be identified with his real biographical self in that particular historic moment, meets the recently dead Futurist impresario: unlike Eliot's passage, there are no recognition problems here, and the dialogue between the two poets begins at once, dealing with warlike activism and political propaganda.

To return to "Little Gidding" II, here are other similarities to Dante. Unable to recognize the ghost at first glance, Eliot strives to identify it, both through the sense of sight, by knitting his brows and winking his eyes:

> And as I fixed upon the down-turned face
> That pointed scrutiny with which we challenge
> The first-met stranger in the waning dusk
> I caught the sudden look of some dead master
> Whom I had known, forgotten, half recalled
> Both one and many; in the brown baked features
> The eyes of a familiar compound ghost
> Both intimate and unidentifiable. (*CPP* 193)

He goes on to interrogate the ghost after the surprised exclamation at the uncertain identification. Then, he almost splits into two roles and personalities:

> So I assumed a double part, and cried
> And heard another's voice cry: 'What! are *you* here?'
> Although we were not. I was still the same,
> Knowing myself yet being someone other—

Finally, he becomes more sure about the shade's identity after hearing its voice (which is also his own): "yet the words sufficed / To compel the recognition they preceded."

It is easy to notice the parallels between this passage and the meeting between Dante and his master Brunetto Latini in *Inferno* 15. However, there are other lines in the *Commedia* rarely if ever mentioned by Eliot's commentators. For example, as regards the theme of recognition through the eyes and the faces of the newly met spirits, here is a similar passage in *Inferno* describing the Usurers—Florentines and Paduans: "When I had set my eyes upon the faces / of some on whom that painful fire falls, / I recognized no one" (17.53-55). Dante also describes the act of deeply looking into the face: "But if you want to know who joins you so / against the Sienese, look hard at me / that way, my face can also answer rightly / and see that I'm the shade of that Capocchio…" (*Inferno* 29.133-137). Another Dantescan description is focused on the recognition through the voice: "when there!—a shade, his eyes deep in his head, / turned toward me, staring steadily; and then / he *cried* aloud: What grace is granted me! / I never would have recognized him by / his face; and yet his *voice* made plain to me / what his appearance had obliterated" (*Purgatorio* 23.40-45, my emphasis to stress the very same words employed by Eliot).

Since, as mentioned above, in Pound's Canto 72 the difficulties of recognition have already been solved, the poet is free to deal with the most urgent topics of the moment, that is politics and history. Both writers, the Italian Futurist and the American Modernist, are indignant for the defeat of Italian regime, and Marinetti, in perfect Futurist style, praises violent intervention and fighting (as quoted above: "All right, I'm dead, / But I don't want to go to Paradise, I want to continue to fight / want your body, with which I could still make war"). Then, in the language—and style—of Fascist rhetoric and propaganda, he prophesies revenge and the return of his faction: "Alamein! Alamein! / We will return / *We* will return!—" ("Annotated Translation" 11).[6]

The other major protagonist of this canto, the spirit of Ezzelino da Romano, joins Marinetti's bombastic delivery in his tirade against enemies of the Past (and of the Present), the Guelfs—and even this "intrusion" is highly Dantesque, resembling, as it does, various episodes in the *Comedy*, when Dante and his interlocutors are interrupted by other souls eager to speak to the pilgrim and tell him their story or their point of view. But let us consider Ezzelino's words:

> Guelf slander, their weapon always
> Was, and is, slander, from far back.
> The ancient war rages in Romagna,
> Excrement climbs as far as Bologna
> With rape and fire,

---

[6] Note how Pound, in the final repetition, also graphically reproduces the typical declamatory style of Mussolini, who used to slowly pronounce and articulate every syllable and every letter in his speeches to the "Italiani!"

...
So that the buried dust is troubled
Deep down, and stirs, and breathes,
And, in order to repel the foreigner, desires
To return to life
("Annotated Translation" 12)

The tyrannical and heretical Ezzelino, whom Dante met in *Inferno* 12, among the violent and the tyrants, following the general opinion of the historiographers of the Trecento, goes on to rails against the Papacy and the successors of St. Peter:

And all their gang
Worthy followers of Peter the denier,
Fattened with usury and excellent contracts!
("Annotated Translation" 13)

Dante himself, in his *Commedia*, had shown no special respect for several corrupt churchmen, Popes included.

Ezzelino finally attacks the so called "Donation of Constantine," in a passage which, from a formal point of view, is undeniably the best wrought and most Dantesque of all, especially as regards its style, rhythm, and music; Pound here composes perfect Italian tercets, and includes a felicitous pun on "Pietro" and "pietra" ("*Né Pietro pietra fu prima che Augusto*"):

if the emperor ever made that donation
Byzantium was the mother of confusion,
He made it without form and against law,
Dividing himself from himself and from the right:
Nor did ever Caesar break himself in pieces,
Nor was Peter a rock before Augustus
("Annotated Translation" 14)

According to the classic models mentioned above (especially Homer and Virgil), after the hero's ritual meeting and dialogue with the souls of the underworld, the latter necessarily must return to their shadowy realm. The two modernist poets, and before them their master Dante, all devise original but traditional scenes to portray such farewells from their guides.

To begin with Dante, the moment of Virgil's leave-taking occurs at the conclusion of the ascent to Mount Purgatorio (*Purgatorio* 27.126-142); the Latin poet takes leave of his pupil with a final memorable speech of praise, encouragement, and "valediction":

My son, you've seen the temporary fire

and the eternal fire; you have reached
the place past which my powers cannot see.
I've brought you here through intellect and art;
from now on, let your pleasure be your guide;
you're past the steep and past the narrow paths.
…
Await no further word or sign from me:
your will is free, erect, and whole to act
against that will would be to err: therefore
I *crown* and miter *you* over yourself. [my emphasis]

Then, he literally disappears, leaving the poet disoriented and weeping. In "Little Gidding" the ghost, after a brief Mallarmean remark on poetry as the means to refine ordinary speech ("Since our concern was speech, and speech impelled us / To purify the dialect of the tribe" (*CPP* 194)), goes to the heart of the matter, that is a particular kind of prediction about Eliot himself. But, unlike traditional expectations, a different kind of prophecy is in store for the contemporary pilgrim. For Eliot, modern(-ist) disciple of the classic and medieval Tradition, the revelation comes neither from a mythic seer (Tiresias to Odysseus), nor from an ancestor (Anchises with Aeneas, and Cacciaguida with Dante) as in the classical epics mentioned above, but from the "ghost" himself, who is also a double of the persona of the poet, as clearly indicated in the line describing the "dédoublement" of the protagonist, speaking and hearing his voice both as his own and as another's at the same time: "So I assumed a double part, and cried / And heard another's voice cry…" (*CPP* 193).

In this ironic re-writing of the classic topos, the revelation is not particularly exciting, on the contrary it is quite disappointing, in its threefold anti-climax perfectly catching, focusing and stressing increasing physical weaknesses:

First, the cold friction of expiring sense
Without enchantment, offering no promise
But bitter tastelessness of shadow fruit
As body and soul begin to fall asunder.

—then the emotional shortcomings:

Second, the conscious impotence of rage
At human folly, and the laceration
Of laughter at what ceases to amuse.

—and finally mercilessly exposing moral failures and mistakes verging on blind *hubris*:

And last, the rending pain of re-enactment
    Of all that you have done, and been; the shame
    Of motives late revealed, and the awareness
Of things ill done or done to others' harm
    Which once you took for exercise of virtue. (*CPP* 194-5)

Virgil's words to Dante, "I crown…you" (and, before him, St. Paul's letter to Timothy), [7] have become, in Eliot, "to set a crown upon your lifetime's effort," to bitterly and ironically conclude and seal one's lifelong (and almost vain) struggles.

However, a kind of prophecy is revealed in the final advice pointing out the way of expiation, the only atonement which can be obtained through the "purgatorial fire"—which is again mainly Dantesque, but also Yeatsian in the image of the dance amid the flames: "From wrong to wrong the exasperated spirit / Proceeds, unless restored by the refining fire / Where you must move in measure, like a dancer." Such a prophecy is not "epic" (heroic, glorious, genealogic) as in Homer and in Virgil, but "ethic," more similar to Dante's, centred on the personal and spiritual aspects and efforts of the Journey of Life: in this sense, the Dantescan meanings are unmistakably the "moral" and the "anagogical." Apropos of the Florentine, one cannot but recall another famous and unforgettable finale, that of *Purgatorio* 26:

El cominciò liberamente a dire:
    "Tan m'abellis vostre cortes deman,
    qu'ieu no me puesc ni voll a vos cobrire.
Ieu sui Arnaut, que plor e vau cantan ;
    consiros vei la passada folor,
    e vei jausen lo joi qu'esper, denan.
Ara vos prec, par aquella valor
    que vos guida al som de l'escalina,
    sovenha vos a temps de ma dolor!"
poi s'ascose nel foco che li affina. [my emphasis]

Arnaut Daniel's is another farewell in which a soul recognizes its own sins, and proclaims its eagerness to atone for them through the purifying fire—and Eliot never forgot that memorable episode. "After such knowledge" imparted to and bestowed upon the "hero," the ghost may finally disappear. Hamlet-like, he takes leave when it begins to dawn and when the all-clear is heard: "He left me with a kind of valediction, / And faded with the blowing of the horn" (*CPP* 195). The role of guide belongs

[7] See 2 Timothy 4:6-8.

now—Beatrice-like—to the late-medieval mystic Julian of Norwich, alluded to in the following sections (III and V), through brief quotations from her *Revelations of Divine Love*, which state and reassure on the positive conclusion of every human journey and of the whole course of earthly History.

Little by little, like his master and model Dante, the modern poet is being prepared for the ineffable heavenly vision of "the fire and the rose." For Eliot, the ritual "katabasis" implies also an "anabasis," thus mirroring Dante's own extraordinary experience. This double process, embracing Past and Present, the guide and the disciple, "the way down and the way up," has been described by a contemporary Italian Dante scholar with this felicitous formula: "from Virgil's old katabasis to Dante's new anagogy," in close semantic connection to the Medieval dictum on the four meanings and interpretative levels of Dante's work: "*Littera gesta docet, quid credes allegoria, Moralia quid agas, quo tendas anagogia.*"[8]

The leave-takings of Marinetti's and Ezzelino's spirits in Canto 72 are notably different. The former, after his final vindication, is silent: "And he seemed to have peace from my answer" ("Annotated Translation" 11) By contrast, the latter warns the poet: "Beware! Beware of me, until I return / In the night" (ibid. 15)—where in fact he does return, for good. The two shades offer no prophecy, no eternal or absolute truths, but only propaganda statements, destined to failure and to historical disproof.

Thus, in Pound's case, which guide replaces Marinetti and Ezzelino after their farewell? If we consider the next canto, 73, it is Guido Cavalcanti who appears and talks to his modern admirer: "I am Guido whom you loved" ("Annotated Translation" 16). But what—or who—after him? It seems that, for Pound, the infernal journey, the "katabasis," had to continue through *The Pisan Cantos* and the following sections (*Rock Drill* and *Thrones de los Cantares*), though tempered, from time to time, by glimpses of heavenly beatitude. On the one hand there is the recognition that a fragmentary Paradise is still possible: "Le Paradis n'est pas artificiel / but spezzato apparently / it exists only in fragments" (74/452); on the other hand the poet himself claims that he sought to re-create it: "and that I tried to make a paradiso / terrestre," and "I have tried to write Paradise /

---

[8] See Cozzoli 86, 70. The fourfold meaning is explained thus: Scripture has a *literal* meaning (what happened), an *allegorical*, or typical, meaning (what one should believe—this means how one should link a historical or Biblical event to another, to see/understand its significance), a *moral* meaning (what one is to do), and an *anagogical* meaning (what awaits one in the next life). Cf. Bell and Lerner 142-43.

Do not move / Let the wind speak / That is paradise" (from the second and third fragments for Canto 117).

However, if one reads and understands the fourth and final fragment for Canto 117 in its most secret (i.e., exoteric) significance, one realizes that Pound also has found his guides:

> Two mice and a moth my guides—
> To have heard the farfalla gasping
> as towards a bridge over worlds.
> That the kings meet in their island,
> where no food is after flight from the pole
> Milkweed their sustenance
> as to enter arcanum.

Perhaps it would be better to say that, in this instance, his guides have found and led him in the final journey.

After this discussion of the two most remarkable passages inspired in the two poets by Dante, let me conclude by lingering over Pound's and Eliot's own reflections on the Italian language and on Dante—first, Pound's "Letter to the Translator," originally published in Italian in October, 1930. In one of the most original passages of this brief essay, Pound writes:

> Italian is rich in opportunities, this new and effective hardness I long for, is not made up with stumps, but with *hard words hammered one against the other. Heritage is a forgotten resource*. The *light and the ironical points springing from a Latin meaning and the current meaning are not sufficiently exploited*.[9] [my emphasis]

Such theoretical statements and acute stylistic considerations will be clearly proved some fifteen years later in Canto 72 with its Dantesque archaisms: "vanitade" (for "vanità" = vanity); "sanza" (for "senza" = without); "combusta" (for "bruciata" = burnt).

In *Carta da Visita* (1942), in the paragraph entitled "Stile," Pound states that the "Ars poetica is divided into phanopoeia, melopoeia and logopoeia"; then, explaining what these characteristics consist in (as in the

---

[9] "L'italiano è pieno di germogli di opportunità, questa durezza nuova ed efficace che voglio, non si fa di mozziconi, ma si fa di parole dure, martellate, una contro l'altra. Risorsa negletta è l'eredità. Non si adopera abbastanza la luce e le punte ironiche che nascono fra significato latino e significato corrente." ("Lettera al Traduttore,"*L'Indice*, Oct. 12, 1930; *Opere Scelte* 1263-66)

famous Imagist Manifesto of 1913), he concludes with this judgment: "in the third Eliot is my superior, in the second I am superior to him." Once again, in the light of the exemplification from "Little Gidding" II and Canto 72, one cannot but agree.

As regards T. S. Eliot, we can not omit his definition of the criterion to evaluate good and bad poets, stated as early as 1920: "Immature poets imitate; mature poets steal; bad poets deface what they take, and good poets make it into something better, or at least something different" (*SE* 206).

Thirty years later, Eliot wrote a no less famous and revealing comment on the Dantescan inspiration and characteristics of "Little Gidding." He begins by introducing a parallel between his early attempts in *The Waste Land*, and his final one: "Twenty years after writing *The Waste Land*, I wrote, in "Little Gidding," a passage which is intended to be the nearest equivalent to a canto of the *Inferno* or the *Purgatorio*, in style as well as content." He then goes on to explain his intention of juxtaposition between the Past and the Present, represented by Dante and by himself, which had moved him, in order "to present to the mind of the reader a parallel, by means of contrast, between the Inferno and the Purgatorio, which Dante visited, and a hallucinated scene after an air-raid." With impeccable reasoning, in "What Dante Means to Me," Eliot also explains the difference between his own two poems (*The Waste Land* and *Four Quartets*), separated by two decades: "[b]ut the method is different: here I was debarred from quoting or adapting at length—I borrowed and adapted freely only a few phrases—because I was *imitating*." Finally, on the theme of imitation, he concludes with a personal consideration on the differences between his own mother tongue and Dante's (and contemporary) Italian: "My first problem was to find an approximation to the *terza rima* without rhyming. English is less copiously provided with rhyming words than Italian" (*TCC* 128).

As a matter of fact, a careful reader cannot help wondering whether Eliot was contradicting himself (in the light of his 1920 statement) or simply had changed his mind on the subject. Or, more ironically, if he was pulling the reader's leg, "playing Possum." Be that as it may, the poem speaks for itself, and stands as one of the most remarkable instances of successful re-creation from another poet and another language.

The two modern poets, in their most exacting confrontation with their master, resort to their own "peculiar genius": linguistic and musical—a genius for imagery, concepts and meanings (the four Dantescan "meanings"). Once again, in Eliot we acknowledge the profound tension towards that "higher dream" he had so much praised and admired in

Dante; in Pound, as always "*il miglior fabbro del parlar materno*" ("the better craftsman of speech," even though not "maternal," as is the case of Canto 72), we remark the masterly treatment of words, vocabulary, rhythms and cadence. As William Carlos Williams said about his friend Pound's unsurpassed musical skill: "It's the best damned ear ever born to listen to this language" (Carpenter 913).

The famous (and last and moving) homage the elderly Pound paid to his lifelong friend "Possum" on the occasion of his death ("His was the true Dantescan voice…"[10]) applies then to both men, since in these two memorable poems—if a final play on words be permitted—"They do Dante in different voices."

[10] Pound's tribute to Eliot (following his death) was printed in the Winter issue of the *Sewanee Review* in 1966 and reprinted later in Pound's *Selected Prose* (464).

CHAPTER TEN

TYPES OF ECSTASY—PARADISE REGAINED IN ELIOT AND AMERICAN MODERNISM

MASSIMO BACIGALUPO

DANTE, ACCORDING TO YEATS'S "Ego Dominus Tuus" (1919), is "the chief imagination of Christendom" (181). The model of the *Commedia* is ambitiously revisited by the Dante scholars among the Modernists, Ezra Pound and T. S. Eliot, who both published influential prose essays on Dante, and who went on to build into their poetic work the structure of a journey from *Inferno* to *Paradiso*. This is especially evident in Pound's *Cantos*, which has early on episodes imitative of *Inferno* and *Purgatorio*, and attempts to follow Dante in its overall structure. But also in Eliot there is a pattern from the *Inferno* epigraph at the opening of "The Love Song of J. Alfred Prufrock" to Dante's "rose" in the final line of *Little Gidding*. It is harder to spot Dante in that stubbornly original American, Wallace Stevens. But it has been claimed, by Glauco Cambon, that "Notes Toward a Supreme Fiction" with its tercets and thirty cantos in three sections, approaches an *Inferno-Purgatorio-Paradiso* structure, besides being Dantesque in its meter and numerology. Stevens also famously said that "The great poems of heaven and hell have been written and the great poem of the earth remains to be written" (*Necessary Angel* 142, qtd. Cambon 108). Though Wordsworth's *Prelude*, I submit, goes a long way towards being "the great poem of earth," Stevens thought of his work as "preliminary minutiae" to that consummation. We know that Dante was equally central to James Joyce and Samuel Beckett, and it has been suggested that after the Inferno of *Ulysses*, *Finnegans Wake* is very much a dream-world Purgatory, and perhaps James Joyce, had he lived, would have gone on to more Paradisal discoveries.

But Dante is perhaps more important to the American poet because the latter has imbibed the ideology of the Promised Land, the Peaceable Kingdom, so he is really "Running to Paradise" (the title of a witty Yeats ballad): he believes that a Paradise can be attained, or that it is his mission to find the way for himself and others. To him also the old images are more available than to a European. So Pound does not hesitate to write a modern parody of *Inferno* in cantos written around 1920 (and published 1925):

> Io venni in luogo d'ogni luce muto;
> The stench of wet coal, politicians
> ....e and .....n, their wrists bound to their ankles,
> Standing bare bum,
> Faces smeared on their rumps,
> wide eye on flat buttock,
> Bush hanging for beard,
> Addressing crowds through their arse-holes... (Canto 14)

I'm not sure that this is a fully adequate response to the horrors of World War I. The politicians (and journalists) were among those responsible for the war, and thus deserved hell, but Pound doesn't make the connection, or leaves it implicit. In any case, he is passing through one hell and is recording what it feels like to him, to the best of his knowledge.

We know that T. S. Eliot took Pound's hell seriously enough to object to it on moral grounds in his controversial *After Strange Gods*. He pointed out that this was "a Hell for the *other people*" (43), suggesting that a poet would do better to look within himself to find evil lurking. (As Eliot notably did in the *Poems* of 1920, among them the suppressed "Ode.") Pound could probably have answered that Dante's hell is also full of *other people*. This doesn't mean that his hell cantos are particularly successful, though on Pound's terms I suppose they are. They say what he thinks, and make no bones about appropriating *sic et simpliciter* Dante's voyage.

My claim is that this would be easier for an American poet, than for a European. It could be objected that in his sequence "Station Island" Seamus Heaney appropriates the Dante form of the poet travelling in a twilight underworld and meeting ghosts. But he has transferred it to an Irish setting and situation (the Lough Dergh pilgrimage). And besides, he has read Pound and Eliot, thus gaining assurance that imitating Dante is feasible.

An American early modernist of lesser statue whose connection with Dante has been obscured is Edgar Lee Masters. The *Spoon River Anthology* is usually said to be a reprise of the *Greek Anthology* with its epitaphs of people from all walks of life. Actually Masters's poems are not written in the form of epitaphs but as confessions from the other side of death in which the deceased tell the truth as they understand it about their lives—a truth often in contrast with conventional pieties. Thus it is more accurate to see Masters as following the model of Dante's encounter with the dead, who urge him to listen to their tale and remember them in the world of the living. So, for example, the ungainly "village poetess" Minerva Jones pleads:

> Will some one go to the village newspaper,
> And gather into a book the verses I wrote?—
> I thirsted so for love!
> I hungered so for life!

In similar fashion, in the *Inferno* Brunetto Latini urges Dante to "read my *Tesoro*"—the book in which he still lives. Another Spoon River character, Lucius Atherton, a lady's man who ended up as "a gray, untidy, / Toothless, discarded Don Juan," reports meeting Dante in person in the limbo he now inhabits:

> There is a mighty shade here who sings
> Of one named Beatrice;
> And I see now that the force that made him great
> Drove me to the dregs of life.

So Dante was as much of a model for the highbrow modernists as for the more demotic and democratic Masters. All these U.S. poets see nothing strange or presumptuous in invoking such comparisons. Europe is to them a new world to be newly discovered. Thus Eliot, that paragon of discretion, doesn't hesitate to print at the beginning of his first collection not one but two invocations of the eagle-eyed Florentine.

Eliot is no less bold than Pound in his appropriation of Dante's example. His pamphlet *Dante* was published in 1929, praising Dante's allegorical technique as leading (among other things) to "clear visual images," and stressing the bareness of Dante's language which he asserts is easier to understand and perhaps to translate than Shakespeare's, the sense of whose images "is more elusive, and...less possible to convey without close knowledge of the English language" (*SE* 244). But Eliot is also interested in Dante's content, and sets it against modern corruption. Speaking of the pageant at the close of *Purgatorio*, he says that "it belongs to the world of what I call the *high dream*, and the modern world seems capable only of the *low dream*" (*SE* 262). In an earlier passage, he had made explicit a moral implication of Dante's "*visual* imagination":

> We have nothing but dreams, and we have forgotten that seeing visions—a practice now relegated to the aberrant and uneducated—was once a more

> significant, interesting, and disciplined kind of dreaming. We take it for granted that our dreams spring from below: possibly the quality of our dreams suffers in consequence. (*SE* 243)

As in his discussion of the mythical method of *Ulysses*, Eliot is always asking himself, "What is there in this for me?" *Ulysses* led eventually to *The Waste Land*. The pamphlet *Dante* led directly to "Ash-Wednesday", which presents a series of visions in clear language: the "high dream." It is a work of *askesis*, reminiscent of Arnaut in *Purgatorio* and particularly of the episode of Matilda. Eliot writes:

> In the Earthly Paradise Dante encounters a lady named Matilda, whose identity need not at first bother us,
>
> *una donna soletta che si gia*
> *cantando ed iscegliendo fior da fiore,*
> *ond'era pinta tutta la sua via* (*SE* 261)

Section IV of "Ash-Wednesday", published in 1930, the year after *Dante*, begins:

> Who walked between the violet and the violet...
> Who walked between
> The various ranks of varied green... (*CPP* 64)

"Ash-Wednesday" is constructed as a series of allegorical dream visions (parts ii-v) framed by an introduction and conclusion in which the penitent in the middle of the journey of his life is introduced with words that echo a famous ballad of Guido Cavalcanti (also mentioned in passing in the *Dante* essay):

> Because I do not hope to turn again...
> ...
> Although I do not hope to turn again... (*CPP* 60, 66)

The theme of conversion which connects the *Dante* pamphlet and "Ash-Wednesday" is also to be found in another poem of 1930, "Marina," an homage to Shakespeare's *Pericles* in Dantean garb. Here Eliot offers a vision of reconciliation—Marina being a figure of love like Matilda and Beatrice—and of the peace that this new life brings:

> ...let me
> Resign my life for this life, my speech for that unspoken,
> The awakened, lips parted, the hope, the new ships. (*CPP* 73)

Eliot believed that with *Pericles,* as with the last cantos of *Purgatorio* and *Paradiso*, literature approaches the condition of ecstasy. He once claimed that "In reading *Pericles* I have a sense of a pervading smell of seaweed throughout" (Knight 490). It is likely that he shared these intimations with his friend Pound, for the Pisan cantos associate within a few lines Eliot, Thomas Lovell Beddoes and "the odour of eucalyptus or sea wrack" (Canto 80). "Marina" opens with the "scent of pine," and contains many words that smack of the sea, its trades and savors.

In "Marina" Eliot evokes the state of surrender to love and God, a dream which is also an intimation of Paradise. In *Dante* (*SE* 265) he quoted the passage about Glaucus becoming "sea-fellow of the other gods," a comparison introduced by Dante to explain his "transcendence of humanity" as he looks upon Beatrice. Pound also cited this passage in *The Spirit of Romance*, explaining: "Nowhere is the nature of the mystic ecstasy so well described [as] here" (141). Actually, Dante doesn't *describe* it, he only refers to Glaucus and his metamorphosis, though he provides that telling detail of "Glaucus tasting of the grass," which is so precise and suggestive. Was Dante aware of the consciousness-expanding properties of some plants? In his greenhorn days Pound even printed an "Ode to Nicotine," being after all an heir to the debauched Nineties. Pound also wrote a poem called "An Idyll for Glaucus," which he omitted from the authorized collection of his early work, *Personae* (1926). Eliot regretted the omission and, when editing the British *Selected Poems* of Pound (1928), reprinted it in an appendix.

The two friends had a shared enthusiasm for certain Dante passages, like Arnaut's soliloquy in Provençal, the Glaucus simile, and the Brunetto Latini episode. Glaucus had to do with a visionary content, the theme of ecstasy or transcendence, which runs through both poets. They were inclined in different ways to an equation of poetry and vision, and they both borrowed from Dante the means to describe these unusual mental states. "Marina" is an example, another is the vision of the mysterious presences in *Burnt Norton*, who seem to fill the empty pool with water and light. But Eliot's visual imagination is already evident in his first collection in "La figlia che piange," an ironic reworking of Rossetti's "The Blessed Damozel," which however manages to redeem the dream, to keep the vision, though it perplexes the modern narrator:

> Weave, weave the sunlight in your hair... (*CPP* 20)

The quasi-Italian title also suggests where Eliot is seeking a safer model than Rossetti (of which he spoke as a youthful love, followed by revulsion, in *Dante*).

Eliot is sensitive to the light which informs Dante's visions. He scatters through *Little Gidding* references to fire:

> The brief sun flames the ice, on pond and ditches,
> In windless cold that is the heart's heat,
> Reflecting in a watery mirror
> A glare that is blindness in the early afternoon.
> And glow more intense than blaze of branch, or brazier,
> Stirs the dumb spirit... (*CPP 138*)

Light is essential to the ecstatic experience. Eliot is as always cautious, while Pound is more declamatory and his enthusiasm can be repellent or infectious or both:

> The light has entered the cave. Io! Io!
> The light has gone down into the cave,
> Splendour on splendour!
> By prong have I entered these hills... (Canto 47)

Pound is here speaking as the potent king who impregnates Mother Earth in a sort of anti-*Waste Land*. Both passages echo Dante, Pound less distinctly, though this canto, written in the mid-1930s, is rich in imagery of birds and local Italian rituals that could be compared with Dante's similes and references to particular local practices (as in the finale of the Brunetto Latini episode).

Pound went on evoking glimpses of an earthly paradise, populating it with figures of his life and imagination. There is even a draft he wrote in Italian during the war in which Eliot is alluded to:

> i canti lieti e ragionar d'amore
> Qui Hylas, qui sono Ione e Flora e Alcmene
> Dione, Hylase e Clymene
> più più profondo ancora, Dirce
> pur del passato vostro son le ombre
> ma non le nuove
> e chi scrisse Felicity Taverner
> e quella di Lencour verrà ed Astrea
> e Verdenal aspetta il suo amico (*Canti postumi* 189)

[the joyful songs and the discourses of love, / Here is Hylas, here are Ione and Flora and Alcmene / Dione, Hylase and Clymene / yet deeper still, Dirce, / these are the shades from your past / the new ones are not / and the author of *Felicity Taverner* [Mary Butts], / and she of Lencour [Brigit Patmore] shall come and Astrea / and Verdenal awaits his friend]

Eliot had spoken of Jean Verdenal to Pound, and so Ezra decided to put him in this earthly paradise in the act of "awaiting his friend." It is worth pointing out that Pound went so far as to imitate Dante in his own language. He was never one to demur.

There is a famous passage in *The Pisan Cantos* of which one could perhaps say what Pound said of the Glaucus episode: "Nowhere is the nature of the mystic ecstasy so well described as here."

> Ed ascoltando al leggier mormorio
> there came new subtlety of eyes into my tent
> whether of spirit or hypostasis
> saw no entire face
> but what the blindfold hides
> or at carnival
> nor any pair showed anger
> but as unaware of their presence
> Saw but the eyes and stance between the eyes,
> colour, diastasis,
> careless or unaware it had not the
> whole tent's room
> nor was place for the full Eidos.
>
> but if each soul lives in its own space and these
> interpass and penetrate as lights not interfering
> casting but shade beyond the other lights
> — nor lose own forms
> sky's clear
> night's sea
> green of the mountain pool
> shone from the unmasked eyes in half-mask's space
> What thou lovest well remains,
> the rest is dross (*Canti postumi* 196-197)

This is an orchestration of elements out of Dante put to use to describe an objective experience, a "high dream" which actually occurs in Pound's tent. Compare Eliot's visitants in *Burnt Norton*, though here the description is much more detailed and Dantesque. Very effectively Pound's most famous line ("What thou lovest well remains") emerges from the vision, from the reassurance, the conversion, it has brought to "a man on whom the sun has gone down," as he calls himself earlier in the sequence.

Dante is essential to this modernist writing of ecstasy, and allows Eliot and Pound to deal with these very private and even "aberrant" situations in an authoritative poetic way. Eliot's meeting with his Brunetto Latini in *Little Gidding* is obviously not ecstatic but rather purgatorial.

Perhaps Eliot is as close as he gets to the ecstatic in "Marina" and "Ash-Wednesday".

Wallace Stevens pursued single-mindedly his vision, making it out of words that are incantations. An example is the long poem "The Rock," which circles around its central image, attempting to reconcile it with the ephemeral life of men and women; another example is the longer and forbidding "The Auroras of Autumn," which could be compared to Eliot's medieval "high dream." Pound speaks of "the medieval dream" in *ABC of Reading* (104), as well. A short late poem Stevens wrote for an Italian journal offers one of his versions of Paradise, and is freely Dantesque in the opening reference to Infernal regions. It is titled "The River of Rivers in Connecticut" and is about the universal life flowing through everything:

> There is a great river this side of Stygia,
> Before one comes to the first black cataracts
> And trees that lack the intelligence of trees.
>
> In that river, far this side of Stygia,
> The mere flowing of the water is a gayety,
> Flashing and flashing in the sun. On its banks,
>
> No shadow walks.... (*Collected Poems* 533)

The form is the Dantean tercet, and the situation is that of arrival, of Glaucus becoming a god after eating the grass. Like Dante, Stevens returns to us from his visionary trip to tell us what he has seen and still sees. And as in a riddle, we are challenged to understand his meaning. There is a background of nothingness and darkness towards which we are all drifting, but while we are "in this beautiful world of ours" (another Stevens phrase) we are in the midst of a universal current, and in some way deathless. The river of rivers is made only of things as they are, it is not an illusion. Men and women are to live in it fully. All the world is America, pervaded by a sense of dedication. Stevens is really addressing some of our fears and reassuring us with Dantesque authority. Like Pound and Eliot, he projects an image in which the mind can find fulfilment, an earthly paradise, an ecstatic vision.

Thus Eliot is far from alone among 20th-century U.S. poets in taking Dante as his model, and this gesture may be placed in the context of America's eclecticism and extraordinary ambition to "make it new." It is precisely because Dante and even Shakespeare are remote figures that the likes of Melville and Whitman can deal with them familiarly, through quotation, allusion and pastiche—even invite comparison. Whitman went so far as to count the lines in the *Divine Comedy* to see if *Leaves of Grass* was any longer, and therefore (I suppose) more substantial. Pound, in his last troubled annotations, felt no qualms about comparing *The Cantos* and the *Inferno*, not unfavorably: "many errors, / a little rightness, / to excuse his hell / and my paradiso" (Canto 116). In the late 20th century James Merrill was still writing a three-part poem of epic ambition, *The Changing Light at Sandover* (1982), consisting largely of colloquies with the dead, Yeats and Stevens among them. Likewise, Charles Wright published three trilogies that mix private experience with reflections (in true "metaphysical," i.e., Dantean, fashion) and homages to dead masters, but (even more than Merrill) was on the lookout for visionary (aesthetic) states based in the everyday, often in Italian settings. In a late poem he describes himself and his contemporaries as "Step-Children of Paradise":

> We live our lives like stars, unconstellated stars, just next to
> Great form and great structure,
> ungathered, uncalled upon. (*Negative Blue* 193)

Even Robert Frost, to return to the high modernist period, can be read in a Dantean light, for he has been "one acquainted with the night" and has "stopp[ed] by woods on a snowy evening," in fact he is a master explorer of Dante's *selva oscura*, in its modern (and changeless) guises. There is not much paradise in Frost, unless it be found in the intensely physical and mental experiences of mowing ("Mowing"), chopping wood ("Two Tramps in Mud Time"), subduing birches as a boy ("Birches"), or in the ironic gift of the chalice of knowledge offered at the end of the testamentary poem "Directive."

On the other hand, when summarizing for his father the subjects of *The Cantos*, Pound listed them as follows: "Live man goes down into the world of Dead... The 'repeat in history'... The 'magic moment' or moment of metamorphosis, *bust thru from quotidien into 'divine or permanent world.'* Gods, etc." (*Letters* 210, emphasis mine). There was clearly a need for transcendence, not so remotely connected with traditional religious training. Consequently, in *The Cantos* we "bust thru" again and again into the Empyrean, the great good place:

> Lay in soft grass by the cliff's edge
> with the sea 30 metres below this
> and at hand's span, at cubit's reach moving,
> the crystalline, as inverse of water
> clear over rock-bed... (Canto 76)

Also Eliot seeks this kind of physical and mental condition, of deep insight, and is willing to create incantations with words and sounds, like "Marina," to reach it. Stevens, finally, often approaches in his poems the condition of prayer:

> Repeating his name with its patient syllables,
> Never forgetting him that kept coming constantly so near.
> ("The World as Meditation," *Collected Poems* 521)

Like Penelope in this poem, Stevens uses repetitions of words and phrases, often oracular in import, as if slowly putting himself to sleep or entering a cocoon of sounds in which all desire is suspended or fulfilled. He spoke of the mind seeking through poetry, i.e., incantation, "what will suffice."

The state of mind evoked by these passages (and by Eliot's epiphanies in *Four Quartets*) may be compared to Wordsworth's description in "Tintern Abbey" of "that serene and blessed mood" in which "we see into the life of things." Pound, Eliot, and Stevens were, like Wordsworth, similarly influenced by Protestant Christianity. The difference, however, is in the means of describing these desirable moods: images of light and water, cultural allusions to other traditions (some of them oriental), exemplary figures, quotations. It is here that Dante's example is essential. He provides a different poetic access to the divine, or to "The Promised Land." The latter is the title of a chapter of Pound's *Guide to Kulchur*—its subject, predictably, Dante's *Paradiso* and how it is still there to be reached in life and art.

PART III:

ELIOT, DANTE, AND THE IDEA OF EUROPE

CHAPTER ELEVEN

DANTE AS GUIDE TO ELIOT'S COMPETING TRADITIONS

RANDY MALAMUD

> Tradition...cannot be inherited, and if you want it you must obtain it by great labour.
> —T. S. Eliot, "Tradition and the Individual Talent" (*SE* 14)

ELIOT'S POETRY INVITES a reader-response approach: first, by challenging the reader to hear, value, and even help establish a tradition amid what may at first seem a prevalent chaotic randomness (and thus devoid of traditional touchstones); and second, by inviting us to recognize a specific predecessor, Dante, as the poet who appears most resonantly, most centrally, in the pantheon of traditions and cultures that surround the reader who enters Eliot's world. Particularly in the case of *The Waste Land*, the reader who most clearly sees and hears Dante amid the cacophony of voices and songs in that poem and who chooses Dante as the guide through this terrain will be the better reader. A profusion of other allusions and myths are, more likely than not, red herrings—wrong choices. Especially in comparison to Shakespeare, we are prompted to venerate Dante's texts as the more useful artifacts of the poetic tradition that will facilitate the reader's task, which is, along with the poet, to shore fragments against the ruins.[1] Two of the key tropes in *The Waste Land*, water and music, offer numerous opportunities to appraise both Dante's and Shakespeare's efficacy in negotiating their own "waste lands." Eliot suggests that Shakespeare's praxis is less effective than Dante's in using these tropes to guide readers toward emergence from a cultural morass (that is, toward the coherent comforting stability that accompanies the discovery and integration of a cultural tradition).

---

[1] I have argued this point in an earlier essay. See "Shakespeare/Dante and Water/Music in *The Waste Land*." In *Time Present and Time Past: T. S. Eliot and Our Turning World*. Ed. Jewel Spears Brooker. Institute of United States Studies/University of London series, vol. 1. London: Macmillan, 2001. 100-112.

Finding water, for instance, is obviously consummately important in surviving Eliot's dry and dusty terrain, but Shakespearean resonances in *The Waste Land* depict characters who misuse or misappreciate water, such as Cleopatra, who foolishly urged Antony on to battle on the water, instead of land, where he belonged, and Ferdinand, who overvalued music—"This music crept by me upon the waters, / Allaying both their fury and my passion / With its sweet air" (*The Tempest* 1.2.392-4)—in the face of a watery storm that demanded a literal rather than an aesthetic response to ensure survival. Dante, on the other hand, by understanding and inculcating sympathy (through Count Ugolino's story from *Inferno* 33, reprised in *The Waste Land* 412-15), facilitates accuracy and control with respect to water: "*Damyata*: The boat responded / Gaily, to the hand expert with sail and oar / The sea was calm...beating obedient / To controlling hands" (*CPP* 49-50). In the first three parts of *The Waste Land*, Eliot undercuts Shakespearean contrivance and clever artificiality; having done that, he finally presents the poem's more effective water-music, what he called the water-dripping song—"Drip drop drip drop drop drop drop" (*CPP* 48)—in the strain of direct Dantean clarity.

Eliot wrote several critical essays about both Dante and Shakespeare. His extensive commentary about these writers, highly self-reflexive and self-conscious, illustrates how he wants us to hear, and use, and respond to their resonance throughout his own poetry. In deciding what we are going to do with the snatches of poetry and allusions we get from these writers, we are also engaging in an overarching methodological exercise that involves detecting various traditions, learning how to appreciate these traditions, and finding guides who will help us navigate these traditions. I will explore how the perception and appreciation of traditions plays out in Eliot's poetry, and how he uses the idea of the guide as a force of organization and revelation in his poetry.

Examples of Eliot's critical juxtapositions of Shakespeare and Dante abound. In *The Sacred Wood*, he writes, "If I ask myself...why I prefer the poetry of Dante to that of Shakespeare, I should have to say, because it seems to me to illustrate a saner attitude toward the mystery of life" (*SW* x). In "Shakespeare and the Stoicism of Seneca," Eliot argued, "none of the plays of Shakespeare has a 'meaning,' although it would be equally false to say that a play of Shakespeare is meaningless"; unlike Shakespeare, Dante "had one coherent system of thought behind him," and in Dante's time, "thought was orderly and strong and beautiful" (*SE 135-36*) In his 1929 essay "Dante," Eliot writes, "gradually we come to admit that Shakespeare understands a greater extent and variety of human life than Dante; but that Dante understands deeper degrees of degradation and higher degrees of exaltation" (*SE* 252). And even more simply: "Shakespeare gives the greatest *width* of human passion; Dante the greatest altitude and greatest depth" (*SE* 265).

These comparative assessments point toward an array of traditions that, Eliot believes, it is the poet's task to arrange, navigate, and adjudicate. Eliot's poetry embodies a plethora of different traditions, competing traditions (*competing* simply in the sense that they are nationally, or chronologically, or in some other way different and exclusive from each other)—for example, a European tradition, an American tradition, an Eastern tradition, a Christian tradition, an agnostic tradition, a philosophical tradition, a Victorian tradition, even a modernist tradition, and so on. Among all these competing traditions in Eliot's poetry, the readers are expected to enter that competition and pick one: align ourselves with a tradition that will seem most valid, most relevant, most effectively a stepping stone in the parade of traditions that leads from time past through time present and into time future.

For Eliot, the understanding and acknowledgment of a tradition apparently proceeds through binary opposition. Dante is played off against Shakespeare. Extrapolating from Eliot's essays quoted above, we might develop this Dante/Shakespeare contrast more elaborately, in terms of, for example, the keen, sharp serious sanity of Dante's poetic epic as opposed to the hectic frivolity, duplicity, and polyphony that Eliot sees infusing Shakespeare's epic drama; the pure courtly love of *La Vita Nuova* as compared with the barren sterility of Elizabeth and Leicester beating oars (an Eliotic commentary on the nature of love and romance at least generally referential to the Shakespearean tradition); and so on.

In examining Eliot's adaptation and transposition of Dante and the European tradition in his own poetry, I want to investigate what Dante means to Eliot; what Europe means to Eliot; and, how we may most clearly understand Eliot's European tradition. Dante's poetry for Eliot seems to be the apotheosis of a valuable, usable, cultural tradition. Dominic Manganiello explains that Eliot followed Dante's example of demonstrating his up-to-dateness, his own version of a *dolce stil nuovo*: revitalizing language, purifying the dialect of the tribe (2). Eliot wanted to emulate Dante's keen visual imagination and his poetic lucidity. In "What Dante Means to Me," Eliot called Dante "beyond all the other poets of our continent, the most European," and Manganiello writes that Eliot, "recalling the *De Monarchia*, [believed] that only out of Europe could a sense of world harmony proceed" (5).

Manganiello's assertion, while convincing, is nevertheless ironic, considering the condition of Europe during Eliot's lifetime—the chaos of the trenches, the shell-shocked soldiers and civilians, the ruined landscape, the no man's land, of the Great War; the sordid depravity after the wilderness of mirrors, *l'entre deux guerres*, that low dishonest decade of the 1930s; and finally, the blitzkrieg, the battle of London, the dark nightmare, the Holocaust of World War II. Perhaps it is precisely this irony that empowers Eliot's poetry and renders such exquisite tension and pathos—that is, the irony that Eliot clings to an idea of Europe as the source of harmony at the precise historical moment when it descends into the whirlpool of discord, turning and turning in the widening gyre. For example, consider the ironic contrast between J. Alfred Prufrock's obsession with his clothing, manners, and dignity, against the manifest display of his foundering haplessness. This illustrates Eliot's characterization of the tension between harmony and chaos. Or again, when Eliot counterpoises the Victorian stability Aunt Helen's household had once enjoyed against the disorderly lust in the poem's last lines, he highlights the ironic pathos in this tableau.

Thus we arrive at the lingering questions, "What does Europe mean to Eliot?" and "Is England part of Europe, in Eliot's opinion?" To answer the second question first, I think not. The tension of Dante vs. Shakespeare that runs through Eliot's poetry actually plays out, often, as Europe vs. England—implying, that is, that European and English cultures are mutually exclusive. How and why did this poet, who so devoutly transformed himself from an American into an Englishman in the 1910s and 1920s, work, seemingly paradoxically, to celebrate a European tradition in his poetry in a way that, frequently, pointedly excluded England?

Even years before he arrived in London Eliot was writing what looked pretty much like English—as opposed to American—poetry, ensconced in the voice, the temperament, the topoi, the aesthetic and history of what would become his adopted country; so where does this Anglophobia come from? What is it doing in Eliot's poetry?

In 1921 Eliot fled England after a holiday at Margate Sands failed to alleviate his psychological and emotional ailments, finding refuge and solace in continental Europe. So, too, his poetry enacts a recurrent dismissal of Englishness in favor of a European aesthetic that is more likely to salve the battered soul. Perhaps rather than an American or an English poet, Eliot is more of a European poet manqué who settled finally, by default, into the role of an English poet, but who retained a wistful devotion to the European tradition. Perhaps if he had been more in control of his life and the world, he would indeed have re-invented himself as a full-fledged European. Remember that in 1914 England was Eliot's plan B: he had hoped to emigrate to Marburg, Germany, but retreated to Oxford in the wake of the outbreak of the war. While his intellectual apprenticeship and development in England during the following years were crucial formative aspects of his experience, the recent work of Nancy Hargrove describes the profoundly important creative influence of his year in Paris, 1910-11.[2]

Eliot's 1927 conversion to Anglo-Catholicism typifies his ambiguous cultural/geographic positioning: it is a religious tradition that is in some ways more European than English, yet still nominally situated in England. The 1928 declaration in *For Lancelot Andrewes* where Eliot famously identified himself as "classicist in literature, royalist in politics, and Anglo-catholic in religion" may be interpreted as a bifurcated attempt to embrace both the English and European Christian traditions (the European out of passion, the English out of necessity). It was a fulcrum in the European-English agon that Eliot weathered for over a decade, which played out in the tensions of his personal life and the wrenched topoi of his poetry from this period, a poetic that alternately approaches and warily deflates the aesthetics of European classicism. Like Anglo-Catholicism, the other terms in Eliot's pithy autobiographical maxim—classicist and royalist—are comparably bifurcated as they relate to his English-European conflict; both *could* connect him culturally to England, but are more extensively the tropes of Europe, where there are more (and more powerful) royals, more (and more ancient) classics.

The years 1927-28 form a turning point in Eliot's cultural consciousness. The "Anglo" of "Anglo-Catholicism" situates Eliot in England, but he accepts the term perhaps with his fingers crossed, at least on one hand; his royalist devotion may be partly to King George V, though it would not be surprising if some extended as well to Spain's Alphonse XIII, Italy's Vittorio Emanuele III, and Belgium's Leopold III. And if Eliot meant to valorize, say, the classicism of Shakespeare, which certainly might have been a *part* of what he thought of when he identified himself as a classicist, still we must certainly see the larger element of his classicist canon as comprising Ovid, Seneca, Euripides, and Aeschylus.

From 1927 on, Eliot's English roots grew deeper: the "place poems" set in Burnt Norton, East Coker, and Little Gidding suggest a more comfortable acceptance of his Englishness; his increasing engagement in verse drama betokens a willingness to follow in the steps of Shakespeare, who seems to become a more credible guide for Eliot, displacing Dante, in the second half

---

[2] See Hargrove's "T. S. Eliot and the Parisian Theatre World, 1910-1911," *South Atlantic Review* 66.4 4 (Autumn, 2001): 1-44; "T. S. Eliot and Opera in Paris, 1910-1911," *Yeats Eliot Review* 21.3 (Fall 2004): 2-20; "T. S. Eliot's Year Abroad, 1910-1911: The Visual Arts," *South Atlantic Review* 71.1 (Winter 2006): 71-131.

of his life and career. Certainly the devastation of World War II solidified Eliot's resolve to come to terms with his immediate community in England.

So Eliot's European affinities, his European cravings, surface most strongly during the 1910s and early 1920s, and then diminishing (though still extant) from the late 1920s on. Perhaps, given that Eliot's early poetic is rooted in alienation, it makes sense that he is wary of the English tradition at the same time that he is planted in England, and so his poetry must strain for a foundation elsewhere—in the textuality of Europe, and Dante.

Eliot's Anglophobia (which is often dialectically opposed to his Europhilia) surfaces whenever Eliot juxtaposes the English and European traditions. For example, he points out in *The Waste Land* that Europeans don't tear down their churches. Eliot's endnote to l. 264 of *The Waste Land* ("The interior of St. Magnus Martyr is to my mind one of the finest among Wren's interiors" [*CPP* 53]), directs the reader to a book called *The Proposed Demolition of Nineteen City Churches*, the title of which suggests that the English insufficiently value their traditions. Eliot's prejudice shows elsewhere in *The Waste Land*, as in section two, where Lil's husband, a soldier in Europe, presumably brave, is reduced to "poor Albert" (*CPP* 41) when he comes home to England, to his drunken wife and his tattered marriage. The dedicatee of Eliot's first book, Jean Verdenal, was French, European—replete with a Dantean epigraph—while Viv, who was merely his wife and did *not* have a book dedicated to her, was English.

Eliot's prominently placed homage to Verdenal is brief but poignant, "mort aux Dardanelles." As throughout Eliot's poetry, we see in this dedication and the following epigraph from Dante ("*Or puoi quantitante comprender dell amor* ...") that poetic discourse specifically associated with the European tradition is resonantly eloquent—frequently, as here, precisely because of a direct association with Dante. Poetic discourse situated in a more explicitly English context, on the other hand, embodies the bleak, stinted banality we see in lines like Vivien Eliot's own direct contribution to *The Waste Land*—"What you get married for if you don't want children" (*CPP* 42)—and painfully deflating mannerliness, as typified in "Portrait of a Lady": "For everybody said so, all our friends, They were so sure our feelings would relate / so closely!..." (*CPP* 11)

The dreary, pedestrian details that are such a famous element of Eliot's aesthetic—"a slice of lemon, and a bitten macaroon"(*CPP* 18); "the damp souls of housemaids"(*CPP* 16); "newspapers from vacant lots"; "one-night cheap hotels / And sawdust restaurants with oyster shells" (*CPP* 3))—seem nearly always indicators of the English temperament, the English milieu. True, banality inhabits the European sphere as well—the "estaminet of Antwerp" (*CPP* 21) in "Gerontion," the rats on the Rialto in "Burbank with a

Baedeker: Bleistein with a Cigar" (*CPP* 24)—but it is the English poetic that is much more heavily littered with this strain, while it is possible to find more easily among the poesis that springs from Eliot's European tradition images and moments that are less inherently sullied, more potentially (you may say) beautiful, as in "La Figlia che Piange": "Lean on a garden urn—/ Weave, weave the sunlight in your hair" (*CPP* 20). Or in "Lune de Miel," "St. Apollinaire En Classe, basilique connue des amateurs / De chapitaux d'acanthe que tournoie le vent." (*CPP* 29)

Evidence of Eliot's Anglophobia recurs throughout his career: Eliot's poetical midwife, Ezra Pound, evacuated London for Europe. Sweeney is from the British isles. Aunt Helen dies, pointlessly, pathetically; but at the end of her poem, the Dresden (i.e., European) clock ticks on. Is Aunt Helen British or American? We might be inclined to regard her as technically American, as she is identified by the technically-American poet as a relative (like Cousin Nancy), but it is certainly easy to imagine her aristocratic household located in Sloane Square or Belgravia. An obvious but, I think, important point is that England and America share the same language, so there is a perhaps intentional blurriness as to whether a particular scene, character, or moment, in Eliot's poetry is culturally English or American. And given Eliot's rejection of America, this potential confusion is a damning one for England, which is tarred with the same brush.

When it's Europe vs. America, even more clearly than when it's Europe vs. England, Europe wins: Europeans read La Rochefoucauld, while Americans, merely, wearily, read the *Boston Evening Transcript*. Yes, both are trite, but the newspaper is more so.

As innocents abroad in Europe, the American and English characters—one might conflate the two by referring simply to the English-language-speakers—are inept and profane. In "Burbank," the English-speakers are boorish, saggy, lusterless...hapless against the backdrop of European elegance, even in its phthisic defunctive decline; Europe's worst tableau still outranks whatever that the Anglophone world has to offer. In "Lune de Miel," the honeymooners from Terre Haute, Indiana, slouching through Europe worrying about bugs and tips are another iteration of Americans who don't understand or appreciate the European tradition. And in "The Love Song of J. Alfred Prufrock," the English-speaking women talking of Michelangelo connote non-Europeans who are out of their depths when trying to broach the European tradition.

The traces of Eliot's competing traditions may be found often in the proper names of places that infuse the poems—New England, Richmond and Kew, Venice, East Coker, Athens, Alexandria, Vienna, London, Himavant. We see competing traditions in the sublimated places that are palimpsestically overwritten: Siena and Maremma; Lausanne; Cambridge, Massachusetts. And we see them in the transposition of places: the early poems that were written in Cambridge, yet seem like London streetscapes; the tableaux in the city of London that reiterate a Dantean landscape; an English garden in Munich; a classical, Mediterranean, European vista, profanely inhabited by, of all people, Sweeney erect.

We perceive the competing traditions that infuse Eliot's poetry as we confront the sense of internationalism throughout his oeuvre—polyglot cosmopolitanism run amok. It is an uneasy, unsettling clash of cultural traditions—for example, Hakagawa bowing among the Titians—where we are being asked, precisely, to unravel and make sense of this confusing fusion of cultures. It is a "Mélange Adultère de Tout"—an adulterous mixture of everything, as the title of one of the French lyrics from *Poems 1920* puts it. The wilderness of mirrors that is contemporary Europe puts us in a chaotic, surreal carnival fun-house and demands that, if we are to remain sane, we must figure out where we are and what enduring, orderly, bona fide European traditions can be salvaged from the dizzying incoherence that pervades the immediate moment of Eliot's poetry.

That dizziness leads us often to ask, when reading Eliot's poetry, where are we? What are the consequences of being in that place? Are we, indeed, closer to a sense of order and harmony if we are in Europe, or if we are heading for Europe, (as Eliot was in his trek from Margate to Lausanne), or if we are thinking about Europe (as, I believe, the gentleman caller in "Portrait of a Lady" is doing when he takes his refuge in the public park, admiring the monuments and drinking his Bock, his dark German beer), or if we are in some other way influenced by Europe, by a European painting (as in "La Figlia che Piange"), or by a European poem (as whenever we hear Dante)?

We may, in these European moments, be closer to what Manganiello calls "a sense of world harmony." Or perhaps I should couch that more tentatively: we may *seem* closer to that sense of order. But still, often, between the idea and the reality, between the emotion and the response, between the desire and the spasm, falls the shadow. We may seem to be closer to the harmonic order, but we may be deluded; or we may find that we experience no more than a Pisgah view of Palestine.

O quam te memorem virgo...: O maiden, by what name shall I know you? The Virgilian epigraph to "La Figlia che Piange" alludes to a stele that Eliot had been advised to see on a trip to Italy, but which he was unable to find. Eliot's poems recurrently present a pilgrim to Europe, a figure who craves to connect with the European tradition, but, for whatever reasons, amid the fragmented confusion of the modern age, may find himself unable to grasp it. This makes the European tradition all the more potent in the imagination, all the more tantalizing, if also all the more elusive and ultimately frustrating.

In "Portrait of a Lady," the gentleman caller's German beer, his little stein full of the European tradition that he imbibes for half an hour, does not redeem him, does not release him, from the English tradition. This scene on a December afternoon occurs at the end of Part I, and of course he must return to the English-speaking lady's drawing room and still endure Part II, in April, and Part III, in October.

How, then, can we know what awaits us, what may redeem us, in this glorious, tormenting European tradition? Certainly a guide would be helpful. The trope of the guide, so central to the structure of the *Commedia*, expresses a cultural tradition. When one visits a foreign country, one hopes to encounter good and reliable guides— knowledgeable local residents, curators, docents, lecturers, steeped in the cultural traditions of their homeland and eager to share this tradition; to dispel visitors' neophyte confusion at the dazzling culture and set them on the right path; to explain it, so that guests may integrate it into their own intellectual consciousness and take it back home with them, and somehow make their excursion a part of the experiences they will have in the future.

Dante is a guide through Eliot's literary landscape, just as Dante himself so importantly imagined earlier writers, Virgil and Statius, as guides through his own comparably complicated landscape in the *Commedia*. At the beginning of *The Waste Land*, it had seemed as if Chaucer might be the guide, but Eliot quickly deflates and discards *The Canterbury Tales* in the first sentence with a burst of unmitigated irony that disqualifies the fourteenth-century Englishman from leading us through the poem, encouraging us to choose instead the thirteenth-century European.

Dante of course honors Statius and Virgil consummately, and yet there are times when he damns them with faint praise, times when he knows better than them what's going on, because they are characters in *his* poem, in his universe, and also because he has had the advantage of living after them. He has social and spiritual insights, concerning, for example, the unique turpitude of Trecento Europe, that they never experienced. As important as his guides are foundationally, he transcends their poetics simply because he has come after them.

The same is true of Eliot with respect to Dante as guide. He trusts profoundly Dante's poetic, his craft, his voice, but Eliot retains the right to modify, to update, even to correct any oversights, or mistakes, that the spirit of Dante, the Dantean tradition, might harbor. When we (Eliot and his reader) follow Dante as guide through the modern iterations of Hell, purgatory, and heaven, we may confront complexities, choices, challenges, that Dante was unable to prepare us for. But finally, I believe—and I concede that this is a reductionist reading of a poet about whom it is certainly a great folly to be reductionist—that Eliot and his audience will find themselves best served by discovering, valuing, and reiterating the steps of the Dantean path that was set out in the *Commedia*: that is, by embracing the guidance of Dante. On this Dantean path, the world is organized into sharply-demarcated and morally-defined circles/pouches/terraces/spheres. Experience is colored with a distinct, exemplary visuality. The guide keeps the reader aligned with the proper spatial orientation (concern, metaphorically, with height and depth, rather than width, in Eliot's Dantean schema) as we proceed through the terrain of the poem. There is the pervasive sense of traversing a landscape, literal, allegorical, moral, anagogical, for a long pilgrimage, as opposed to traipsing around gaily and melodramatically spinning circles and spouting pithy soliloquies for an afternoon (as we would do if Shakespeare were our guide).

At the same time, though, paradoxically, we must see that Dante-as-guide, besides being an inspiration, a companion, a colleague, even a father-figure for Eliot, is also, importantly, a figuration of the other: the European other. Eliot the American, or Eliot the Englishman, may passionately aspire to follow or emulate his European guide, but may be fated to fail in this, as in his poems the European tradition so often proves elusive to the English-language consciousness. The scraps and shards of Dante in Eliot's poetry are, finally, just that: incomplete, inadequate.

Does the guide ultimately *give* us what he is showing us? Do we become (at least a little bit) Dantean, European, Florentine—or is the guide showing us something that is finally his and not ours, something that we experience for the length of the tour, the length of the epic, which then dissipates after the guide returns to his domain and the visitor, the reader, the tourist, departs? I think a conclusive answer to this important question of what Eliot expects and receives from his guide is elusive. The experience is different in different moments throughout Eliot's canon: sometimes the poet and reader succeed in gleaning and integrating what the guide has to offer, and at other times our own cultural limitations and the anti-cosmopolitan forces of the modernist zeitgeist inhibit us from tapping into the European tradition, shoring those fragments against our ruins. Though I feel unable to formulate a definitive thesis on the efficacy of the Eliotic guide, still, the question bears important consideration as we try to understand how Dante and the tradition of Europe resonate in Eliot's poetry.

CHAPTER TWELVE

T. S. ELIOT'S EUROPEAN TRADITION: THE ROLES OF DANTE ALIGHIERI AND MATTHEW ARNOLD

PAUL DOUGLASS

> That corpse you planted last year in your garden,
> Has it begun to sprout? Will it bloom this year?
> —T. S. Eliot, *The Waste Land* (*CPP* 39).

WHILE DANTE MAY BE FOUND blossoming under the gardener's watchful eye in almost every corner of T. S. Eliot's sacred wood, Matthew Arnold seems to be more of a weed. Eliot explicitly wished to root out certain principles of Arnold's critical works and sometimes also denigrated him as a poet. For example, in *The Use of Poetry and the Use of Criticism* Eliot characterizes Arnold's poetry as having "little technical interest" and denies Arnold's claim that "poetry is a criticism of life" (*UPUC* 105, 111). He accuses Arnold of other offenses, such as over-emphasizing feelings, neglecting the poem itself, and of having too little awareness of "the boredom, and the horror, and the glory" of life (*UPUC* 106). Eliot also rejected Arnold's suggestion that poetry could fill the cultural gap left by a receding religious faith. And yet Arnold also seemed to grow on Eliot, for Eliot also said that "Arnold is a poet to whom one readily returns" (*UPUC* 105), and Eliot's 1923 essay, "The Function of Criticism" echoes the title of Arnold's famous 1864 essay, "The Function of Criticism at the Present Time."[1] As late as 1933 Eliot wrote that "we are still in the Arnold period" of literary criticism (*UPUC* 129). And it appears that Eliot generally follows Arnold in thinking of criticism as seeking "to learn and propagate the best that is known and thought in the world" ("Function" 282), even if that project takes on a more severe tone in Eliot's hands.

[1] "The Function of Criticism at the Present Time" originally appeared in *The National Review* in November 1864.

Eliot also seems to follow his predecessor in believing that criticism should keep away from what Arnold called "the practical view of things" and follow "the law of its own nature, which is to be a free play of the mind on all subjects which it touches" ("Function" 270). He also apparently likes Arnold's notion that literature, like philosophy and science, tries "to see the object as in itself it really is" (ibid. 3). *The Sacred Wood* (1920) states unequivocally that, "Language in a healthy state presents the object, is so close to the object that the two are identified" (*SW* 149). Eliot carried the torch for this view into the mid-twentieth century, influencing the "New Criticism" as developed and propounded by John Crowe Ransom, R. P. Blackmur, Cleanth Brooks, and I. A. Richards. Perhaps it is the Arnoldian legacy in Eliot's criticism that gave him such an ambivalence toward its foundational importance in the New Criticism—particularly was this so in relation to Richards, whose intellect he admired. Yet Eliot distinctly disliked "the intense religious seriousness of Mr. Richards's attitude toward poetry" (*UPUC* 132), which he connected to Arnold. Arnold and Richards would seem to differ drastically on several key points, including their attitudes toward science. Richards divides history into 1) a 10,000 year epoch of human belief in a "magical [i.e., *religious*] view" of the universe, and 2) a brief recent emergence of the "scientific view" that characterizes rational evaluation of the cosmos (see chapter five of *Science and Poetry*).

Yet Richards also believed that science simply could not provide emotional satisfactions to humanity, however powerfully it might render the cold beauty of the universe. The "magical view" of the universe, which supplies answers to what he called "pseudo-questions," quickly coalesces with poetry itself in his discussion, so that, in a sense, Richards has "simply allowed poetry to assimilate religion," as Jerome Schiller explains it (124), and indeed his concept of science functions eerily like Arnold's in his theory of poetry. Science, he argues, offers us only a lifeless collocation of "facts" that answers little to the richness and the hunger for meaning that characterize emotional life. As Arnold wrote in "The Study of Poetry," "More and more mankind will discover that we have to turn to poetry to interpret life for us, to console us, to sustain us. Without poetry, our science will appear incomplete; and most of what now passes with us for religion and philosophy will be replaced by poetry" ("The Study of Poetry" 161-62). In the same vein, Richards uncouples religious dogma from its poetic expression in order to reify the latter as consolation. He follows Arnold in arguing, in the seventh chapter of *Practical Criticism* (1929), that modern readers "are little disturbed by even a direct opposition betweeen their own beliefs and the beliefs of [a] poet" like Dante

(*Practical Criticism* 271). And in *Science and Poetry* (1926), Richards quotes the opening paragraph of "The Study of Poetry" (a self-quotation of Arnold's): "The future of poetry is imense.... Our religion has materialised itself in the fact, in the supposed fact; it has attached its emotion to thje fact, and now the fact is failing it. But for poetry the idea is everything" (*see* epigraph to *Science and Poetry* and Arnold's "The Study of Poetry" 161). As Eliot asserted in *The Use of Poetry and the Use of Criticism*: "[W]hat [Richards] is trying to do is essentially the same as what Arnold wanted to do: to preserve emotions [of religious faith] without the beliefs with which their history has been involved. It would seem that Mr. Richards, on his own showing, is engaged in a rear-guard religious action" (134-35).

In asking poetry to "give religious and philosophic satisfaction, while deprecating philosophy and dogmatic religion," Arnold and Richards had "embrace[d] the shadow of a shade," according to Eliot. Arnold, he thought, "cared too much for civilisation, forgetting that Heaven and Earth shall pass away, and Mr. Arnold with them, and there is only one stay," by which Eliot apparently meant real—not recycled or renovated—religious faith (*UPUC* 118, 119). Eliot's rejection of Arnold's hope that poetry could compensate for loss of religious faith intensified in Eliot's later work, after he made his oft-discussed avowal in *For Lancelot Andrewes* (1928) of being an Anglo-Catholic in religion, a classicist in literature, and a royalist in politics. Many studies have shown, however, that Eliot had embraced conservative and reactionary beliefs much earlier in his career. For example, John Harrison's *The Reactionaries: A Study of the Anti-democratic Intelligentsia* (1966), a piece of 1960s academic radicalism, charted a course that William Chace would follow with *The Political Identities of Ezra Pound and T. S. Eliot* (1973), which is a carefully argued case for the reactionary tendency of modernism that set the trend for later criticism. Ronald Schuchard has also argued effectively that Eliot was deeply influenced by T. E. Hulme's reactionary cultural politics from about 1915.[2] Eliot's rejection of Arnold's positions on culture, anarchy, religion, and the role of poetry may be contextualized, then, as part of his more general rejection of modernity.

And yet, Arnold is not expelled from the garden. Far from it. Eliot's dismissal of Arnold as a School Inspector who was too concerned with "civilisation" and mistook poetry for communion must be further contextualized. Who, for example, among the English-speaking writers of

---

[2] See Schuchard's "Did Eliot Know Hulme? Final Answer," in the *Journal of Modern Literature* 27, no. 1/2, Modern Poets (Autumn, 2003): 63-69.

the twentieth-century, cared more than Eliot about culture, anarchy, and civilization? Who wrote more about the issues that obsessed Arnold? And who set a more intensely religious tone in his mature poetry, reaching for what Arnold described as an "accent of high seriousness, born of absolute sincerity…." (*Essays 2nd Series* 48, 184)? No—Eliot knew that he and Arnold were of one kidney. And that is perhaps the reason he instinctively sought to dispatch him in the first place.

But this he could only do if he followed Arnold's own path into the Sacred Wood. Remember that the title of *The Sacred Wood*, Eliot's first book of criticism, is drawn from Frazer's *The Golden Bough*, and that it refers to a myth in which the priesthood is secured through the murder of the incumbent priest. Eliot's attitude toward Arnold exhibits double-vision, the anticipation of Arnold's inevitable return in the very moment he is laid to rest. It is as if Eliot had already, in the act of burying Arnold as symbolic of the last century's mistaken faith in "progress," affirmed Arnold's permanence. It is as if Eliot had experienced what Harold Bloom defined (though referring to poets, not critics) as "*apophrades*, the dismal or unlucky days upon which the dead return to inhabit their former houses, [which] come to the very strongest poets, but with the very strongest there is a grand and final revisionary moment that purifies even this last influx" (141). Eliot's quest to supersede Arnold proceeds with full awareness of the continuities of their work.

For example, he follows his predecessor in believing that the future of criticism and literature will be *European*. Arnold wrote, "[T]he criticism I am really concerned with [...] regards Europe as being, for intellectual and spiritual purposes, one great confederation, bound to joint action and working to a common result; and whose members have, for their proper outfit, a knowledge of Greek, Roman, and Eastern antiquity, and of one another" ("Function" 284). Arnold assumes European ownership of the classical past through the physical and intellectual custody of its artifacts and texts, seemingly without regard to nations, but really from the perspective of the great powers of the eighteenth and nineteenth centuries, who took so much of "antiquity" by force: Germany, France, the Netherlands, England. A strong nationalistic impulse lies behind Arnold's statement, which goes on to say, "Special, local, and temporary advantages being put out of account, that modern nation will in the intellectual and spiritual sphere make most progress, which most thoroughly carries out this programme [of European cultural unity]" (ibid.). I shall return to this British chauvinism, which Eliot both adopted and decried, but suffice to say that Eliot shared Arnold's vision of European unity. He was contemplating his own transplantation to England in 1918, as well as the career of Henry James, when he wrote that, "It is the final perfection, the consummation of an American to become, not an Englishman, but a European" ("In Memory of Henry James" 2). Later, in a different context, he would argue, "We cannot understand any one European literature without knowing a good deal about the others" (*NTDC* 112). And, as John Xiros Cooper argues in the present volume, Eliot would come to think of himself as a European public intellectual and cultural figure.

In fact, Eliot took up Arnold's challenge to cultivate European unity. As Eliot knew, Arnold believed that the first truly European literature was Italian, and that Dante and Petrarch were the first "to strike the true and grand note, and to bring forth... classics" (Arnold, *Essays In Criticism, 2nd Series* 24, 172). As we know, Eliot repeatedly praised Dante as the best of poetic craftsmen, the most self-sacrificing of artists, and as a poet who was "certainly greater than Milton, and at least as great as Shakespeare" (*NTDC* 110), a view he already held in 1920, when he wrote to his friend R. C. Trevelyan, "Dante seems to me so immeasurably greater in every way [than Milton], even in the control of language, that I am often irritated by Milton's admirers" (*Letters* 426). Most importantly, For Eliot, as for Arnold, the "incontestable fact" is that "Dante is, beyond all poets of our continent, the most *European*" (*TCC* 134). Eliot had carried a little Italian edition of the *Divine Comedy* in his pocket starting in 1911, studying the Italian alongside the English prose translation (*SW* xi; *Letters* 338n; *TCC* 125).This was when he first enrolled as a graduate student at Harvard and began composing "Prufrock," which famously takes a passage from the *Inferno* as an epigraph and concludes in terza rima. I shall return to Arnold's and Eliot's views of Dante shortly. At this point, however, I wish to focus upon the fact that Eliot's choice of Dante as culture-hero was strategic, forming part his plan to follow Arnold—in a sense, to supplant him in the twentieth century, though also to join him ultimately as one of the indispensable critics of history.

Eliot was embarking on a career, and he chose his allies and affiliations consciously. As mentioned earlier, Schuchard pointed out long ago that his Oxford University extension course syllabus for winter 1916 asserts, "A classicist in art and literature will therefore be likely to adhere to a monarchical form of government, and to the Catholic Church" ("T. S. Eliot as an Extension Lecturer" 165). In short, Eliot was drawn both to the "Classics" personified in Dante, and to an idea of British culture personified in Arnold. Moreover, Eliot was deeply interested in the idea of a blooded aristocracy rather than a meritocracy. He was thinking hard about how to gain aristocratic credentials from at least the period of his marriage in 1915. In March of that year, he writes his cousin, Eleanor

Hinkley, "Do tell Aunt Susie that the Miss Rhyss' are the most charming persons I have met in Oxford—certainly the most aristocratic," and in a chatty tone he goes on to lament that "a cultivated aristocracy is sadly to seek even in England, but God knows it is far better here than in our Slater-ised society" (*Letters* 91-92). Samuel Slater was the English-born founder of the American cotton manufacturing industry. The desire to escape identification with such mercantile American transplants and be accepted in an aristocratic realm—even a debased one—seems to motivate Eliot as he differentiates, in this same letter, various Oxford and Cambridge acquaintances. He says he has met two Irishmen, who "rather raised my opinion of the race," and several Indians, whom he prefers to the English, though he reports that "Bertie" (Bertrand Russell) "says they give him the creeps." He ranks himself above the over-serious Cambridge and Oxford students, the best of whom he compares to "the clever Jew undergraduate mind at Harvard; wide but disorderly reading, intense but confused thinking, and utter absence of background and balance and proportion. I should expect it to be accompanied by a philistine aristocracy" (*Letters* 92). As a colonial returning to the seat of empire, Eliot adopted the prejudices as well as the tastes of his target class, perfectly illustrating Edward Said's observation that the colonial personality models itself on the imperial one (74). A further insight into Eliot's desire for acceptance in elite circles may be gleaned from a letter to his mother in 1920, in which Eliot described a meeting with American writer Maxwell Bodenheim: "I told him of my history here, and left him to consider whether an American Jew, of only a common school education and no university degree, with no money, no connections, and no social polish or experience, could make a living in London. Of course I did not say all this; but I made him see that getting recognized in English letters is like breaking open a safe" (*Letters* 392). Bodenheim returned to America. Eliot's simile, however, is an assessment of his own situation.

Eliot's desire to emulate the British upper class probably began in his Harvard graduate years, if not before. He had been made to feel, one thinks, how difficult the transformation from colonial to imperial would be. Bertrand Russell was his teacher in 1914, and he commented in a letter to Lady Ottoline Morrell that "One [of my students], named Eliot, is very well dressed and polished," but he "obviously has not been taught the minute thoroughness that we practise in England" (Russell 2:237). When he finally arrived in England, Eliot tried perhaps too hard to impress. When he visited Lady Ottoline Morrell in summer, 1916, he made his host ill at ease and put her off with "ostentatious learning" (Gordon 83). Aldous Huxley described him in 1916 as "just a Europeanized American, overwhelmingly cultured, talking about French literature in the most uninspired fashion imaginable" (ibid.). Eliot's awareness that he was himself a "safe-cracker" helps explain his reaction to Bodenheim in 1920. David Spurr observes, "The fear of being perceived as a philistine in upper-class English society may partly account for, though hardly excuses, the malevolent portrayal of Jews in Eliot's early poems" (273). Unfortunately, the anti-Semitism persisted. As Anthony Julius has said, Eliot was "civil to Jews he knew, offensive to those who merely knew him through his work," and in general wounded the sensibilities of his Jewish readers, who read his work with the sense of being "appalled, and impressed" (Julius 1, 40).

Eliot's adoption of British attitudes, as well as his ambition to break into British letters, certainly affected the role he assigned to Matthew Arnold in *The Sacred Wood* (1920), which is primarily a compendium of previously published essays and reviews, prefaced by a significant introduction.[3] The book has two epigraphs: one from Petronius' *Satyricon*, the other from Byron's "Italy versus England." The latter choice implies Eliot's preference for Italy. The former satirizes an old white-headed man of letters who believes himself a writer of "genius" simply because he has received the laurels of his generation—an obvious Arnoldian figure. Here is the passage, with the parts left out by Eliot in brackets

> *[But lo! while I am thus complaining to the winds of heaven,]* there entered the colonnade an old white-headed man, with a thought-worn face, that seemed to promise something mysterious and out of the common. Yet his dress was far from imposing, making it evident he belonged to the class of men of letters, so ill-looked upon by the rich. *[This man now came up to me, saying,]* "Sir! I am a poet, and I trust of no mean genius, if these crowns mean anything, which I admit unfair partiality often confers on unworthy recipients."[4]

---

[3] Eliot somewhat misleadingly acknowledges that "certain of these essays" had already appeared in various periodicals. In fact all but three of the seventeen had been printed earlier, and significant revision had been done on scarcely any. The new writing in the book consisted of the Introduction, three essays ("The American Critic," "The French Intelligence," and "Blake") and a new introductory passage on Paul Valéry for his "essay" on Dante, which is really just a book review.

[4] See Petronius' *Satyricon*, 63: [83] [Ecce autem, ego dum cum ventis litigo,] intravit pinacothecam senex canus, exercitati vultus et qui videretur nescio quid magnum promittere, sed cultu non proinde speciosus, ut facile appareret eum <ex> hac nota litterat<or>um esse, quos odisse divites solent... "Ego, inquit, poeta sum et, ut spero, non humillimi spiritus, si modo coronis aliquid credendum est, quas etiam ad imperitos deferre gratia solet..."

I have already suggested that the title of *The Sacred Wood* is a tip-off to Eliot's designs on Arnold, confirmed in the Introduction, which expresses Eliot's pleasure that he can finally "make amends" to Arnold, "whom [Eliot] has vaguely depreciated for some years." He first praises Arnold for condemning the Romantic poets as "empty of matter," "incoherent," and "wanting in completeness and variety" (*SW* xii). He then concedes that Arnold was engaged not so much "in establishing a criticism as in attacking the uncritical," and that he is not to be blamed for "wast[ing] his strength" in trying to address the problems of literacy and education in Britain rather than exercising his prodigious talents in proving, for example, that Stendhal is a more serious writer than Dickens (*SW* xiii). It seems as though Eliot has now whipped Arnold and put him in the corner. He confessed as much in a letter: "I am using Arnold a little as a stalking horse, or as a cloak of invisibility-respectability to protect me from the elderly. I wanted him as a scarecrow with a real gun under his arm" (*Letters* 406).

"A gun?" the reader may wonder. "What sort of gun?" I suggest one might think of it as loaded with ammunition intended for anyone with a modern slant on literature, for Eliot goes on to say, "It is part of the business of the critic to preserve tradition—where a good tradition exists. It is part of his business to see literature steadily and to see it whole; and this is eminently to see it *not* as consecrated by time, but to see it beyond time; to see the best work of our time and the best work of twenty-five hundred years ago with the same eyes" (*SW* xv-xvi). Here Eliot has made Arnold his ventriloquist's dummy, using his voice ("see [it] steadily and see it whole," an allusion to Arnold's poem, "To A Friend"). Eliot acknowledges as much by complaining that Arnold must be excused for giving the erroneous impression that the great writers are "canonical"—i.e., part of history—rather than masters who have transcended Time, a view that is supposed to contrast—one doesn't quite see how—with Eliot's own in "Tradition and the Individual Talent." What, after all, is Eliot's notion of an enduring pantheon of great poets, if not a version of Arnold's own idea that there are authors of "touchstone" works to which a reader must return in the quest for the truly excellent and *enduring* works of her own era. To this end, compare Eliot's idea that new work must be "judged by the standards of the past... [and] its fitting in is a test of its value—a test, it is true, which can only be slowly and cautiously applied, for we are none of us infallible judges of conformity" (*SE* 15) with Arnold's stipulation that one should "have always in one's mind lines and expressions of the great masters, and to apply them as a touchstone to other poetry" ("The Study of Poetry" 168). Even Eliot's idea of the escape from personality sought by the true poet, expressed in this early essay (*SE* 21), echoes Arnold's concession in "Resignation" that

> The poet, to whose mighty heart
> Heaven doth a quicker pulse impart
> ....
> Fate gave, what chance shall not control,
> His sad lucidity of soul. (*Poems* 96-97).

In the first essay of *The Sacred Wood*, "The Perfect Critic," Eliot, however, portrays Arnold not as a thinker in pursuit of a "clearer, deeper sense of the best in poetry" ("The Study of Poetry" 163), but rather as someone easily distracted by social and political problems: Arnold "was rather a propagandist for criticism than a critic," he says, and turns his attention to attacking emotionality in criticism and poetry.

Here, as in "Tradition and the Individual Talent," Eliot was laying down his notion of impersonality, "The end of the enjoyment of poetry is a pure contemplation," he writes, "from which all the accidents of personal emotion are removed; thus we aim to see the object as it really is and find a meaning for the words of Arnold" (*SW* 15). Why does Eliot pretend to stumble across a meaning for Arnold's famous phrase from the opening paragraph of "The Function of Criticism at the Present Time"? It appears that he wishes to put Arnold's name and works in play on many levels, and to make Arnold say something that is not quite his original meaning but suits Eliot's purposes. Arnold is deployed here as a poet who is also a critic. In a letter to *TLS* of 22 April 1920, Eliot asserted that "with one or two exceptions in remote antiquity, all the best criticism of poetry is the criticism of poets," mentioning Dryden, Coleridge and Arnold (*Letters* 380-81). He obviously proposes himself for that tradition, while distancing himself from Arnold's achievements in public critical debates. In the second essay in *The Sacred Wood* titled "Imperfect Critics," he praises Paul More and Irving Babbitt for having followed Arnold in studying French literature, because it brought them "much nearer to the European current" (*SW* 39). More and Babbitt—of whom Eliot later said that they were "the two *wisest* men that I have known" (qtd in Margolis, 144-5)—each made significant contributions to Eliot's thinking. He particularly admired Babbitt for having a greater ability "than any critic of equal authority in America or England to perceive Europe as a whole" (*SW* 42).

Eliot praises Paul More for a different reason, one that reminds us again how Arnold's name and works are being deployed in Eliot's arguments on different levels. More is important to Eliot because he has "pointed out... there is a vital weakens in Arnold's definition of criticism as 'the disinterested endeavour to know the best that is known and thought in the world, irrespectively of practice, politics, and everything of the kind'" (*SW* 42-43). What more has discovered, from Eliot's perspective, is that Arnold has confused a quality of the critic (namely "disinterestedness" with what ought to be a quality inherent in criticism. That makes Arnold, in Eliot's words, more "the Briton rather than the European" (*SW* 43). And so it goes throughout this essay, with Arnold praised on one hand as the only rival England can boast to the great French critics, a man of great intelligence, yet condemned on the other hand as having "lacked the active resistance which is necessary to keep a mind at its sharpest" (*SW* 45, 46). Arnold is apparently both indispensable and too "facile" and imprecise (*SW* 43). He comes to the aid of Eliot when he wishes to critique Swinburne, cuff the Romantics, or define poetic language (see *SW* 149); but Arnold serves as a negative example just as often—primarily as a foil for the collision between time and the timeless.

If Arnold's role in *The Sacred Wood* is ambivalent, Dante's is not. Whenever he is mentioned, he is praised as the apex of European classicism—Blake, by contrast, was a mere "genius" (*SW* 158), who created a perfect order of continually present "art emotions" (*SW* 57), admittedly "the most comprehensive, and the most *ordered* presentation of emotions that has ever been made" (*SW* 168). But genius cannot compete with an artist who epitomizes a culture's organism of thought, emotion, and doctrine. Dante is a sturdy tree of heaven in the sacred wood compared to Blake's impressive, but sprawling profusion of emotions. "More can be learned about how to write poetry from Dante," Eliot said, "than from any English poet" (*SE* 252).

But note once again that Arnold plays a significant positive role in Eliot's choice of Dante, for Arnold has already blazed the path of "touchstone" passages which was in a sense applied in the poetics of *The Waste Land* and then elaborated in Eliot's subsequent criticism, with special reverence for Dante's line from *Paradiso* 3.85: "In la sua voluntade e nostra pace" [In His will is our peace]. That line, which is quoted three times in Arnold's "The Study of Poetry" (169, 176, 184), is also quoted by Eliot in his 1927 essay "Shakespeare and the Stoicism of Seneca," and twice in his long 1929 essay "Dante" (*SE* 136, 265, 270). It also appears in English translation in the final lines of "Ash-Wednesday":

> Blessèd sister holy mother, spirit of the fountain, spirit of the garden,
> Suffer us not to mock ourselves with falsehood
> Teach us to care and not to care
> Teach us to sit still
> Even among these rocks,

Our peace in His will.... (*CPP* 67).

Dante's great line also echoes in his 1935 verse-drama *Murder in the Cathedral*'s first part, in the lines of the Tempter, who explains that acting and suffering are both "fixed"

In an eternal action, an eternal patience
To which all must consent that it may be willed
And which all must suffer that they may will it,
That the pattern may subsist, that the wheel may turn and still
Be forever still. (*CPP* 193)

Eliot sought for a modern expression of Dante's simplicity and profundity, the power of that touchstone line, which (to repeat the point) Arnold described as, "The accent of high seriousness, born of absolute sincerity...." (*Essays 2nd Series* 48, 184).

Having laid down his critical and artistic program in *The Sacred Wood*, Eliot had the extraordinary good fortune to publish *The Waste Land* in 1922, a turning point following the turmoil and crises of the first World War that saw events as disparate and as significant as the publication of James Joyce's *Ulysses* and the discovery of the tomb of King Tut. Eliot had immense talent, but his rise to become the most important English poet of the early twentieth century also involved this good luck, upon which he capitalized. In 1922 he not only published *The Waste Land*, but he founded the *Criterion*. He had bonded strongly with conservative British culture, and just a year later would describe himself as "an old-fashioned Tory," saying, "I am all for empires." He would also soon make use of his editorship of the *Criterion* to applaud T. E. Hulme's "classical, reactionary, and revolutionary" poetics as "the antipodes of the eclectic, tolerant, and democratic mind of the end of last century."[5] Did he mean Arnold, among others? if so, he must have known he was in some respects the reincarnation of that major mind of the previous century. Sounding altogether like a School Inspector he would write in 1925, "Neglect of Greek means for Europe a relapse into unconsciousness."[6]

In the end, Eliot articulated not only the mind of an epoch, in his poem seemingly about the disintegration of the British empire and the decline of the West, but also the nexus of British power in the triumvirate of church, letters, and state. *The Waste Land* derived its power from

[5] See the *Transatlantic Review* (Jan. 1924) and *Criterion* II (1924): 231.
[6] See the *Criterion* III (1925):341-44.

traditional literary forms: blank verse, terza rima, Chaucerian and heroic couplets juxtaposed in a jagged, non-linear structure studded with artifacts from the Indo-European Literary Tradition. Eliot had found the perfect expression of a modern aesthetic of wreckage. *The Waste Land* satirizes tarot-card readings, séances, and working-class pub-talk, and it also expresses a right-wing social perspective, with fears of deracination and corruption. The lynchpin of *The Waste Land* is the curse on the land. It is a poem imbued with a lucid Arnoldian pessimism of the kind delineated by Alan Grob in his study, *A Longing Like Despair*—a "metaphysical pessimism" which was already well-formed by the time Arnold had published "Resignation" in 1849 (Grob 75).

Like many whose education started with the New Criticism, I came later to wonder why Eliot's work had defined "literary modernity" as a recoil against the modern? Why not HD's modernism, which included classicism (but not Anglo-Catholicism or royalism)? Why not Gertrude Stein's? The surrealists'? Why, particularly, this version of modernity for America? Why not Williams's? Frost's? Stevens's? Moore's? The answer, apparently, is that Eliot propounded his point with compelling language and fierce loyalty to his cause, and others followed. Already by 1918 he had formulated the pattern of elitism in which he sought to take his place: "[T]he forces of deterioration are a large crawling mass, and the forces of development half a dozen men" ("Observations" 69). Already he had embraced the belief later expressed in "Little Gidding" that "History is now and England" (*CPP* 145). Already by 1920 he had turned the greatest critic of the previous century on his lathe, shaping him to his purposes. Already he had embraced the influence of Dante, the poet of the three levels of Catholic theology. I do not agree with Irish poet and critic Tom Paulin that Eliot's notion of tradition is "an artificial and polemical construct that... still weighs like a nightmare on English literary studies" (290). Admittedly, though, Eliot was craftier than he let on.

There is a saying that the wise man "knows where all the bodies are buried." And now I think I know where at least one may be found: Matthew Arnold's... in *The Sacred Wood*.

CHAPTER THIRTEEN

T. S. ELIOT'S *DIE EINHEIT DER EUROPÄISCHEN KULTUR* AND THE IDEA OF EUROPEAN UNION

JOHN XIROS COOPER

THE CRITICAL ATTENTION paid to T. S. Eliot exceeds that given to most other twentieth century literary figures. Every area of his life and work has had extensive commentary over the years, every area except one. The one exception is the period after his Nobel Prize in 1948 when he became one of the most celebrated authors of his time. These later years are often treated in a perfunctory manner.[1] The work produced, though good, did not, according to some, have the bite and savour of the previous four decades. After the publication of *Four Quartets* in 1944, Eliot turned his attention fully to verse drama. He met some contemporary success in the theatre with *The Cocktail Party*, but it's clear that he was no longer on the artistic cutting edge. By 1953, the literary situation had changed dramatically. In that year, Beckett's *En Attendant Godot* was the talk of Paris, London, and New York and not Eliot's *The Confidential Clerk*. After the war, his major literary work was largely in prose. Indeed, his Nobel Prize in 1948 was awarded for the publication of *Notes towards the Definition of Culture*, although it's clear the award was given to celebrate his whole career up to that point. But it is at that point that *critical* interest in Eliot begins to decline. The commonplace view is that his greatest work in poetry and criticism was behind him. And what lay ahead was a good deal of public acclaim, some mildly interesting work for the theatre, and a good deal of prose. Eliot, by 1948, had become a public personality, perhaps the

[1] It was not neglect that Eliot suffered in the post-war but a kind of reputational 're-positioning'. Eliot was not the only artist who, having achieved a great deal in the pre-war period, found him- or herself 're-positioned' after the war. "Until recently there has been little recognition that pre-war artists had post-war existence. Modernist survivors disliked their relegation, as Igor Stravinsky put it, "to an annex of the nineteenth century, and they did not, on the whole, admire what Stravinsky called 'post-contemporary' art" (Perl 343).

last time a poet and critic in our era has been able to achieve such wide approbation and respect.[2] He was featured in a nine page spread in the February 1, 1954, number of *Life* magazine (56-64). There he shared space with the latest news from the war in Indochina where the French were about to meet another Waterloo at Dien Bien Phu and a colour spread of swimwear for the upcoming summer resort season in "newly popular Puerto Rico." His public appearances were always events of importance and were usually standing room only. One might even think of him as the last Victorian sage, Matthew Arnold's twentieth-century successor. But the acclaim he achieved was not limited to Great Britain and America. He achieved in those later years a much wider reputation and indeed saw himself and, I believe, should be considered, as a European cultural figure.

The European dimension of Eliot's later career has not been sufficiently appreciated. He was, according to most, a two-nation author, either an American poet living in Britain or a British poet who hailed from America. What we have not fully appreciated was his position as a notable European, a persona he explicitly cultivated from quite an early period, and I mean the 1920s when he began editing the *Criterion* with the hope that it would become a periodical with a decidedly European perspective, "a vital conduit of European intellectual currents" (Harding 205). Indeed in later years when he came to talk about the *Criterion*, he was always careful to refer to it in those terms. That this was not an ambition comprehensively realized is not the point. The review aimed, as he recalled in 1946, at providing a place for the best thinking and writing from all European countries. Of course, it was to be an English language production, meant primarily for an English speaking readership, but it was not going to be narrowly provincial. Non-English contributions would, of necessity, be translated in order to facilitate the widest circulation of foreign ideas in the English-speaking world. It was, he wrote, "an ordinary English periodical, only of international scope" (*NTDC* 115). *The Criterion* was only one aspect of his international, and specifically European, perspective. A good deal of his prose writing after 1945 engaged with the wider dilemmas affecting Europe, a continent devastated by political extremism, war, and genocide.[3]

His critical prose in the later years of his life did not have the same or a similar impact on letters as his earlier critical interventions, but its

[2] Perhaps only Vaclav Havel and Alexander Solzhenitsyn have achieved similar standing in the West, but these are rather different cases.

[3] I have explored in more detail Eliot's reaction to the moral and ethical situation of Europe at the end of the Second World War in my 1996 book on *Four Quartets* (122-141).

importance in areas beyond the compass of literary criticism has not been sufficiently acknowledged. And it is precisely in its European context that the insufficiency is most evident. His sense of himself as a European came late. There was a European focus from the beginning, as his avid interest in certain French poets and in Dante makes clear. Dante especially became a key figure in his thinking about Europe after the Second World War. In his first engagement with the great Italian, Eliot concentrated on his work and its relevance to our time. Dante's period was one of the three great moments of 'metaphysical' poetry in the literary history of Europe, namely, the Trecento, the metaphysical poets in England in the late sixteenth and early seventeenth centuries, and the *symbolistes* in late nineteenth-century France. The post-1945 Dante was still a great poet, but Eliot had begun to understand him in a more extended role as an important cultural figure for the whole of Europe. He was most assuredly a Tuscan poet, but he was also a European poet. I will return to this post-war Dante later, but first let us consider briefly the place of Europe in Eliot's thinking.

When he first went to Europe during his so-called 'gap year' in 1910-11, he went as an American. Later when he resided in England, he visited the continent as an Anglo-American, often, more Anglo than American. But he never lost sight of the larger picture. It is there in the background of his work from when he first encountered the teaching of Irving Babbitt at Harvard and when he first read Arthur Symons on the symbolist movement in French literature. But before going any further let me put aside one misunderstanding that may arise around the topic of Eliot and Europe. I do not mean to rehearse what Eliot may or may not have meant by the phrase "the mind of Europe" in "Tradition and the Individual Talent." There he invoked something he called the "European tradition" and made the point that this collective "mind" was, as A. D. Moody has put it, "much more important than any writer's own private mind" ("The Mind of Europe" 13). This "mind," it seems, combined significant ingredients from a recipe of literary and philosophical ideas that when well cooked by an individual talent produced a dish of European savour. Eliot's youthful engagement with "Europe" was more or less a lovely fantasy, an idealizing of the influences he had acquired from his educational experiences and his reading. It was not primarily an engagement with a real, historical Europe. That would come later.

Space does not allow a comprehensive working through of those early encounters to the later evolution of his ideas of Europe and of European civilization and his own sense of belonging to the culture. It is a story that has not been fully told yet. And it is a story that is worth telling well. In this chapter, however, I want to focus on one particular episode in this story, an episode that I believe contributed to the political and cultural resurrection of Europe after 1945. I mean the three radio talks he broadcast to the Germans after the war, the talks that appeared first in German translation in 1946 and in English in 1948 as an Appendix to *Notes towards the Definition of Culture*. Their English title is "The Unity of European Culture." You will notice that in my chapter title I have used the term "Union" in reference to these broadcasts rather than "Unity." This is a deliberate move. Clearly the words "union" and "unity" are related, but they carry, I believe, two rather different implications. Unity suggests an ideal, an abstraction, a kind of Bradleyan idea of the Whole. Union, on the other hand, implies something more practical, something down to earth. It also invokes the new political order of Europe after the Treaty of Rome in 1957, first as "common market," then as a "community," and now as a union of nations working out the practical, i.e., institutional, implications of an evolving federation.

The three talks hold the two words, unity and union, in a silent balance. Eliot's sense of the *unity* of European culture is one thing, but these talks to the Germans address the practical problems of maintaining the *union* of European cultures. Before looking more closely at these texts, let me briefly sketch the relevant context. The idea of a unified or integrated Europe did not suddenly appear after the war. The idea goes back quite far, some might even say as far back as the founding of the Holy Roman Empire in the tenth century. The fact that this entity was neither Roman nor Holy, nor even an Empire emphasizes its notional character. That it begins with an actual historical event, the crowning in 962 CE of Otto the Great as King of the Romans, does not gainsay the Holy Roman Empire's luminous whimsicality. That the 'Empire' was also responsible for much, only too real, political and military conflict over the next several hundred years only shows how powerfully present even whimsy can be in the mind. Eight centuries after Otto, Napoleon Bonaparte brought another kind of socio-political definition to the concept of Europe as a whole, with post-Revolutionary France as its epicentre. This time, however, there was more than whimsy at work. As in the transformation of France itself during and after the Revolution, Napoleon's armies brought with them new juridical and socio-political institutions. These did not entirely disappear with the recession of French military power after Waterloo, or even after the Congress of Vienna had done its work of restoration. The idea of Europe and its embodiment in certain practical forms continued into our time.

More recently the conversation about European integration began in earnest in the period between the two world wars. It was placed on the political agenda by the French Prime Minister Aristide Briand in the late 1920s. He broached the topic in Madrid in June 1929 in a private conversation with Gustav Stresemann, the German leader, by referring to the need for creating a "kind of European federation" as a step towards the "final liquidation of the [Great] war" (Stirk 34-35). But serious agreement was impossible to reach in the aftermath of Versailles. The tensions among the Great Powers as a result of the inequities and perceived injustices visited on the Germans by the Allies could not be assuaged that easily. As long as these bitter resentments persisted, the idea of a federal Europe, as a French idea, was seen simply as a tactic for maintaining the Germans in their weakened position. The Kellog-Briand Pact of 1928 by which "the signatories renounced war as an instrument of state policy" was the only concrete achievement of the Briand initiative (Stirk 34). Subsequent events in Europe underlined the unreality of this 'achievement'. But this failure did not deter others from pursuing the idea of unity in socio-cultural and philosophical terms.

The search for European self-awareness animates Paul Valéry's *La Crise de l'Esprit* (1919), a work widely read and translated into every major language in the 1920s. This remarkable book, incidentally, reads like a prose commentary on *The Waste Land*, *avant le lettre* of course. Valéry wrote and lectured on this theme for the last years of his life. He gave his most important formulation of the idea of European unity in a speech at the university in Zurich in 1922 (Jarrety 532-533). Different elements of culture, Greek, Roman, Christian, the idea of individual responsibility, etc. had fused into what today we might call a European mind-set. Other authoritative voices took up the theme of a common culture, Hermann Keyserling, for example, in his good-natured and witty *Das Spektrum Europas* published in Heidelberg in 1928 (trans. also in 1928 as *Europe*) , or Ortega y Gasset's widely read *La Rebelión de las Masas* (1930; trans., 1932, and rpt. as *The Revolt of the Masses*, 1961) in which he speaks of individuals being "more influenced by what is European in us than by what is special to us as Frenchmen, Spaniards, and so on...four-fifths of the average European's spiritual wealth is the common property of Europe" (137).

The idea of Europe as possessing a common culture carried on into the war itself, in two competing formulations. One was German and it originated with the National Socialist idea of a unified Europe under the leadership of Germany. Unity could only be manifested if there were one hegemonic power. Here is Goebbels on this theme in 1943: "The aim of our struggle must be to create a unified Europe. Only the Germans can really organize Europe" (*Continental Plans* 12). Karl Megerle, the official in charge of information matters in the Reich Foreign Ministry, developed a number of talking points on "Europe" to guide media discussion about integration. The memorandum was written in the Autumn of 1941 and is particularly interesting because the National Socialist definition of Europe is almost entirely negative, posited in opposition to forces seen to be alien to Europe: certainly Bolshevism in the East was seen to be the principal enemy of not only Germany, but Europe as a whole. But, in addition to Russia, Britain and America are also named as alien threats to the 'new Europe'. Megerle writes as his first point that

> The unification of Europe, which was already showing itself to be an inevitable development in accordance with the iron laws of history, has been strengthened and accelerated as a result of the war imposed on Germany and Italy by the continent's old enemy, England.

His second point looks to the enemy in the East.

> The new Europe has received its baptism of fire on the Eastern battlefields: the new order has been consecrated by the testing of almost all European nations on the Eastern front against the common enemy of the West.

And, finally, in his eighth point, he looks beyond the Atlantic in the West to the new power rising in America.

> The alien invasion of Europe and the adulteration of its culture by aggressive Americanism will no longer be tolerated. Europe will belong to the Europeans alone, and its crowning glory will be to preserve and revive Western civilization. (*Continental Plans* 95)

This new order in Europe will be "protected," Megerle goes on to say, by Germany and Italy, who will regard this mission "as a solemn duty." This is only one of many documents in the German archives of the National Socialist period that take up the European theme. But what is striking about these German ideas of unification and integration is that they speak usually in political and cultural abstractions. Precious little is said about the economic unification of Europe except in one respect: the economic life of the new Europe would be under German control and, above all, serve German interests. That this vision of a unified Europe was little more than an ideological screen for naked aggression, occupation, and exploitation was lost on very few; even high-placed German officials could see that the European theme in National Socialist policy was, as

Ernest von Weizsäcker (State Secretary in the Foreign Ministry) noted in his diary on the 23rd of November 1941, "chiefly a matter of propaganda" (*Continental Plans* 98). On the 26th of October 1940 he was even more frank: "Ideological unity in Europe is confined to Germany, Italy, and Spain: attempts are being made to extend it further, but in fact it is only imported in the baggage-train of our armies" (98). So much for the National Socialist contribution to the discussion.

The other line on European integration came primarily from the resistance movements operating under German occupation during the war. Many of these pronouncements were little more than ideological wish-fulfilment. Take for example this extract from the "Theses on 10 April 1945" of the Trotskyist group in Vienna known as the Karl-Liebknecht-Bund: "The proletariat...directs its implacable revolutionary struggle against the Austrian bourgeoisie with the purpose...of creating an Austria of workers' councils...as a member of the United Socialist States of Europe, which can only be set up under the leadership of the Fourth International" (*Continental Plans* 213). Happily, many in the resistance movements across the continent were far more thoughtful than this. For one thing the physical reconstruction of Europe, and hence the need for economic co-operation, took precedence over political and ideological concerns. The mainly clandestine publications in which the matter of Europe's future was discussed emerged from the resistance movements in many countries and there is a rather large archive of materials available that make fascinating reading in light of subsequent developments on the road to integration: the European Coal and Steel Community in 1951, the Treaty of Rome in 1957, and more recently the founding of the European Union after Maastricht. Although the focus in the 1940s was understandably on creating economic institutions, the debate about politics and culture did not lag far behind. For example, several senior students of the *Lycée Henri IV* in Paris issued a crudely printed sheet entitled *Volontaires de la Liberté* of which 99 numbers were issued from June 1941 to August 1944. On October 8th, 1943 in bulletin number 63, the students sounded the larger theme in terms that came to be familiar in the next six decades.

> What Europe wants is not [only]...economic unity, ... but a cultural and moral community which must be transformed by the war into a political and social one.... Economic problems may play a part in European union, but not the most important one, and that union is not to be thought of as an instrument of Russian or German industry in opposition to American industry, but as the point of departure of a new political and social organization. (*Continental Plans* 319-20)

It is interesting to note that the term "European union," in its more contemporary sense, may have perhaps been used for the first time in this humble resistance broadside. The terms in which it is expressed suggest as much: the "cultural and moral community" needs a "new political and social organization" in the interests of advancing the prospect of "European union." Technocrats and politicians recognized that Europe would need to be rebuilt physically by concrete economic measures, not by invoking grand abstractions and idealizations. Correspondingly, cultural workers came to understand that an ensemble of concrete practises and institutions would create a tangible moral and cultural union as opposed to the weightless magnificence of fine-sounding ideals. What is different and progressive about the thinking of the *lycéens* is their distrust of the abstract and their focus on the particulars of union. It is a similar shift in thinking that marks Eliot's engagements with Europe after 1945. This pragmatic turn in Eliot has been little noticed, critics and scholars preferring to hold on to the idealizing tendencies of the younger Eliot. There may be a root idea or ideal of unity somewhere in the background, but the task in the post-war will need to be more bluntly practical.

Eliot's "The Unity of European Culture" was written in the immediate aftermath of the war and broadcast in English as three radio talks to Germany in early 1946. The German translation was issued as a pamphlet, *Die Einheit der Europäischen Kultur*, some months later. The talks and the pamphlet had a specific and concrete purpose. In 1945-46, Germany was prostrate. Divided, occupied, its major cities in ruins, its urban population barely able to feed itself and to find shelter, it lay mute, vulnerable, and desolate. Germany had achieved instead of the conquest and leadership of Europe, utter alienation from the larger homeland. Eliot's talks had three goals. One was to contribute to the Allied de-Nazification process that began soon after the end of the war. A second was to bring the Germans, especially the German intelligentsia, back into vital contact with, what Eliot had called in an earlier engagement, "the mind of Europe." And third, as Valéry had done in 1922, Ortega y Gasset in 1929, and the *Lycée Henri IV* students in 1943, to affirm the 80% of the culture of individual Europeans that is common to all of them. The third, and most important goal, was to liberate the discussion about European unity from both the damage down to it by the ideologues of right and left and from those who limited their thinking to economics. In this respect Eliot had more in common during the war with the *Lycée* students than with most others.

In his first broadcast, Eliot discusses the unity of European culture through a consideration of how language and poetry draw the nations of Europe into a common culture. English is offered as an example of language embodying a concrete cultural unity as opposed to a conceptual ideal. To the Germanic foundation, there was added a Scandinavian element after the Danish invasions. The Normans brought French influences and as a result, through them, Latin and Greek entered the cultural mix. These influences brought with them more than a few new words. New ideas, new manners, new kinds of sensibility entered the culture of England through these linguistic contacts. They modified the literary culture, especially the writing of poetry, and joined England to the European homeland, not as a vassal nation to Rome as in the past, but as a specific intersection in a network of European peoples drawn together by mutual contact. Halfway through this first broadcast, Eliot gives a concrete example. He talks of the importance of French poetry in the nineteenth century for all Europe, the poetry from Baudelaire to Valéry, and finds it best embodied in three exemplary twentieth-century Europeans, W. B. Yeats, Rainer Maria Rilke, and himself (*NTDC* 112). "And, so complicated are these literary influences," he writes, that "we must remember that this French movement itself owed a good deal to an American of Irish extraction: Edgar Allan Poe." This leads him to pronounce what he calls an "important truth about poetry in Europe."

> This is, that no one nation, no one language, would have achieved what it has, if the same art had not been cultivated in neighbouring countries and in different languages. We cannot understand any one European literature without knowing a good deal about the others. When we examine the history of poetry in Europe, we find a tissue of influences woven to and fro. There have been good poets who know no language but their own, but even they have been subject to influences taken in and disseminated by other writers among their own people. Now, the possibility of each literature renewing itself, proceeding to new creative activity, making new discoveries in the use of words, depends on two things. First, its ability to receive and assimilate influences from abroad. Second, its ability to go back and learn from its own sources. (*NTDC* 112-113)

He develops these two points by warning, firstly, of the negative effects on their work of poets being limited to reading literature only in their own language. His second point, he writes, requires particular emphasis. Every European literature brings together sources that are both peculiarly its own and sources which are shared in common; he names these as the literatures of Rome, Greece, and Israel. But these affirmations of continental mutuality must not lead to continental parochialism. Eliot acknowledges that the influences on his poetry went well beyond the physical and mental borders of Europe. He cites "the influence of Indian thought and sensibility" and believes permeable frontiers, more generally, can benefit the receiving culture. But history does make a difference. "Those countries which share the most history, are the most important to each other, with respect to their future literature" (*NTDC* 114).

Eliot's second broadcast moves from seeing the unity of European culture as illustrated by the arts, poetry in particular, to unity illustrated by the circulation of ideas. Here he invokes again his own practical experience as editor of a quarterly review in the period *entre deux guerres*. He emphasizes the importance for European culture of intellectual contact across national boundaries, He suggests that one of the best ways of assuring that this contact occurs at the highest intellectual level leads through the medium of the independent literary review. He lists a number of them, including two German ones, which during "the years of peace" made it possible to maintain the movement of ideas "while they were still fresh" across national boundaries (*NTDC* 116). Important as well is personal contact among the editors and regular contributors of cultural institutions such as the literary review; they should, he says, "be able to get to know each other personally, to visit each other, to entertain each other, and to exchange ideas in conversation" (*NTDC* 116). It is in passages such as this that the tension between 'unity' and 'union' is most evident. Recognition of the unity of European culture as an idea is one thing, but integration can only be realized through the union of actual institutions. The idea needs to be brought down to earth and realized both at the institutional level, the literary review for example, and over dinner as well. Eliot here brings together in vital tension the two sides of the discussion about European integration in the twentieth-century. Valéry, Keyserling, and Ortega had fleshed out the idea, but it is Eliot and the students of the *Lycée Henri IV* who show the way forward to how the idea is made real. Here is precisely the process in the domain of culture that paralleled what Europe's political leaders undertook in bringing about the European Union. Of course, they started with the production and circulation of coal and steel and moved on from there. Eliot's parable about the *Criterion* in his second broadcast does not end as a story of triumph but of defeat, attributable he says, "to the gradual closing of the mental frontiers of Europe" in the 1930s (*NTDC* 116).

Eliot's third broadcast enlarges the theme of the practical inter-relationships that characterize the history of Europe, relationships back and forth across the various nationalities and ethnicities. We should not underestimate the intellectual commerce among diverse European communities. To this web of associations and contacts one must acknowledge the fact of Christianity as a great unifying force in the culture, though like politics it has the power to divide and fracture community. But Christendom inherits more than religious faith: through Christianity the arts, for example, have evolved into secular pursuits without completely abandoning their earlier orientations as embodiments of mind, feeling, and spirit. Moreover, we cannot forget other common elements, standards of aesthetic evaluation, for example, or Roman law, the grounding of politics in ethics, and many other aspects of heritage from the ancient civilizations—Greece, Rome, and Israel—from which Europe traces its descent. After these generalities, the talk approaches, very carefully, the catastrophic moment in history in which it is being spoken. What I mean by this is that Eliot has stayed well clear of the fraught topic of politics up to this point. It was political blindness, the rise of political extremes in the 1920s and 1930s, and the weakness and corruption of the democracies that led to the abyss of war, genocide, and ruin. He contrasts cultural unity and political unity. Culture, he says, permits diversity and a multiplicity of unities, indeed on the cultural level Europe constitutes what we might call a *union of unities*. Politics, on the other hand, demands singularity and conformity.

> The unity of culture, in contrast to the unity of political organisation, does not require us all to have only one loyalty: it means that there will be a variety of loyalties. It is wrong that the only duty of the individual should be held to be towards the State; it is fantastic to hold that the supreme duty of every individual should be towards a Super-State.... We may hold very different political views: our common responsibility is to preserve our common culture uncontaminated by political influences. It is not a question of sentiment: it does not matter so much whether we like each other, or praise each other's writings. What matters is that we should recognise our relationship and mutual dependence upon each other. (*NTDC* 123-24)

He has said earlier in the third talk that we need to

> be clear about the distinction between the material organisation of Europe, and the spiritual organism of Europe. If the latter dies, then what you organise will not be Europe, but merely a mass of human beings speaking several different languages. And there will be no longer any justification for their continuing to speak different languages, for they will no longer have anything to say which cannot be said equally well in any language: they will, in short, have no longer anything to say in poetry. I have already affirmed that there can be no 'European' culture if the several countries are isolated from each other: I add now that there can be no European culture if these countries are reduced to identity. We need variety in unity: not the unity of organisation, but the unity of nature. (*NTDC* 119-20)

Here is the unity / union dichotomy restated in terms of, first, organisation and organism and at the end of the passage, organisation and nature. Now I realize that in cultural studies we have all been trained to spot the constructedness of terms like 'organic' and 'nature', but it should be clear that Eliot is using the terms here not to assert that culture is natural in the bad sense and politics is not, but that culture will have certain specific characteristics that are also found in the natural world, a multiplicity of forms and a (bio)diversity of expressive possibilities that politics does not usually have and if it has it, it's probably not politics but something else. At this point it would be useful to turn to the chapters in *Notes towards the Definition of Culture* in which Eliot discusses in more detail, and more generally, precisely this balance or tension of Unity and Diversity in a variety of areas: class, region, religion (as in Sect and Cult), culture and politics, and in education. They develop more fully the themes of the three broadcast talks to the Germans. In those chapters, Eliot argues for the recognition of local communities as a counterweight to the centripetal force of statist centralism. National or trans-regional political, economic, *and* cultural institutions are necessary but not at the expense of vigorous regionalism. A society's and, by extension, a continent's rich diversity of nations, regions, provinces, counties, and towns needs to persist in those historically rooted traditions of self-recognition, self-government, and difference for two reasons: as social and political forms resistant to statist totalitarianism and as potent links to cultural memory. The principle underlying the tension between nation and region, or the tension between classes, lies in established interdependencies of rights and obligations. These cannot be created or maintained by legislative measures alone. They are knit into the social fabric as threads or skeins of experience in the cultural memory of peoples. Lastly, it is necessary for societies to recognize civil and human rights not only as abstractions cloistered in constitutions and other legislative documents, but in practice, that is to say, as rights seriously exercised at every level of society. Finally, Eliot expands on the need to recognize that the frontiers between nations are not impervious or static, they are permeable and fluid. They allow for the historical contacts between nations that have characterised the history of Europe hitherto. In many ways this is the heart of Eliot's vision of post-war European unity. There can be no 'European' culture if the nations of Europe are isolated from each other. The forms of union must needs recognize the uniqueness of regions, classes, literatures, and faiths. There is no other way that a union can endure.

This may remind us of another talk given by Eliot after the war. It was given at the Italian Institute in London on July 4, 1950 on the topic of

"What Dante Means to Me." To the Germans he had talked briefly about certain literary figures who seemed to him to embody exactly the balance he has sought to maintain between unity and diversity or, from another angle, the tension between the idea as a union of local realities, that is to say, three figures who are deeply immersed in their local cultures but whose work also reaches out across the union of localities that make up the continent of Europe: Shakespeare, Goethe, and, of course, that "most *European*" (*TCC* 134) of poets, Dante. He ends the essay with these words:

> What I have been saying...is not irrelevant to the fact — for me it appears incontestable fact — that Dante is, beyond all other poets of our continent, the most *European*. He is the least provincial — and yet that statement must be immediately protected by saying that he did not become the 'least provincial' by ceasing to be local. No one is more local; ... (134-5)

Eliot concedes that there is much in Dante's work that requires an intimate, even native, knowledge of the Italian language. But a foreign reader "is less *aware*," he writes, "of any residuum that must for ever escape him, than any of us is in reading any other master of a language which is not our own" (135). Dante's Italian is in many ways "*our* language." Dante has much to teach us about the craft of poetry, poetic speech and what Eliot calls the "exploration of sensibility." These are models which anyone, no matter what their native tongue, can learn and take into his or her own poetic practice.

'No one is more local'. This praise of the particulars of place may remind us of an incisive formulation about language and politics in the fifth chapter of *Notes towards the Definition of Culture*. Eliot there writes about the virtues of a decentralised society, "in which the majority of problems were local problems on which local populations could form an opinion from their own experience and from conversation with their neighbours" (*NTDC* 87). This he feels, as does George Orwell in "Politics and the English Language," would tend to make political speech more concrete, and more clear, and be more difficult to misinterpret. "A local speech on a local issue is likely to be more intelligible than one addressed to a whole nation, and we observe," he adds, with an ear attuned to the windy cant of ideologists of all stripes in his time, "that the greatest muster of ambiguities and obscure generalities is usually to be found in speeches which are addressed to the whole world" (*NTDC* 87-88).

For a poet who has a reputation for being a philosophical idealist and universalist (think of the way Eliot's concept of tradition is read as an idealist construction), it may seem odd to hear Eliot recommending the particular and local, the diverse, the multiple and of seeing the matter of the unity of European culture in terms of the union of particular places brought together by the specifics of historical contacts, by well-defined inherited commonalities, and by the creation of practical institutions for the maintenance of the union. In this Eliot is in step with the most progressive and the most pragmatic thinking in post-war Europe.[4] There is a tradition in criticism of misreading or misinterpreting Eliot's thought, of turning him into a lofty, idealizing, pompous straw man. But it is thinking of the sort I've tried to make manifest that brings Eliot into line with the best thinking after the Second World War on the realities of creating, out of the abyss, a European community and, beyond that, a European Union.

[4] Compare Eliot's vision with one enunciated by the post-war Dutch federalist movement, Europeesche Actie, in their Hertenstein Programme in 1946: "Europe's mission does not lie only in the intellectual sphere; it lies just as much in the sphere where political and economic life is shaped. It is part of its very essence that one has to seek the wealth of diversity and to reject the overwhelming pressure in favour of uniformity…; that one rejects the postulate of a tyrannical community as much as one rejects the kind of abstract individualism which would like to release man from all communal ties. The political expression of this attitude is federalism" (quoted in Lipgens 1:23).

CHAPTER FOURTEEN

T. S. ELIOT AND DANTE: THE ANXIETY OF ROMANTIC CONTAMINATION

MAFRUHA MOHUA

MIDWAY INTO HIS 1926 CLARK LECTURES T. S. Eliot pauses to remind his audience, that he is "concerned with poetry, not with modern Europe and its progress or decline." Such a reminder, however, would not be felt to be necessary if Eliot himself had not been aware that his theory of the "disintegration of the [European] intellect," an avatar of the earlier and more famous theory of the "dissociation of sensibility," is as much a theory of the disintegration of European culture as it is of poetry (*VMP* 158). It becomes apparent, in the Clark Lectures, that between the period of Dante, who is seen to be the supreme metaphysical poet, and that of Donne, European sensibility suffered a sea-change by being "romanticized." Such a profound transformation led to a disintegration of the ontological, or classical, point of view of the medieval Europe of Dante, and brought about the psychological, or romantic, point of view of the post-medieval Europe of Donne and later poets. The difference between the ontological, or classical, and the psychological, or romantic, points of view marks the difference in the degree of sophistication of medieval Europe and its poets and of seventeenth century Europe and its poets. The superiority of Dante's poetry to that of Donne is, therefore, an indication of the superiority of the civilization of Europe during the Trecento compared to that of the *Seicento*. The term metaphysical, consequently, is used evaluatively not only in relation to the merits and demerits of poetry but also of the culture that facilitates the production of such poetry.

Although Eliot distinguishes metaphysical poets by their ability to present an image through the fusion of thought and emotion, this fusion, for him, is best exemplified by Dante and his contemporaries. There is a clarity and precision in Dante's imagery where "adjectives are chosen as they might be in a scientific treatise" (*VMP* 120-21). Dante's images are objective and impersonal, and therefore their suggestive power has the same effect on all readers. During the Renaissance, on the other hand, language, infused with the eccentric mental habits of the writer, loses its objective clarity. To clarify his point regarding the opacity of language during the Renaissance, Eliot cites an image from the sixteenth-century Martin Marprelate tracts where a certain Puritan says of Bishop Cooper that he "[h]as a face like old wainscot, and would lie as fast as a dog would trot." "It is meaningless," Eliot says, "to compare rapidity of lying to rapidity of dog's trotting" and furthermore, the image of the Bishop's face as that of an "old wainscot" is a "variable one," for it will suggest "different things" to different readers. In contrast to such images with variable suggestions, Dante's images are "exact and the same for everybody" (*VMP* 121-22).

What is curious about the above analogy is Eliot's choice of texts; that he should compare a thirteenth-century literary text with a bellicose text composed by sixteenth-century Puritans unhappy with Queen Elizabeth's inability to rid the Church of England of Catholic influences. This is not a fortuitous choice on Eliot's part, for there is a reason behind his use of a text of theological dissent to characterise the language of the Renaissance. Unlike the 1921 essay "The Metaphysical Poets," the Clark Lectures of 1926, a year before Eliot's conversion to Anglicanism, establish an explicit relationship between theology and metaphysical poetry. To contrast the opacity of an image from a sixteenth-century theological text with the clarity of Dante's image serves a useful purpose in Eliot's interpretation of the process of disintegration of metaphysical poetry, for the obscurity of Donne's images is, according to Eliot, an outcome of the theological battles that dominated post-medieval Europe. According to Eliot, both the ontological and psychological points of view, characterising Medieval and post-Medieval European sensibility, emanate from specific religio-philosophical systems which provide the metaphysical poet with a "schema of the universe," by which he tries to comprehend man's "part and place in the universe" (*VMP* 48). The disintegration of European culture, and its effect upon poetry, is therefore related to the disintegration of the European religio-philosophical system. The clarity of Dante's poetry, his ability to represent reality as an objective, communal entity, in other words, in an ontological manner, is, Eliot tells his audience, the product of a unified Roman Catholic Church which provided medieval Europe with a "*sensus communis*" within which disinterested enquiry was possible (*VMP* 78). The "architectonic" nature of Dante's poetry, with its straightforward development of ideas, is a manifestation of the orderly and rational organisation and structure of the medieval religio-philosophical system. The obscurity of Donne's poetry, on the other hand, emanating from various conflicting and not necessarily believed in, but merely entertained, systems of thought, is the consequence of the disintegration of the Roman Catholic Church and the rise of "Protestant schismatics" (*VMP* 75). Devoid of a *sensus communis*, post-medieval Europe was vulnerable to various contaminations, chief amongst which was Romanticism. In the course of the Clark Lectures, Eliot nominates several culprits responsible for the "romanticization" of European culture. If we were, however, to place the personages and events in this process of contamination in chronological order we would observe that the point of origin is St. Ignatius and the Society of Jesus. Jesuitism, for Eliot, marks the beginning of the disintegration of the Roman Catholic Church and, therefore, of Europe. And, not surprisingly, Donne's mind, Eliot tells his audience, was "infused with Jesuitism" (*VMP* 89).

Although the subsequent 1932 Turnbull Lectures, delivered in Johns Hopkins University, do not present a new interpretation of metaphysical poetry, Eliot introduces a reference to research on Dante by the Spanish scholar Miguel Asin Palacios and the English scholar Christopher Dawson:

> More recent and more scholarly writers—such as Señor Asin and Mr. Christopher Dawson—lead us to believe that this Dantesque conception of love is due ultimately to Arabic influences; but I am not here concerned with its origins. My point is merely that in the poetry of Dante and his group we do find a philosophical passion—not a passion for philosophy but an alteration of human passion by philosophy. (*VMP* 254)

Asin Palacios's book *Islam and the Divine Comedy* is perhaps the first serious study of Dante's relationship with the Arabic tradition of Europe. Palacios not only points to the presence of the work of the Arab philosopher Averroes behind Dante's *Divine Comedy*, he claims that the plot and the structure of the poem were borrowed from the popular Islamic text known as *Kitab al miraj*, *The Book of the Ladder*, which describes Muhammad's journey, under the guidance of the Archangel Gabriel, to hell and heaven. Although Palacios's claim that Dante was familiar with the classical Arabic text of the prophet's journey to the other world is highly unlikely, it is not improbable that Dante should have been familiar with the story of the prophet's miraculous travels through the numerous Latin and vernacular versions that were readily available in Italy. Since the English publication of Palacios's book in 1926, the year that the Clark Lectures were delivered, the perception of a Graeco-Christian Medieval Europe has been modified to accommodate a far from minor presence of an Arabic tradition that spread to Italy through Frederick II's court in

Sicily, and through the University of Bologna, where Dante studied, which was, as Maria Menocal says, "an intellectual hotbed of Averroism" (122).

Had the audience in Johns Hopkins University been familiar with Eliot's earlier Clark Lectures, they would have been perplexed and perhaps even amused by this reference to a possible Arabic influence on Dante, for this tangential reference to the presence of Arabic tradition in the work of the writer whom Eliot presents as the pre-eminent metaphysical, and the greatest European poet, seems to conflict with Eliot's interpretation of the poetry of Dante.

The passage just quoted, taken from the Turnbull Lectures, appears to imply that Dante's "conception of love" can be separated from its philosophical origin. Yet in the Clark Lectures Eliot never fails to remind his audience that there is a fundamental connection between Dante's conception of love and his philosophy. The expression of love as "contemplation of the beloved object" in the Italian poets of the Trecento is described as "Aristotelian" and "Platonic" (*VMP* 107). The representation of love as a struggle between the body and the soul by poets of the seventeenth century embodies, on the other hand, a "far cruder state of philosophical speculation" (114).

The philosophy of medieval theologians like Aquinas and Richard of St. Victor, whose religio-philosophical systems provided Dante with his "schema of the universe," and therefore, with his "conception of love," representing the ideals of order, reason and restraint, is, according to Eliot in the Clark lectures, in the direct line of the classical philosophical tradition of Europe. It is a tradition from which the Society of Jesus is explicitly excluded:

> [T]he Society of Jesus … has nothing to do with classicism, but is on the contrary, what I … would call Romantic … The fact that the Society of Jesus is of Spanish origin is an indication that it is outside of the Graeco-Roman classical tradition. There is plenty of evidence that its founder St. Ignatius was a romantic … There is some evidence, too, that he drew his inspiration, and the constitution of his order, not from Christian but from Mohammedan examples. Its principles are non-Aristotelian and are surprisingly like those of certain Moslem orders flourishing in Spain in Ignatius' time. (*VMP* 76)

The "psychologism" of Spanish mysticism, due no doubt to the non-Aristotelian tradition of the Arabs, is for Eliot a "spiritual haschisch, a drugging of the emotions" whereas the philosophy of Richard of St. Victor and Aquinas and Dante, whose "*origin* [italics mine] is in the *Metaphysics* of Aristotle 1072 and elsewhere, and in the *Nicomachean Ethics*," is an "intellectual preparation for spiritual contemplation" (*VMP* 106, 99). What becomes clear in the Clark Lectures is that the "ontologism" of the twelfth century, the "acceptance of one orderly system of thought and feeling [which] results in Dante and his friends, in a simple, direct and even austere manner of speech" (*VMP* 120), was, in the sixteenth century, destroyed by the "psychologism" of the Spanish mystics:

> I believe that Jesuitism was one of the most significant phenomena of Donne's time … and I tried to show that in Jesuitism the centre of philosophical interest is deflected from what it was for the Middle Ages, and that this marks an important alteration of human attitudes. (89)

The Society of Jesus is seen by Eliot as a factor in the "destruction of [European] civilisation" (158). The Spanish mystic St. Ignatius sowed the seeds of this process of destruction, in the form of romanticism:

> I wish to draw as sharply as possible the difference between this mysticism of Richard of St. Victor, which is the mysticism also of St. Aquinas and of Dante, and the mysticism of the Spaniards, which … is the mysticism of Crashaw and the Society of Jesus. The Aristotelian-Victorine-Dantesque mysticism is ontological; the Spanish mysticism is psychological. The first is what I call classical, the second romantic. (*VMP* 104)

Romanticism is, therefore, non-European, an alien import from Arabia via Al Andalus.

Eliot's interpretation of Dante as the supreme metaphysical poet, and therefore the supreme European poet, rests on his belief that Dante was the product of a sophisticated religio-philosophical system and that this system was the product of a unified Church: "For the Church was one; it was not occupied with polemic or defence against other churches. The systems of philosophy were hardly of a nature to inflame whole races to heresy" (*VMP* 77). The unified Church therefore produced a common philosophy from which, Eliot says, Dante derived not only his style of writing but his conception of love as well. With the ascendancy of "Protestant schismatics," the unity of the Roman Church was lost, which resulted in the disintegration of the common culture of medieval Europe, for the various factions of Protestantism were as Eliot says "identified with ... powerful nationalism" (*VMP* 75). Within this chaotic situation the church, concerned with combating heresy, could no longer provide the environment needed for the pursuit of objective truth. It is from this confused theological environment that, according to Eliot, Donne's poetry imbibed its "catabolic tendency" (*VMP* 76).

The medieval Church was, however, hardly as unified as Eliot leads his audience to believe. The papal approval in 1252 of the use of torture for religious disobedience following Innocent III's brutal crusade against the Albigenses cannot be described as the act of a church not disturbed by heresy and dissent. Eliot maintains that, once the "Albigensian heresy was done away with," the church was no longer "occupied with defence or polemic" (260). But during Dante's lifetime the Church was in constant conflict with the Albigenses. Furthermore the theological environment was not as unified as Eliot presents it. The system developed by Aquinas, which began to reconcile the philosophy of Aristotle with medieval Christian theology, did not always agree with Augustinianism, mainly represented by Franciscan thinkers who were determined to combat the growing influence of Aristotelian philosophy. Averroism, a movement led by Siger of Brabant and Boethius of Dacia, which took a radical Aristotelian approach to philosophical problems was deemed dangerous by the Church. In 1270 the ecclesiastical authority led by Bishop Stephen Tempier condemned Averroism and both Siger and Boethius were charged with heresy. In 1277 Bishop Tempier would also ban certain parts of Aristotle's *Physics.* Eliot's depiction of Aristotelian philosophy as being harmoniously fused with medieval theology is, therefore, a simplification of the church's ambivalent attitude towards Aristotle.

Eliot also fails to take into account that the Muslim presence which influenced St. Ignatius was even more prevalent during Aquinas's time. Arabic influence was not confined to Spain, the whole of Medieval Europe was infused with Arabic texts, myths, literature, and music. The philosophy of Avicenna and Averroes was as prevalent during Dante's lifetime as it was, later on, during Donne's. Both Aquinas and Dante grappled with the works of Avicenna and Averroes, at times accepting their ideas and at times rejecting them, but the intellectual reach of these Arab philosophers was such that it was impossible to ignore their works. Bologna, the university which Dante attended, was, as Maria Menocal says, "permeated with the revolutions of thought and learning produced by the preceding two centuries of contacts, translations, and absorptions of texts from al-Andalus and other sources of knowledge of Arabic texts, such as Sicily" (124). The philosophy of Aristotle, and particularly his *Nicomachean Ethics*, which was translated into Latin from an Arabic edition, and which Eliot cites as the source of twelfth century philosophy, was introduced to Dante's generation by the Arab philosopher Averroes. And although, as Menocal says, it was "horrifying" and "discouraging" for Dante to see the spread of Averroism in Bologna and the influence it had on many of the intellectual avant-garde of the period, especially on his close friend Guido Cavalcanti, Dante himself was not free of such influence (125). As Paul Cantor has pointed out "sometimes [Dante] speaks of Averroes approvingly and even cites him as an authority he accepts, sometimes he appears to be critical of Averroes, but even just to mention him by name was a daring act in Dante's day" (145). In his political treatise *De Monarchia*, copies of which were burned in 1329 on the order of Pope John XXII, Dante appears to accept Averroes's idea of the Possible Intellect. By presenting, in the Clark Lectures, Dante's intellectual background as existing wholly within the classical European tradition, therefore, Eliot opens himself to the accusation that he simplifies it. Dante's mind, in fact, though not infiltrated by, appears to have been fully exposed to elements of the chaotic. Unlike Donne's mind, however, which Eliot describes as "a mind of the trecento in disorder, capable of experiencing and setting down many super-sensuous feelings, only those feelings are of a mind in chaos, not a mind in order," Dante's mind never descends into disorder nor his poetry into obscurity (*VMP* 133).

It is indeed possible that in 1926 Eliot was unaware of the presence of a non-European tradition in Dante's work. His reluctance, however, to acknowledge the existence of an Arabic tradition in Medieval Europe, and his unwillingness to alter his Graeco-Christian perception of the Trecento in the Turnbull Lectures, displays a degree of anxiety of influence.[1] The medieval Europe represented in the Clark and Turnbull Lectures, where the hegemony of the Roman Catholic Church is portrayed as being absolute, appears to have undergone a form of cultural cleansing. Eliot's disapproval of the impact of Al Andalus on Europe and his disappointment with the Jesuits susceptibility to the influence of the Arabic tradition of Al Andalus, an influence which Eliot says can be discerned in the "Europe of 1914" (*VMP* 74), is, perhaps, expressive of an anxiety of the "Other" infiltrating the culture of Europe, and his need to filter out non-Graeco-Roman elements from the Trecento is a manifestation of the further need to possess an idea of an authentic and pure European culture uncontaminated by alien influences. If this is so, then there appears to be a hidden, or perhaps ulterior, agenda in Eliot's interpretation of metaphysical poetry. In praising the poetic style of Dante Eliot is endorsing more than the literature of the Trecento. Through his politics of reading Eliot is attempting to provide a definition of European identity circumscribed by the Roman Catholic Church. In presenting the second variation of metaphysical poetry, represented by the English poets of the seventeenth

[1] The T. S. Eliot collection in Houghton Library contains evidence that as early as 1915, in J. A. Smith's course on Logic, Eliot was introduced to the works of the Arab philosophers and their impact in medieval Europe. Professor Smith, in one of his lectures states that St. Aquinas was familiar with the works of Averroes and Avicenna.

century, as inferior to that of Dante's generation, Eliot is voicing more than literary disapproval—he is pointing to the supposed contribution of the poets of the seventeenth century, through an alien romantic contamination, to the destruction of European civilization. It is, therefore, to be expected that in the later Turnbull Lectures Eliot would not want to dwell on the Arabic origins of Dante's work, for it would undermine the argument of the Clark Lectures, where Eliot explicitly states that Dante's ability to transform thought into emotion, and emotion into thought, to present poetry as the perfect equivalent of a religio-philosophical system, is the natural result of the *origin* of Dante's ideas which, embodied within the philosophy of such medieval theologians as Aquinas and Richard of St. Victor, were in the "direct, classical Aristotelian tradition" (*VMP* 84).

CHAPTER FIFTEEN

OUR OWN FIELD OF ACTION: T. S. ELIOT, VERSE DRAMA, AND THE MIND OF EUROPE

PATRICK QUERY

T. S. ELIOT'S POETIC PERSONAE announce an arrival on the European scene with something more of a whimper than a bang. "The Love Song of J. Alfred Prufrock" finds a young man wading, one might say—the bottoms of his trousers rolled—at the edge of Europe's literary heritage: the epigraph from Dante's *Inferno*, the tentative references to Elizabethan drama, to Donne and Marvell, the exploratory inclusion of lines from Laforgue, and the women who "come and go / Talking of Michelangelo." But even these shallow waters end up drowning Prufrock in the end. Undaunted, Eliot dives in 1922 into the deep water: Ovid and the Old Testament, Shakespeare, Shackleton, Sappho, Spenser, and St. Augustine, Wagner, Webster, and Weston, Milton, Hesse, Day, and Dante again. *The Waste Land* is a poem thrashing about trying to keep its head above the surface while the roiling European waters batter and beat it, until it finally washes up on shore, dazed, moaning "Shantih...." Together, "Prufrock" and *The Waste Land* are the clearest early articulation of a theme that runs throughout Eliot's work: the desire to find a literary form capable of expressing what he called "the mind of Europe" (*SW* 51). The proposition that Europe is united by a common "mind" was in Eliot's time deeply fraught with contradictions, and each new shift in European relations argues afresh that such may forever be the case, particularly (as the present moment highlights in economic terms) when the proposition involves marrying up Europe's northern and balky southern traditions. It was audacious in the extreme for Eliot—no European by birth—not only to proclaim the possibility of such a marriage but to commit himself as a young man to its poetic realization. The later stages of his career in which he became officially ensconced in Europe—or at least in England—evince the same commitment to the European idea but with an increased feeling for the local and with a different literary emphasis: writing for the stage.

A. David Moody's essay "The Mind of Europe in T. S. Eliot" includes a fine articulation of the notion of Eliot's early poetry, specifically *The Waste Land*, depicting the mind of a young poet overwhelmed by a mind of Europe it cannot fully grasp. Moody limits his discussion of the ways Eliot dealt with this problem to Eliot's poetry and prose, whereas the question of Eliot's coming to terms with the mind of Europe requires going one step further: into the dramatic project that occupied Eliot's attention for the bulk of the interwar years and beyond. As is being increasingly well argued—by Randy Malamud, David Chinitz, and others—Eliot's work as a dramatist, which has long fit with comparative awkwardness into the critical picture of his career and legacy, merits a central, not a peripheral place in that picture: by virtue of its volume, to be sure, but also its relevance to understanding Eliot's complex relation to culture.[1] The dramatic work is further relevant for the light it sheds on Eliot's evolving engagement with the European question. Were "Prufrock" and *The Waste Land*, those two famous forays into European tradition, Eliot's last word on the subject of European cohesion, one might assume the futility of his search for a literature of European unity. As Moody acknowledges, they are not the last word, although they do represent the end of one phase of that search in Eliot's career. The next phase would see Eliot increasingly looking to verse drama as his medium and not to polymathic Europe but to the safe harbor of the local—England—as his primary point of reference. At first, these seem unusual choices—too narrow, too peripheral—for a writer in search of a coherent European identity, but the example of Dante begins to explain why, for Eliot, they may have been the best ones.

In his 1950 lecture "What Dante Means to Me," Eliot identified as one of the several kinds of poetic influence those "poets who have been at the back of one's mind, or perhaps consciously there, when one has had some particular problem to settle, for which something they have written suggests the method" (*TCC* 127). It is well known that Dante was consciously in Eliot's mind in trying to settle the problem of how to imagine a common European identity and, as evidenced in "Ash-Wednesday" and "Little Gidding," in addressing very acute challenges of imagery and versification. It also appears likely that Dante was one of those poets in the back of Eliot's mind as he worked towards a modern form of verse drama.

[1] See for example David Chinitz's *T. S. Eliot and the Cultural Divide* (2003).

In a famous line from his 1929 essay, Eliot wrote "Dante, none the less an Italian and a patriot, is first a European" (*SE* 239). Even that seemingly casual, straightforward assertion is loaded with the fundamental paradox of the European idea—unity in diversity—and, in the context of Eliot's later thought on language, culture, and European identity, it may be somewhat misleading. In an October 1937 *Criterion* "Commentary," he wrote that "I cannot think of art as either national or international...but as racial and local; and an art which is not representative of a particular people, but 'international,' or an art which does not represent a particular civilization, but only an abstract civilization-in-general, may lose its sources of vitality" (82). His own art being literature, he added that "it is obvious that the limitation of a particular language is the condition of a writer doing anything at all" (83). While by the 1950 essay Eliot was still insisting on Dante's Europeanness, he had shifted the emphasis of the earlier formulation somewhat, asserting that Dante "did not become the 'least provincial'" of European poets "by ceasing to be local. No one is more local" (*TCC* 135). Indeed, the emphasis on the local becomes so important to Eliot's thinking—about Dante and about Europe—as his career progresses that one could imagine him saying, instead of that "Dante, none the less an Italian and a patriot, is first a European," rather that Dante: "none the less a European...is first an Italian and a patriot." The desire to represent Europe as one coherent thing—to imagine its unity—began to take a backseat to the necessity and the advantage of representing an aspect of its diversity. As he continues to be influenced by Dante, Eliot begins to move farther and farther away from the ambitious but ultimately abortive European unions of his early poetry to the seemingly provincial sphere of domestic verse drama in English. Nothing is more local than Eliot's plays, and yet, to insist on the paradox once more, those plays represent his best stab at the European.

Eliot admired and was fascinated by the ability of Dante's mind and language to encompass virtually the whole mind of the West, an advantage not afforded proportionately to modern English poets like himself. In the 1929 essay, Eliot lamented that "in Dante's time Europe, with all its dissensions and dirtiness, was mentally more united than we can now conceive" (*SE* 240) and, further, that "Dante's advantages are not due to greater genius, but to the fact that he wrote when Europe was still more or less one" (*SE* 242). No matter at which historical point one begins to track Eliot's poetic evolution, such was simply not the case for him. The bold pronunciations about the coexistence of the literature of Europe in "Tradition and the Individual Talent" notwithstanding, and even with his own multilingualism, Eliot never was able to operate creatively from a position of European linguistic commonality, and he knew as much. The solution to how to write the European mind lie, paradoxically again but perhaps inevitably, in the territory of locality.

In attempting to think European, Eliot initially saw the condition of English particularity as a hindrance, or at least a limitation. "The language of each great English poet is his own language," he argued; "the language of Dante is the perfection of a common language" (213). What, then, are "Prufrock" and *The Waste Land* but a demonstration of his own impossible distance from that "common language" of the Dantean condition? Those poems' untranslatability (particularly that of *The Waste Land*) signals the inevitable provinciality, even in attempting to be supremely international, of a poetry that tries to squeeze the European universe into a ball and roll it towards the overwhelming question of unity in diversity. Where, then, was the poet to go?

In a 1932 "Commentary," still yearning for "that higher community which existed...throughout the middle ages," Eliot asked, "Would it not be better at present for each people to concentrate attention on what it can do at home?" (271). What Eliot could do at home was write poetry. More specifically, he could write poetry for the stage because the stage, he believed, was the best delivery system for poetry and the best means to instill the idea of a common language so key to his conception of a healthy and unified culture. Eliot's choice of poetic drama was related to his envisioned restoration of Europe's "higher community" in the way that writing a single poem is related to the condition of all poetry: a relationship the complex reciprocity of which no one has argued more memorably than Eliot.

In *The Use of Poetry and the Use of Criticism*, Eliot posited that "[E]very poet would like...to be able to think that he had some direct social utility.... He would like to convey the pleasures of poetry, not only to a larger audience, but to larger groups of people collectively; and the theatre is the best place in which to do it" (154). Whether or not every poet shares Eliot's hankering for the stage is less important than the idea, expressed in no uncertain terms in "The Social Function of Poetry" (1943), that poetry "makes a difference to the society as a whole...it makes a difference to the speech, to the sensibility, to the lives of all the members of a society, to all the members of the community, to the whole people, whether they read and enjoy poetry or not" and that the deterioration of language resulting from the absence of great poets invariably leads to the deterioration of culture (*OPP* 8-12). The more contact ordinary people have with the great poetry in their language, Eliot argued, the more direct will be the positive difference poetry can make in society; the theatre, by virtue not only of its larger audiences but by its necessarily intimate relationship with ordinary speech, has the greatest potential to affect the living language and thus the sensibility of a public. Ideally, poetic drama will "bring poetry into the world in which the audience lives and to which it returns when it leaves the theatre" (*OPP* 87). Rather than "transport the audience into some imaginary world totally unlike its own, an unreal world in which poetry is tolerated," poetic drama should do the opposite: transport poetry into the daily life of the audience, that their speech, their sensibility, and their local culture might be revitalized.

Eliot tried, through verse drama, to create a culture in which his own work could truly be "the perfection of a common language," by getting his audiences to recognize both their own speech and his verse as flourishing in the same hedgerow, as it were. Taking his poetry into the theatre signals Eliot's acknowledgement that he needed help in achieving the unified condition in which Dante's poetry thrived. Specifically, he needed something like what Malamud refers to as the communities that drama affords. Dante wrote in allegory, and, lucky for him, according to Eliot, "He not only thought in a way in which every man of his culture in the whole of Europe then thought, but he employed a method which was common and commonly understood throughout Europe.... [A]llegory was not a local Italian custom, but a universal European method" (203-05). The same could not be said of verse drama in the twentieth century, but then by Eliot's day the terms of the problem had changed. As he wrote in *East Coker* (1940), "There is only the fight to recover what has been lost / And found and lost again and again: and now, under conditions / That seem unpropitious" (*CPP* 128). For Eliot, there is little possibility of tapping into a common European pattern of thought, so the question becomes instead how to do the best one can at home, hoping that it serves the interests of the European whole, if only by delayed or unperceived connections.

Conveniently for Eliot, he believed that his adopted home of England provided the best purchase in the collective mind of Europe. In a wartime address to the Anglo-Swedish Society on "The Nature of Cultural Relations," he suggested that "London, as the capital of a country which has the Celtic world on its border from the south-west to the north, the Scandinavian to the east, the plattdeutsch to the south-east, and the Latin to the south, is suited to be one of the great *entrepôts* of culture for Europe" (15). In the postwar Berlin lecture, he gave his full, but diplomatic, support to the claim "that English, of all the languages of modern Europe, is the richest for the purposes of writing poetry" (*Christianity and Culture* 187). The primary reason for this richness is not any feature that isolates

English from other European languages, but rather "that it is a composite from so many different European sources," from Greek and Latin to Germanic, Anglo-Saxon, and Celtic (189). It is, in Eliot's view, precisely English's status as the repository of so much European linguistic history that privileges it as the vehicle for poetry. In its breadth and variety, English contains more of the mind of Europe than the more narrowly derived languages of the continent. Thus Eliot uses English, as in a line from *Murder in the Cathedral*, "That the pattern" of Europe "may subsist" in one of its particular manifestations (*CPP* 182).

How to use English most effectively was, of course, the great question of Eliot's life and one that acutely exercised him when it came to writing plays. Just as there is an observable trajectory in Eliot's poetry from the anxious linguistic maneuvering—in English and in other languages—in the early poems to the assured cadences and diction of *Four Quartets*, there is a trajectory in the evolution of Eliot's dramatic verse, one that entails increased balance between the appeal of local and contemporary speech and the European mind with all its riches over which the English language is a steward. This is the most cursory description of the evolution, but it hopefully helps to explain something of the direction Eliot's verse drama took from the avant-garde and intensely local linguistic experimentation of *Sweeney Agonistes*:

> There's no telephones
> There's no gramophones
> There's no motor cars
> No two-seaters, no six-seaters,
> ....
> I seen it in the papers
> You seen it in the papers
> They *dont* [sic] all get pinched in the end. (*CPP* 80-83)

to the weightier, more retrospective versification of *Murder in the Cathedral*, and then, gradually, to the increasingly transparent verse of his later plays from *The Family Reunion* onward.

To suggest this progress, a very brief example must suffice from *Murder in the Cathedral*, a play that represents a pivot on which Eliot's dramatic writing turns. The "literary" weight of much of the play's idiom is not merely, as was assumed early on, the result of a temperamental high seriousness attendant upon Eliot's newfound orthodoxy after his conversion to Anglicanism. It is the music produced by the strategic use of his native language's capacity to suggest order. The English language's richness subsists, according to Eliot, in its ability not only to assimilate new material, but to maintain the linguistic tradition behind "the mind of Europe." In "The Music of Poetry" (1942), he argues that the

> music of a word...arises from its relation first to the words immediately preceding and following it, and indefinitely to the rest of its context; and from another relation, that of its immediate meaning in that context to all the other meanings which it has had in other contexts, to its greater or less wealth of association. (*OPP* 25)

In this sense the lines of *Sweeney Agonistes* appear definitely impoverished, while it is clear from a glance at any page of *Murder in the Cathedral* that Eliot has selected a vocabulary with a far greater "wealth of association":

> Now is my way clear, now is the meaning plain:
> Temptation shall not come in this kind again.
> The last temptation is the greatest treason:
> To do the right deed for the wrong reason.
> The natural vigour in the venial sin
> Is the way in which our lives begin.
> Thirty years ago, I searched all the ways
> That lead to pleasure, advancement and praise.
> Delight in sense, in learning and in thought,
> Music and philosophy, curiosity,
> The purple bullfinch in the lilac tree,
> The tilt-yard skill, the strategy of chess,
> Love in the garden, singing to the instrument,
> Were all things equally desirable. (*CPP* 196)

Even this short passage is shot through with the accumulated signification of centuries. The word-group *temptation*, *sin*, *tree*, *garden* evokes the core myth of Western civilization. The litany of pursuits—*learning*, *music*, *philosophy*, nature, sport, *love*, even *chess*—speaks to the West's more earthly imagination of itself. Even the music of the line "The purple bullfinch in the lilac tree," balanced between soft Latinate adjectives (*purple*, *lilac*) and sturdy Anglo-Saxon nouns (*bullfinch*, *tree*), captures the rich order in diversity behind Europe and inside English. The language suggests how much respect Eliot accords the English language's cultural inheritance, on the level of rhythm, tone, and the individual word.

Of course, Eliot never wrote another play like *Murder in the Cathedral*. *The Family Reunion*, first performed in 1939, boasts some similarly weighty verse, but it also begins to indicate his dissatisfaction with a language so far from that of *Sweeney* as to miss much of the utility of the everyday. *The Cocktail Party* (1949) and each subsequent play, while continuing in the direction of everyday speech for the verse, do retain the foundation established at the outset of Eliot's dramatic career of a local English scene and recognizably English characters. One feels, it is true, a long way in reading *The Confidential Clerk* and *The Elder Statesman* from any very broad idea of Europe. At the same time, the last plays are about the difficulties of identity, coming to terms with what appearance contains and conceals, and the ways in which shared memory creates subtle unities. Their immediate subjects and forms are emphatically local, but they tantalize with the suggestion of unseen bonds of commonality.

Eliot's dramatic ideas and his idea of Europe were inseparable. The relationship is necessarily more deliberate, more arduously sustained than in the case of Dante and allegory, but the example of Dante is nonetheless present, suggesting how a poet goes about being European by being local in the richest, most purposeful way. For Eliot, Europe, like history, is "now and England" (*CPP* 145). Unity in diversity is the characteristic European ideal and problem, but in Eliot's mature work he was able to see it more precisely in the dynamics of the local, writing, for example, in *Little Gidding*, that

> ...love of a country
> Begins as attachment to our own field of action. (*CPP* 142)

For Eliot, the love of Europe, the idea of Europe, arrives at rather than begins as the love of one's own field of action, one's country. He was convinced equally of Europe's inherent unity and of the fact that only by poetry's work in nourishing local language could local culture be preserved. Therefore, he could set about writing poetic plays in his native language, confident that that language contained more than any other of the mind of Europe, and that in his service to his own language, he was doing all that one might for European culture.

CHAPTER SIXTEEN

"*DANTE, E POI DANTE*": T. S. ELIOT, WENDELL BERRY AND "EUROPE'S EPIC"

DOMINIC MANGANIELLO

AFTER SEVEN CENTURIES Dante remains a luminous presence, a catalyst of literary renewal. The warm reception accorded the *Commedia*, from its first appearance down to the present, has made him very much the lionized author. "Dante-mania"[1] particularly infected canonical modernists such as Pound and Joyce, who referred to the medieval masterpiece as "Europe's epic" (Gorman 74). Chief among these writers was T. S. Eliot, who, when asked about his favorite period in Italian literature, replied, "Dante, and then Dante, and then Dante" (Manganiello 1). The Florentine master, he believed, remained the "least provincial" and "most European" of poets (*TCC* 134-5). That the moderns rekindled their interest in Dante in the process of "making it new" should come as no surprise. No poet has been so fascinated with every nuance of innovation, from the title of his early *Vita Nuova* to the triple use of the word "new" at the end of the *Purgatorio,* where Dante likens his spiritual rejuvenation to new trees sprouting new foliage.[2] This accentuation of what Hans Robert Jauss (184)

---

[1] Dorothy L. Sayers described herself as being in "the grip of Dante-mania" in her correspondence with Charles Williams (*Letters* 76). This apt phrase can be equally applied to a number of the major canonical modernists.

[2] Allen Mandelbaum (331) makes this point in "Dante as Ancient and Modern." Teodolinda Barolini also reminds us that "Dante's hallmark is his never-ceasing experimentalism, his linguistic and stylistic voracity" (26). Barolini claims that Dante's invention of dividing his epic into cantos rather than into the long books Virgil used in the *Aeneid* reflects "Dante's obsession with the new; the division into cantos renders the spiralling rhythm of new dawns and new dusks, the incessant new beginnings and endings that punctuate the line of becoming, the *cammin di nostra vita*"(32). For example, Dante extends language to the limit in the *Commedia* by coining numerous neologisms (see 160-162, 221).

calls the "evergreen" of the medieval imagination allowed Dante to shape the reception-history of his work for posterity. As Osip Mandelstam has observed, "It is inconceivable to read Dante's cantos without directing them toward contemporaneity. They were created for that purpose. They are missiles for capturing the future. They demand commentary in the *futurum.*" Consequently, Mandelstam concludes, Dante's contemporaneity is "continuous, incalculable and exhausting" (420).

The main impulse behind Dante's great poem should not be misconstrued, however. The medieval poet never promoted, in Solzhenitsyn's striking phrase, the "relentless cult of novelty" for its own sake (3). Nor did he foster that "parochialism in time"[3] typical of the modern mind which judges the past by the absolute standard of the present. The reason for Dante's enduring relevance lies elsewhere. The "alterity"[4] of the *Commedia* challenges the horizon of expectations of both contemporary and future readers alike: "if I am a timid friend of truth, / I fear I may lose my life among / those who will call this present, ancient times" (*Paradiso* 17.118-120). Eternal truth, Dante claims, keeps his art in the perpetual calendar by constantly illuminating the new intellectual vistas he opens up: "we cannot satisfy our mind unless it is enlightened by / the truth beyond whose boundary no truth lies" (*Paradiso* 4.124-126).[5] The timelessness of Dante's vision accounts for its timeliness.

Because English writers since the Romantics have articulated rival versions of this transcendent vision, at least two Dantes emerge at the birth of modernism. The first Dante, fashioned by Gabriele Rossetti and later embellished by Ezra Pound, is a heterodox poet presiding over a mystical underground church of poetic tradition whose "secret history" stretches back to pagan antiquity. As master of the "initiated" in accordance with a

---

[3] Bertrand Russell described "parochialism in time" as one of the great faults of the modern age. See Dawson, xx. In this connection, most modernists, like Joyce, dismissed what they considered to be "the unfortunate prejudices of Dante" (Joyce 101), while Eliot, on the other hand, praised Dante for being the "least provincial" of poets, the principal literary model for overcoming the prejudices of one's own place and time (*TCC* 134-5).

[4] Jauss (187) identifies the hermeneutic concept of alterity as "the particular double structure of a discourse which not only appears to us as evidence of a distant, historically absent past in all its surprising "otherness," but also is an aesthetic object which, thanks to its linguistic form, is directed toward an *other*, understanding consciousness—and which therefore also allows for communication with a later, no longer contemporary addressee."

[5] Grandgent (225) glosses Dante's verses as follows: "the mind is satisfied only with that truth which contains within itself every other truth."

private gnosis, Pound's Dante experiences a "new life" of esoteric eroticism (Surette 106, 119). Based on this gnostic reading of the *Comedy*, the Middle Ages becomes the site of what Umberto Eco calls an "*ironical revisitation*" (69). In stark contrast, the second Dante sponsored by T. S. Eliot acts as the principal exponent of the mind of Europe, a universal poet whose unified sensibility keeps tradition and the search for novelty in dynamic balance. This more orthodox figure believes that recognizing the reality of sin ushers in a "New Life" (*SE* 427), celebrates human love as a step to the divine, and never confounds the two. By foregrounding the unity of European culture reflected in Dante's work, Eliot succeeded in establishing the terms of engagement for several generations of English readers of the *Comedy*.

One of the most compelling responses to this Eliot-inspired portrait of Dante has come recently from the pen of Wendell Berry. On receiving the T. S. Eliot Award for Creative Writing in 1994, this contemporary American writer paid tribute to the great modem poet as one of his principal sources of hope ("The Country Writer" 14-15). Eliot's "pilgrimage of works," stretching from "The Love Song of J. Alfred Prufrock" to *The Elder Statesman,* presents a "dismembered humanity, each one eccentric, alone, anxious, and troubled, tottering on the margin of an emptiness that is both within them and around them." Although redemption eludes them at first, these hollow men never yield to total despair. By "different stages," they move out of the shadows of the wasteland and into the light of what Berry calls "a love far greater, more compassionate, and more forgiving than their own." As transfigured pilgrims in a divine comedy, they discover the transcendent in the "small things" of ordinary life such as family relationships. Berry's fragmented figures in *Remembering* (1988) and *Jayber Crow* (2000) also follow a hopeful trajectory towards the wholeness of membership. A sojourner like the characters in his fiction, Berry the "country writer," no less than Eliot the city poet, wends his way to "the very heart of his faith and his tradition." The importance of passing on a vital tradition originating from Europe forms the core of Berry's literary project and reflects his active exchange with Eliot's famous pronouncements on the subject, to which I now turn.

Tradition and Contemporaneity

"Make it new"—the celebrated slogan of modernism—has been understood primarily as an exhortation to throw off the "burden of the past" in an attempt to locate a "true present," a new point of origin. Eliot himself contributed to this widespread impression in "A Preface to Modern Literature," an essay published in *Vanity Fair* the year after *The Waste Land,* with the tautological reminder about "how exceedingly new... is the newness of anything really new" (118). An inherent irony, however, arises from such a view. When writers "assert their own modernity," Paul de Man reckons, "they are bound to discover their dependence on similar assertions made by their literary predecessors, their claim to being a new beginning turns out to be the repetition of a claim that has always already been made" (de Man 161). Eliot realized that novelty could never be advanced at the expense of discarding tradition. Rather, he imagined a society, under ideal conditions, building up a "living tradition" with "the good New growing naturally out of the good Old" (*TCC* 184). The modernist "abandons nothing en route," Eliot insisted in his most well-known essay, since the "historical sense" compels him to write "not merely with his own generation in his bones" but also with the whole of European literature from Homer onwards in mind (*SE* 14). As opposed to Nietzsche, Eliot did not subject the cultural past to a "ruthless forgetting" or dissolution (cf. de Man, 147). "The unending quest for what is new and fresh," Solzhenitsyn observed, "does not deprive our grateful memory of all that came before" (3). In a similar vein, Eliot envisaged canon-formation as involving a process of constant addition and complication that would preserve the newcomer from "the error of pure contemporaneity" (cf. *TCC* 119). Because dead authors are what we know, they interact with the living to such an extent that "the most individual parts of [a recent] work may be those in which his ancestors... assert their immortality most vigorously." Even avant-garde art derives its "complete meaning" when placed, for purposes of comparison and contrast, in relation to the classics. This double vision of the timeless and temporal together, of the presence of the past, allows for "conformity between the old and the new." It is precisely this appeal to tradition, paradoxically, that makes a writer "most acutely conscious of his place in time, of his own contemporaneity"(*SE* 14).

Berry also stresses the interplay between tradition and contemporaneity. The "modern cult of originality," he points out, seeks "to replace the old with the new" and to foster a thoughtless "preoccupation with the present" (*Standing* 13-14). This aim contradicts, however, what Pound meant by his traditional instruction. "The new must come from the old, for where else would you get it?"(*Life* 71), Berry asks pointedly. To remove the "sense of continuity" with what came before would leave us with no cultural identity: "If we fail to see that we live in the same world that Homer lived in, then we not only misunderstand Homer; we misunderstand ourselves. The past is our definition" (*Standing* 14). To recover our cultural memory does not mean, as Nietzsche would have it, "to gain a past a posteriori, from which we might spring, as against that which we do spring" (Nietzsche 21), with each individual becoming his own origin. Nor should it necessarily lead one to adopt an "adolescent critical theory" such as the "anxiety of influence," Berry argues (*What are People for?* 165) with its Freudian family romance of a weaker son condemning and killing the stronger father. The "indispensable correction" to such an attitude for Berry comes from the pen of William Blake (and later Eliot): "I cannot think that Real Poets have any competition."[6] Literary tradition restores the familial bonds between a paternal precursor and a filial latecomer, as can be witnessed in "Spenser's filial admiration for Chaucer, or Dante's for Virgil"(*What are People for?* 165). (Even Harold Bloom (122-3) contrasts the deliberate revisionism of post-enlightenment writers with the "generous" influence or "sharing-with-others" in Dante). Contemporaneity, in the sense of being "up with the times," Berry insists, is of "no value" whatsoever (*Standing* 93). Returning to one's origins is what makes a writer truly "original," in the root sense of the word (*Long-Legged House* 177). Tradition does not imply, of course, standing still or indulging in sterile repetition. Berry likens authentic renewal instead to a process of grafting that adds the new to the old: "Why cannot the critical faculty, in poets and critics alike, undertake to see that the *best* of the new is grafted to *the best* of the old?"(*Standing* 18). All art is "communal" ("Country Writer" 14) since it provides a "common ground" that "joins all the sharers of literature, writers and readers, living and dead" (*Standing* 10). Berry equates tradition with democracy and invokes here the first principle enunciated by Chesterton: "the essential things in men are [those] they hold in common, not [those] they hold separately" (*Orthodoxy* 47). By extending the franchise to those disqualified by "the accident of death," the "democracy of the dead" or the "consensus of common human voices" (*Orthodoxy* 47) allows the commonalty to "commune with, to speak with" each other against and across time (*Standing* 14). This "great community of recorded human experience," that includes great writers and the

[6] Berry quotes this passage in "The Country Writer," 14. Eliot expressed a similar idea in *East Coker* V: "there is no competition…/For us, there is only the trying. The rest is not our business" (*CPP* 128).

accumulated wisdom of the past,[7] opens up a truly democratic vista of a world in which "all wakeful and responsible people, dead, living, and unborn, are contemporaries." And that reality, Berry affirms, is "the only contemporaneity worth having" (*Standing* 13).

Berry takes his cue for the idea of a continuous communal dialogue taking place between the living and the dead across the ages from Eliot's seminal essay. The modernist poet found a similar sense of diachrony at work in the *Comedy*, especially in *Inferno* 4, where Dante follows Virgil into the company of the great poets of antiquity, Homer, Horace, Ovid, and Lucan (cf. Manganiello, *Eliot and Dante* 124-5). Eliot commended his great precursor for displaying an historical sense in the *Comedy* by including "real men, his contemporaries, friends, and enemies, recent historical personages, legendary and Biblical figures, and figures of ancient fiction." All are "transformed in the whole," and "all become of the same reality and contemporary" (*SE* 248). Berry follows suit by imagining human reality in Dantesque fashion as a series of interdependent concentric circles with a divine center: nature, culture, community, marriage and the family (Weinreb 29).

The contemporary American writer takes his place alongside Eliot and Pound by sustaining their effort to "reweave the tattered garment of culture" (*Home Economies* 142). This cultural task has become increasingly urgent given the postmodern tendency to leave the threads of the older "textile" or text dangling and barely recognizable.[8] In the words of Jacques Derrida,

> This interweaving, this textile, is the *text* produced only in the transformation of another text. Nothing...is anywhere ever simply present or absent. There are only, everywhere, differences and traces of traces. (Derrida 26)

The postmodernist privileges "the Penelope work of forgetting," to use Walter Benjamin's phrase, the unraveling of tradition over "the Penelope work of recollection"(*Illuminations* 202). The reverse holds true for Eliot: "the great poet is...one who retwines as many straying strands as possible" (*UPUC* 85) into a seamless and "living whole" (*SE* 17) that forms an open-ended book of memory. Berry concurs. When "a communal order of memory" re-collects the scattered fragments of our common story, it produces, in his view, a wholesome or "healthy culture" (*Unsettling* 43).

---

[7] Berry adopts this phrase from Wallace Stegner (see *What are People For?* 50).

[8] Walter Benjamin points out that the Latin word *textum* means "web" (*Illuminations* 202).

Berry foregrounds the act of purposive remembering in his ecological aesthetics, calling for a double recovery of culture and nature (*Home* 142). These tasks complement one another for, as Pound explained, "a return to origins invigorates because it is a return to nature and reason" ("The Tradition" 92). Berry views creation as "one continuous fabric," a "universe, a whole, the parts of which are all 'turned into one'" ("Health" 91; *Unsettling* 46). The world "subsists, coheres, and endures" by divine love ("Health" 89). Ecological responsibility requires human beings to extend charity not only towards each other but also to try "to love all Creation in response to the Creator's love for it" (*Gift* 273). To love one's neighbor entails, in this broader sense, taking care of the land on which his life depends, and preserving "both inheritances, the natural and the cultural"(*Home* 17). As charity grows, Creation's "neighborhood" expands in both time and space. Membership is not restricted just to those who now live "next door," but includes "the dead who have bequeathed the land to the living, and...the unborn to whom the living will in turn bequeath it" (*Gift* 272). All become members of one body.[9] Charitable stewardship, then, ensures the survival of local culture, whereas "despising Nature and her goodness,"[10] to quote Dante, threatens it. Doing violence against God's handiwork, Berry adds, dismembers the neighborhood and exiles the individual from his rightful place in the order of Creation. Those who lack "carità per natio loco" ("love for one's native place," *Inferno* 14.1) wander aimlessly in an infernal no man's land: "We are lost in the 'dark wood' of Dante—dark, I think, not because the wood itself is dark—but because we cannot see where we are. We are lost in our own error" (*Standing* 193). Only the light of divine love can help people rekindle "affection for the place and respect for it" (*What are People For?* 166),[11] and thereby remember the road that leads back home.

The Cocktail Party

Finding one's way back home appears as a central trope in *The Cocktail Party*. Eliot echoes Chesterton's modern variation on the famous opening scene of the *Comedy*: "Man…has always lost his way; but now he has lost his address" (*What's Wrong* 77). The principal characters in the

---

[9] Berry conceives of culture as "one body" (see *Unsettling* 43).

[10] Berry cites this phrase from *Inferno* 11.46-48 in *Sex, Economy, Freedom and Community* (98).

[11] Berry adds, "the local culture will carry on the knowledge of how the place may be well and lovingly used, and also the implicit command to use it only well and lovingly" (*What are People For?* 166).

play recover their sense of direction and identity after experiencing the vicissitudes of love. Eliot dramatizes the process of illumination they undergo by referring to a key point Virgil makes in his great discourse in *Purgatorio* 18.22-26, as a main subtext of their interaction: love directs its attention to an image of someone who exists outside the self. The true lover beholds, in other words, a real person, not a phantasm generated by one's own perception and desires. To mistake the phantasmal for the real is to inhabit an illusory world. Edward Chamberlayne pinpoints the infernal quandary everyone faces in *The Cocktail Party* with a striking dictum: "Hell is oneself, /Hell is alone, the other figures in it /Merely projections" (*CPP* 342). Sartre believed that hell is other people, but in this passage Eliot restores the somewhat starker original meaning of Dante's underworld. Each set of paired lovers at the play's opening suffers the isolation resulting from seeing others exclusively from their private optic. Celia, for example, admits she has loved an image of Edward she invented on first meeting him:

> The man I saw before, he was only a projection—
> I see that now—of something that I wanted—
> No, not *wanted*—something I aspired to—
> Something I desperately wanted to exist. (*CPP* 327)

Unsure about whether she can love only someone she has fabricated in her own imagination, Celia is troubled, like Edward, by the frightening consequence of withdrawing into the solitary self: "Then lover and beloved are equally unreal / And the dreamer is no more real than his dreams" (362). To contextualize Celia's fear further Eliot invokes the disturbing implications of Dante's dream of the siren. Initially ugly in appearance, the enchantress becomes increasingly beautiful as Dante gazes on her (*Purgatorio* 19.7-15). Dorothy L. Sayers explains that the siren is "the projection upon the outer world of something in the mind: the soul, falling in love with itself, perceives other people and things, not as they are, but as wish-fulfillments of its own: i.e., its love for them is not love for a "true other," but a devouring egotistical fantasy, by absorption in which the personality rots away into illusion" ("Introduction" 220). The siren appears, in short, as a false image of Beatrice (Williams, *Figure* 165-166). Sayers's supplementary gloss on this episode of the *Purgatorio*, drawn from a spiritual writer, illuminates Celia's predicament as well as Dante's: "If you exalt the objects of your love until your picture is a false one; if you idealize them; *if you project upon them your own ideal self;* then you are loving not a real person but a dream" (*Purgatorio* 19.58-9, Sayers trans. 221). There are, of course, two ways of finding the road back to real personhood (cf. *CPP* 341). One is to go through a human agent, the other through a divine. For Celia this means discarding the false image of the self fashioned by her narcissism in order to seek the face of her mystical spouse, the ultimate Image whose imprint all human creatures bear, and thereby experience "the delight of loving" without fleshly desire (cf. *CPP* 363). To break out of his perceptual prison Edward, for his part, must change his point of view and learn to see himself through the eyes of the beloved (*CPP* 340). The corrective lens of the consort brings the true self into clearer focus, facilitates mutual understanding, and allows affection to grow into the charity that ennobles eros.

The gradual process that leads to the reconciliation of Edward and Lavinia signals their entry into a new life. Just as Beatrice welcomes back Dante as her "prodigal lover" (Sayers, "Introduction" 28), so too the Chamberlaynes patch up their differences to save their marriage. By making both husband and wife culpable for their brief separation, Eliot privileges an idea only hinted at in the *Commedia*. In the words of Charles Williams, "Dante's spiritual movement is the pattern of [Beatrice's]; reverse the names, and it holds" (*Figure* 182) The principles of Dante's way can apply to any human love, whether in family or in friendship, but marriage affords a unique opportunity of seeking wholeness or holiness (Williams, *Outlines* 92, 111). Accordingly, Edward and Lavinia undertake the affirmative way together, determined to renew contact with their estranged partner, and to revive their mutual love, each playing the role of Beatrice to the other's Dante. So when Lavinia finally notices that Edward is like a child lost in a forest, as Celia pictured him (363), she proposes that he spend some time recuperating in a hotel located in a symbolically charged area called the New Forest (352). With this image Eliot evokes not only the dark wood Dante finds himself in at the start of his journey but also the moment he stands at the edge of the world's first forest before two streams, Lethe and Eunoe: the former removes the memory of sin, while the latter restores the memory of good (*Purgatorio* 28.127). Like Dante, the Chamberlaynes resolve to live with the memories of their failings and "make them / Into something new." Only by accepting the past will they alter its meaning (385) and look forward to the future. Their commitment to sanctifying the "common routine" of family life (363) marks a new beginning; the child Lavinia is expecting constitutes its visible proof. Through an act of exchanged marital love new life (literally) exists.[12] By following the way that leads from human to divine love, Eliot's characters re-enact Europe's epic theme as epitomized in *The Divine Comedy.*

Remembering

Like Edward Chamberlayne, the hero of Berry's *Remembering* descends first into a fragmentary world of shadows before he can ascend to the realm of light and find his way back home. His little pilgrim story therefore recapitulates in miniature the epic dimension of Dante's journey from hell to heaven. Berry's novel opens with Andy Catlett lying in bed alone at night in a hotel room in San Francisco, far from his native Kentucky, plunged in an ominous nightmare. As the phantasmagorical scenario unfolds, he sees his hometown, Port William, being destroyed by bulldozers. A fat man gnawing at his own flesh, symbolic of the modern agriculture businessman consumed by his own greed, supervises the operation. The wholesale destruction of landmarks in the familiar surroundings, even the names on churchyard gravestones, turns the neighbourhood into a veritable wasteland.

The prospect of being uprooted from the world he knows leaves Andy with a heightened fear of losing everything that connects him to his past and to the present. The loss of his personal and cultural identity pains Andy to such an extent that he feels just as "disformed and naked" (*Remembering* 3, 5) as the blessed plot of earth (where he once lived and worked) that man-made machines have now trampled. The unbearable ache in his body awakens Andy from his deep slumber, prompting him to ponder the meaning of the dark epiphany. The focus shifts from exterior to interior landscape, a *paysage intèrieur*, with the illumination that he has made a barren waste of himself. As Berry puts it, "Not knowing where you are, you can make mistakes of the utmost seriousness: you can lose your soul or your soil, your life or your way home"(*Standing* 103). Andy boarded a plane to California instead of returning to his farm after attending a university conference in the Midwest. The geographical dislocation reflects his moral impasse. The gentleman farmer likened his participation in the academic proceedings to entering "a place of eternal

[12] The fact that Lavinia is expecting a child is not indicated in the stage directions as such but by Eliot himself (Coghill 281). In Eliot's poetry, from "Marina" to *Burnt Norton,* the laughter of unborn children is an image of new promise, of hope. In *The Cocktail Party*, to sanctify the common routine means not only to beget and bear a child. The next step, Eliot explained, is for parents to try to "understand what they have created" ("Aims of Poetic Drama" 16).

hopelessness" (22), like Dante's hell. Although Andy "damned" proponents of modern "agribusiness" for practising what he called "an agriculture of the mind" (23, 25), the dream, ironically, makes him realize that he is the victim of a mental hell of his own making. His self-imposed exile from Port William involves a "displacement of mind or heart" that strands him in "no place that he knows" (21). The reason for escaping to this ambiguous no man's land becomes readily apparent. Having lost his right hand in a farming accident, Andy cut himself off from his family and his neighbours in the farming community:

> His right hand had been the one with which he reached out to the world and attached himself to it. When he lost his hand he lost his hold. It was as though his hand still clutched all that was dear to him—and was gone. All the world then became to him a steep slope, and he a man descending, staggering and falling, unable to reach out to tree trunk or branch or root to catch and hold on. (28)

Andy finds himself like Dante in the dark wood,[13] unable to connect with the people that matter most in his life, especially his wife Flora: "his hand knew her as a man knows his homeland. Now the hand that joined him to her had been cast away, and he mourned over it as over a priceless map… [that was] forever lost" (28). Although he pines for his "body's wholeness" (28), the estranged husband remains a broken man living in "the little hell of himself alone," (45) apart from his better half.

The life of infernal solitude causes the loss of communion between persons and poses a threat to marital fidelity. As he goes through the "gate of Universal Suspicion" to check in his baggage at the airport, Andy is a "no man going nowhere," falling prey to the sensual charms of beautiful women who pass by him. Like J. Alfred Prufrock, he fails to make contact with these sirens, however, since they refuse to sing to him. Lost in thought, the blank faces in the crowd of passengers are "all turned inward," appearing "each in the world alone." The timely reminder of his own solipsism provokes a poignant memory of the universal dance of membership that symbolizes, as in *East Coker*, the concord between man and woman as well as cosmic order. Andy realizes that he has a Beatrice, like Dante did, to steer him away from temptresses and back on course towards a higher love (*Purgatorio* 31.43-5), but the possibility of being reunited with his faithful companion seems remote, for the "dance that

---

[13] I probe various allusions to Dante in my article, "Dante and Wendell Berry's Modern Book of Memory."

would bring her back again is broken" (93-5). The missing link that would join him to his wife, home, and community is love (cf. *Standing* 60).

Berry uses this familiar word not in the sense of an egotistical impulse, but with reference to the Dantesque idea that the love of the Good is increased "by partnership." To illustrate his meaning Berry critiques elsewhere what he considers to be Percy Shelley's misapplication of the principle in *Epipsychidion*. The Romantic poet translates the main point he takes from *Purgatorio* 15 in the following verses: "True Love in this suffers from gold and clay, / That to divide is not to take away." Berry comments:

> Love of the Good undoubtedly does increase the more it is shared or divided. Familial and neighbourly love increases by division the same way—though here there may be a limit. But Shelley is writing about what is properly called "a consuming passion" and the growth of that sort of love by division seems extremely doubtful. (*Standing* 157)

Berry finds Shelley's corollary to his central argument, contained in the lines "If you divide pleasure and love and thought, /Each part exceeds the whole," to be extremely perplexing: "The …statement…not only misuses Dante, but turns him upside down….[I]f the divided part exceeds the whole, then the whole has no standing and its existence implies no restraint" (*Standing*, 158). Shelley's paean to free love destroys the marriage bond, according to Berry, because it releases love from "gold and clay," and, once divided from their relation to each other, all three elements wander aimlessly and dangerously (*Standing* 159). Shelley fails to acknowledge the fact, as Dante does, that divine love came to down to meet human love, to heal it, to redirect it, and to raise it to a higher plane (*Paradiso* 7.30-3). Sexual attraction, like every natural desire, finds its issue in the love of God (*Paradiso* 7.142-4). Eliot dramatized this belief, as we have seen, in *The Cocktail Party*. Before Andy Catlett makes the same discovery in *Remembering*, Berry shows the deleterious effects of living in the prison-house of marital discord.

The first chapter reveals how he became estranged from Flora. Initially their quarrels were always about "two longing to be one, or one dividing relentlessly into two." This "duality" that divided them would eventually bring them together again in the "only way that fragments can be rejoined"(34-35). Then their quarrels opened up "an infinite cold space" between them (35) because they focused exclusively on their "division" rather than on their reciprocal relationship. There seemed to be no way to stop the fall into "the world of his distrust," a hell "bottomless and forever dark" (34). The memory of a conversation with Flora, however, serves as the antidote to his despair (35). The suggestion that he forgive himself before seeking the forgiveness of others infuriates Andy at the time, but later, on reflection, the exchange teaches him that "to trust is simply to give oneself" and "once given, the self cannot be taken back" (110). He comes to the realization that "his anger, his loneliness, his selfish grief, all have been wrong," and that Flora was indeed right (113). The memory of Flora's commitment to him prepares Andy to receive, above all, divine mercy.

Berry deliberately keeps the couple's reunion low-key by having it occur off stage. Their reconciliation is achieved through a brief exchange of handwritten notes left on the kitchen table. On his arrival Andy finds the house empty; Flora's message informs him that she has taken the children to pick beans at a neighbor's farm. Her simple question, "you're back?" signed with her "love," touches Andy. Recognizing the "blessedness" of his home for the first time, he responds by begging his wife's forgiveness (119). He then steps outside to perform his usual chores.

Berry foregrounds the grandeur of ordinary life in this domestic scene. It re-enacts on a small scale the epic/biblical pattern of return in the context of marriage. In his fiction Berry artfully modulates the notion of heroism commonly found in stories about the "extraordinary actions of 'great men' "who display physical or moral courage in "extreme circumstances" (*Gift* 276-277). While such exceptional cases bear universal significance, the "drama of ordinary or daily behaviour" also raises issues of courage, skill, and especially perseverance in a more complex way (*Gift* 277). To love one's spouse in the trivial occurrences of each day, while less spectacular, can be more demanding than performing a remarkable feat once in a lifetime: "It may, in some ways, be easier to be Samson than to be a good husband or wife day after day for fifty years" (*Gift* 277). The story of a faithful marriage, woven from prosaic details, contains a hidden heroic dimension. The humble find strength, paradoxically, in their weakness. Despite the problems that inevitably crop up during the conjugal life of the Catletts, their effort to remain faithful to each other leads them to experience the joy of "union, communion, atonement (in the root sense of at-one-ment" (*Unsettling* 122).

Remembering closes appropriately with a "high dream" of membership in counterpoint to the "low dream" of fragmentation that opens the novel.[14] A light from heaven grants Andy "a change of sight" which enables him to go back to his native place and offer its inhabitants the aid

[14] Eliot indicates that the "high dream" is inspired from above, while the "low dream" springs from below. See Eliot's "Dante" (*SE* 243, 262).

of "the restored right band of his joy" (*Remembering* 124). Healed, he takes part in "the feast of Creation" (*Unsettling* 104). The remembered landscape shines in its pristine splendor, while birds sing in unison with Andy's own people, now all transformed into translucent flowers. "The song of the many members of one love" (*Remembering* 122-123) provides a bright contrast to the eerie silence of hell he had experienced earlier.

Love sets in motion "the great dance that joins [people] to [their] home, to each other, to other creatures, to the dead and the unborn" (*Standing* 60; cf. *Remembering* 60, 94-95). Berry alludes here to the enchanting image of the matrimonial dance in *East Coker* that serves as a tribute to the ideal of a harmonious community. The transformation of the Port William membership into floral figures, moreover, recalls the souls of the heavenly city who blossom forth into the manifold petals of a white rose in *Paradiso,* Canto 30. Dante's vivid emblem of *caritas* shows "*everyone* is in love," as Peter S. Hawkins (84) says: "the exclusive affection of earthly married couples that the *Commedia* on one occasion celebrates (*Purgatorio* 25.134-5) becomes in Heaven a corporate and inclusive partnership" of the blessed. Berry affirms this Dantesque principle of expansive love in the visionary ending of his novel.

Other intertextual echoes from Eliot and Dante abound in the final tableau of *Remembering*. Initially, when Andy floundered in the darkness of his self-made hell, both "the dead and the living... departed from him" (125). His contemporaries reappear once "he sees that he lives in eternity as he lives in time" (123). Andy's renewed vision recalls Eliot's Dantesque insight in *The Rock*, "In every moment you live at a point of intersection, / Remember living in time, you must also now live in Eternity" (52). Some poignant verses from *Little Gidding* also haunt Andy as he enters the passageway beyond the temporal world: "See, they depart and we go with them./ We are born with the dead:/ See, they return, and bring us with them" (*CPP* 144). Andy communes with his loved ones, who are no longer "mere thoughts or memories but presences" that have "the luminous vividness of new grass after fire" (*Remembering* 117, 124). Marx believed "the tradition of the dead generations weighs like a nightmare upon the brain of the living" (146). Berry's hero carries no corpse of ideas he intends to bury deep in the recesses of his memory, but feels reinvigorated by gaining access to the wisdom of the ages. This dynamic process of engaging a living body of tradition liberates the mind from being its own place or sole point of reference, and reintegrates the whole person into the bigger world that becomes his native town. Andy comes to share the conviction the chorus articulates in *The Rock*: "There is no life that is not in community" (*CPP* 101). In his hopeful dream vision,

Andy imagines himself living in "the company of immortals" (cf. *A World Lost*, 150-1), the dead ancestors who awaken and traverse the glowing fields of his imagination. The familiar faces of the past merge with those of the present to "become renewed, transfigured, in another pattern," as Eliot would put it in *Little Gidding* (*CPP* 142). The power of remembering these resurrected figures with gratitude helps to foster a meaningful dialogue, a veritable "convocation of the voices of predecessors" (*Remembering* 18), for, in Eliot's words from *Little Gidding*, "the communication / Of the dead is tongued with fire beyond the language of the living" (*CPP* 139). The end of Andy's journey, like that of Eliot's traveler, leads him back home where he started, a trajectory that allows him to "know the place for the first time" (*CPP* 145). Even in a transitory world the eternal design appears. A member of two households (cf. Eph 2:19), Andy passes freely from the "country remembered" of Port William to the "true country" of eternity.[15] Berry's strong historical sense compels him to connect the local with the universal according to the pattern established by Dante in "Europe's epic" and revived by Eliot in his modern visions.

Jayber Crow

The eponymous hero of Jayber Crow also takes Port William as the point of departure for his journey towards what Dante calls "una vera cittã" (*Purgatorio* 13.95), the true city, but the path he follows is not as straightforward as that of his medieval predecessor:

> If you could do it, I suppose, it would be a good idea to live your life in a straight line—starting, say, in the Dark Wood of Error, and proceeding by logical steps through Hell and Purgatory and into Heaven…Often what has looked like a straight line to me has been a circle or a doubling back. I have been in the Dark Wood any number of times. I have known something of Hell, Purgatory, and Heaven, but not always in that order. (133)

Jayber reveals that his itinerary has tended to be circular rather than linear, and goes on to describe himself as an "ignorant pilgrim, crossing a dark

---

[15] Flannery O'Connor comments in *Mystery and Manners* that the word "country" suggests "everything from the actual countryside that the novelist describes, on to and through the peculiar characteristics of his region and his nation, and on, through, and under all of these to his true country, which the writer with Christian convictions will consider to be what is eternal and absolute" (O'Connor 27).

valley," (133), but one who can see in retrospect the light of providence guiding his steps. He has a keen sense of being "led" particularly along "the way of love" (cf. 247-260) that takes him away from the "futility and absurdity" of "self-begotten desire" towards a hope of being "possessed by something greater, no longer at all belonging to himself" (198).

Jayber embarks upon this way when he experiences the "Beatrician moment" that Charles Williams defined as "a moment of revelation and communicated conversion by means of a girl" (*Figure* 123). The young girl in question is Mattie Keith, whose beautiful eyes impress Jayber the first time he sees her one spring afternoon from the open door of his barber shop. The impact is immediate and unforgettable: "The brief, laughing look that she had given me made me feel extraordinarily seen, as if after that I might be visible in the dark" (10). Mattie plays Beatrice to Jayber's Dante by coming to the aid of a man who finds himself in a dark and pathless wood.

Although Mattie ends up marrying another man, Troy Chatham, she remains Jayber's love interest (9). The threads of their lives continue to interweave in unsuspected ways, especially when Jayber discovers that Troy has been unfaithful to his wife. The discovery places the town barber in an awkward position, sparking a lively internal debate which concludes with his decision to be "the faithful husband of a woman who is already married to an unfaithful husband" (243). Why would Jayber choose to make a vow in secret and enter into a "strange marriage" which no one knows about, including Mattie herself? Realizing that some would consider his imaginary proposal foolish, Jayber nevertheless insists he is no Agamemnon or Jephthah (259), the classical and biblical characters respectively who sacrificed their daughters because of the rash promises they made. Berry has his protagonist allude here to the passage in *Paradiso* (5.68ff) where Beatrice maintains that one should not be obliged to fulfill a vow made in jest or one that will have an evil outcome. Solemn vows such as the religious or spouses make, on the other hand, should never be broken on one's private judgment. Berry comments that although in some instances a promise should be reneged, the breaking of a vow "can tell us nothing of what is meant by making and keeping one. Divorce is the contradiction of marriage, not one of its proposed results" (*Standing* 202). Jayber accordingly provides the following rationale for his action:

> I was married to Mattie Chatham but she was not married to me, which pretty fairly balanced her marriage to Troy, who became always less married to her, though legally (and varyingly in appearance) he remained her husband.

> Young lovers see a vision of the world redeemed by love. That is the truest thing they ever see, for without it life is death. I believe that Mattie had seen that vision in the time of her falling in love with Troy, and that she kept it still and honored it. And so I honored it. But the answering vision, which ought to have been his, was mine. And my marriage to Mattie was validated in a way by Troy's continuing invalidation of his marriage to her. (258)

For Jayber, as for Andy Catlett, a vow of fidelity unites not just a man and a woman with each other but also each of them with the whole community (cf. *Recollected Essays* 302). Though a bachelor, Jayber is, as Berry described him in an earlier novel, the "most married" man in Port William because he embraces a communal ideal of marriage. His vision of the heavenly city would see each household inhabited by two people who might "care for each other and know each other better than enemies, and better than strangers" (*A Place on Earth* 68-9).

In the earthly city of Port William, however, Jayber falls far short of his ideal. His intense hatred for his rival contradicts his most cherished belief: "in [Troy's] presence I was in perfect absence, the night shadow, of the charity I sought for and longed for" (337). Jayber realizes the failure to love somebody constitutes the essence of hell (354), the place Dante lies "in danger of ending up," as Berry points out (Weinreb 34), at the beginning of the *Comedy*. Hatred often triumphs in this world, Jayber observes, because it claims to act in the name of the sacred even as it destroys the things of time by every profane means available (249). Hell itself is "a creature of time" bereft of light and hope. Love, on the other hand, is, paradoxically, "in the world but is not altogether of it. It is of eternity. It takes there when it most holds us here" (249). The intersection of time and eternity allows Jayber to experience purgatory by taking upon himself the suffering of his beloved. He comes to the realization that when one member of Port William suffers, the health of the whole membership is adversely affected, for "We are all involved… in all and any evil," he says (295). Through his private pledge of fidelity to Mattie, then, Jayber attempts to make up for Troy's lack of corresponding love as well as his own shortcomings. In a defining moment that occurs towards the end of this long and arduous process, Jayber stands face to face with the man he has hated for forty years, and declares, "I did not hate him. If he had acknowledged then what he finally would not be able to avoid acknowledging, I would have hugged him"(361). Jayber looks forward with hope to the time when "I would be, in the small ways that were possible, his friend…For finally he was redeemed, in my eyes, by Mattie's long abiding love for him, as I myself had been by my love for her" (361).

Mattie's charity guides Jayber towards an understanding of love's mercy just as Beatrice's salvific greeting in the *Vita Nuova* humbled Dante to the point that he forgot all wrongs committed against him (*Vita Nuova* 36). This poignant act of atonement, or at-one-ment, sets the stage for the dramatic climax of the novel. Earlier Jayber admits that he could not imagine Mattie giving him "a look, a smile perhaps, of consent" to his clandestine marriage proposal (196-7). But, in the culminating epiphany, as Mattie lies dying with Jayber standing by her bedside, she gives her visitor "the smile that I had never seen and will not see again in this world, and it covered me all over with light" (363). The signature smile of Jayber's Beatrice transforms a story potentially about Hell into what he calls a "book about Heaven" (354).

Berry takes inspiration for this uplifting denouement, I suggest, from the way Eliot replayed the Beatrician moment in *The Elder Statesman*. *The Divine Comedy* resonated in Eliot's mind with an enhanced tonality while writing his final play. An important change in his personal life stirred the aging playwright to sound the familiar Dantesque epic theme in a new key. The dedicatory poem to his wife Valerie stands as Eliot's most explicit testimony to the affirmative way and to what Beatrice calls "the holy and glorious flesh" (*Paradiso* 14.43), or the sanctity of the body. The consummation of his second marriage in 1957, Eliot agreed, made him feel like Dante did after he had passed into paradise (Gordon 248). The rebirth of human love seems a late occurrence in Eliot, but the event is foreshadowed, as far back as 1930, in the finely chiselled verse in "Marina": "the awakened, the lips parted, the hope" (*CPP* 73). Over the next several years the imaginative exposure to *The Divine Comedy* continued to make a profound impression. There is no doubt that a number of characters who appear in Eliot's early poems are tormented by disordered sexual desires both within marriage and outside it. Like Dante the pilgrim, these unhappy souls need to be rescued from drowning in the sea of perverse love by a Beatrician figure who will then guide them towards the shore of a truer love (cf. *Paradiso* 26.62-3). Eliot accordingly considered the manifestation of the divine in ordinary life from a fresh perspective, focusing especially on how a couple's attempt to balance eros and agape in their troubled relationship can provide propitious grounds for marriage's renewal. The possibility of loving someone for who she is, even with her frailties, the idea that it is never too late to change and be reconciled to God's will, and the meaning of the death of a loved one: these elements, and more, recur in the later plays. Eliot engages them fully in *The Cocktail Party* and with renewed energy in *The Elder Statesman*. Lord Claverton, for example, discovers in his twilight years that it is enough to confess the truth about himself to one person to keep his soul "safe." Then "he loves that person, and his love will save him" (*Elder Statesman* 102). A young couple ratifies the saving power of love as the curtain falls. Claverton's death, Charles says, gives birth to a "new person" who is both lovers together. And death itself no longer dismays Monica since she is firmly rooted in "the certainty of love unchanging" (132).

"If the play were just a love story," Berry comments, "it might be accused of sentimentality, but it is not just a love story: it is the story also of deception and confession, separation and atonement, sin and forgiveness" ("Country Writer" 15). The mutual exchanges of love and compassion that restore fractured family relationships propel Berry's characters within the ambit of the far greater Love that moves all things and especially the human heart. Eliot had closed his career with this Dantesque affirmation. The experience of both a moment and a lifetime confirms that what is true of Eliot is also true of Berry: "Love reciprocated is always rejuvenating" (Hewes 32). With his choice to found his work on the validity of Dante's themes, Berry has reaffirmed the importance of "Europe's epic" in the "New World," underscoring the possibility that the European tradition—the "idea of Europe" propounded by Arnold and then Eliot—may endure and thrive beyond anything its originators imagined.

BENEDICTION: *THIS LEFT HAND OF MINE*

RICHARD BERENGARTEN

This left hand of mine now packing this page with script
and this right hand steadying the same page's edge
together reach out to your hands that hold and turn
the same copy in another time entirely your own
or click or flick an icon to resurrect its appearance

which curiously means that exceedingly far
across time and space and despite our mortalities
you and I join hands through poetry in a kind
of peace and harmony that is unshakeable and this
is a bond and a pledge and a gift

WORKS CITED

Alighieri, Dante. *See Dante.*

Allott, Miriam. "The Bronzino Portrait in Henry James's *The Wings of the Dove." Modern Language Notes* 68 (1953): 23-25.

Ardizzone, Maria Luisa, ed. *Dante e Pound.* Ravenna: Longo, 1998.

Arnold, Matthew. *The Poems of Matthew Arnold.* Ed. Kenneth Allott; 2nd ed. ed. Miriam Allott. London and New York: Longman, 1965, 1979.

—. "The Study of Poetry." *The Complete Prose Works of Matthew Arnold.* Ed. R. H. Super. 11 vols. Ann Arbor: U of Michigan P, 1960-77. 9:161-88.

—. "The Function of Criticism at the Present Time." *The Complete Prose Works of Matthew Arnold.* Ed. R. H. Super. 11 vols. Ann Arbor: U of Michigan P, 1960-77. 3:258-85.

Auerbach, Erich. *Dante: Poet of the Secular World.* Trans. Ralph Mannheim. New York: New York Review of Books, 2001 [1929].

Bacigalupo Massimo, "Ezra Pound's Cantos 72 and 73: An Annotated Translation." *Paideuma* 20.1-2 (1991): 9-41.

Barolini, Teodolinda. "Dante and the Lyric Past." *The Cambridge Companion to Dante.* Ed. Rachel Jacoff. Cambridge, Mass.: Cambridge UP, 1993. 14-33.

Baudelaire, Charles. "The Seven Old Men." Trans. Barbara Gibbs. *An Anthology of French Poetry from Nerval to Valery in English Translation.* Ed. Angel Flores. New Rev. Ed. Garden City, New York: Anchor Books, 1958. 34-35.

Bell, Vereen, and Lawrence Lerner, eds., *On Modern Poetry. Essays Presented to Donald Davie.* Nashville: Vanderbilt UP, 1988.

Benjamin, Walter. *Illuminations.* Ed. Hannah Arendt. Trans. Harry Zohn. New York: Schoken Books, 1973.

Berry, Wendell. "The Country Writer." *Chronicles* 19 (June 1995), 14-15.

—. *The Gift of Good Land: Further Essays Cultural and Agricultural.* San Francisco: North Point P, 1981.

—. "Health is Membership." *Another Turn of the Clock.* Washington: Counterpoint, 1995. 86-109.

—. *Home Economics.* San Francisco: North Point P, 1987.

—. *Jayber Crow.* New York: Counterpoint, 2000.

—. *Life is a Miracle: An Essay against Modern Superstition*. Washington: Counterpoint, 2000.

—. *Long-Legged House*. New York: Harcourt, Brace, and World, 1969.

—. *A Place on Earth*. San Francisco: North Point P, 1983.

—. *Recollected Essays 1965-1980*. New York: North Point P, 1981.

—. *Remembering*. New York: North Point P, 1988.

—. *Sex, Economy, Freedom and Community*. New York: Pantheon Books, 1993.

—. *Standing by Words*. San Francisco: North Point P, 1983.

—. *The Unsettling of America: Culture and Agriculture*. San Francisco: Sierra Club Books, 1986.

—. *What Are People For?* New York: North Point P, 1990.

—. *A World Lost*. Washington: Counterpoint, 1996.

Bhagavad Gita. Tr. Juan Mascaro. Harmondsworth: Penguin, 1962.

Bloom, Harold. *The Anxiety of Influence: A Theory of Poetry*. New York: Oxford UP,1973.

Booth, Wayne C. *A Rhetoric of Irony*. Chicago/London: The U of Chicago P, 1974.

Bradley, F. H. *Appearance and Reality: A Metaphysical Essay*. 2nd ed. Oxford: Clarendon P, 1897.

—. *Essays on Truth and Reality*. 1914. Oxford: Clarendon P, 1950.

Braga, Corin. "'Imagination', 'imaginaire', 'imaginal'. Three Concepts for Defining Creative Fantasy." *Journal for the Study of Religions and Ideologies* 6.16 (2007): 59-68.

Brooks, Cleanth. *Modern Poetry and the tradition.* Chapel Hill NC: U of Carolina P, 1939.

Bullaro, John J. "The Dante of T. S. Eliot." *A Dante Profile*. Ed. Franca Schettino Los Angeles, U of Southern California P, 1967. 27-37.

Bush, Ronald. *T. S. Eliot: A Study in Character and Style*. New York: Oxford UP, 1983.

Cambon, Glauco. "Wallace Stevens's Dialogue with Dante." *Dante Among the Moderns*. Ed. Stuart Y. McDougal. Chapel Hill: U of North Carolina P, 1985. 102-127.

Cantor, Paul A. "The Uncanonical Dante: *The Divine Comedy* and Islamic Philosophy" *Philosophy and Literature* 20.1 (1996) 138-153.

Carpenter, Humphrey, *A Serious Character. The Life of Ezra Pound.* London-Boston: Faber and Faber, 1988.

Charity, A. C. "T. S. Eliot: The Dantean Recognitions." *The Waste Land in Several Voices*, ed. A. D. Moody. London: Edward Arnold, 1974. 117-62.

Chesterton, G.K. *Orthodoxy*. New York: Image Books, 1959.

—. *What's Wrong with the World?* in *The Collected Works of G.K. Chesterton*. Volume 4. San Francisco: Ignatius P, 1987. 33-224.

Chinitz, David. *T. S. Eliot and the Cultural Divide*. Chicago: U Chicago P, 2003.

Cleophas, Sister M. "Ash Wednesday: The *Purgatorio* in a Modern Mode." *Comparative Literature* 11.4 (1959): 329-339.

Coghill, Nevill. "An Essay on the Structure and Meaning of the Play." T. S. Eliot, *The Cocktail Party,* ed. Nevill Coghill. London: Faber and Faber, 1974. 237-291.

Continental Plans for European Integration, 1939-1945. Ed. Walter Lipgens. Berlin: Walter de Gruyter, 1985. Vol. 1 of *Documents on the History of European Integration*. 3 vols. 1985-1988.

Cooper, John Xiros. *T. S. Eliot and the Ideology of* Four Quartets. Cambridge: Cambridge UP, 1996.

Copley, J. H. "Plurilingualism and the Mind of Europe in T. S. Eliot and Dante." *Yeats Eliot Review: A Journal of Criticism and Scholarship*. 22:1 (2005 Spring): 2-24.

Corbin, Henry. *L'imagination creatrice dans le soufisme d'Ibn Arabi*, Paris: Flammarion, 1958. Trans. Ralph Manheim. *Creative imagination in Sufism of Ibn 'Arabi*. Bollingen Series XCL, Princeton: Princeton UP, 1969.

—. "Mundus Imaginalis: or the Imaginary and the Imaginal." *Spring* (Dallas, Texas) 1975: 1-19. Originally published as "Mundus Imaginalis ou l'imaginaire et l'imaginal." *Cahiers internationaux de symbolisme* 6 (1964): 3-26. http://hermetic.com/bey/mundus_imaginalis.htm

Couliano, Ioan. P. *Eros and Magic in the Renaissance*. Chicago: University of Chicago Press, 1987. Originally published as Ioan. P. Couliano. *Eros et magie de la renaissance*. Paris: Flammarion, 1984.

Cozzoli, Vittorio, *La Guida delle Guide. Dante secondo Dante*. Trieste: Battello Stampatore, 2007.

Dante [Alighieri]. *The Divine Comedy. 1: Hell*. Trans. Dorothy L. Sayers. Harmondsworth: Penguin, 1949.

—. *The Divine Comedy. Inferno*. Trans. John D. Sinclair. Oxford: Oxford UP, 1939.

—. *The Divine Comedy of Dante Alighieri: Inferno*. Trans. Allen Mandelbaum. New York: Bantam, 1980.

—. *The Divine Comedy of Dante Alighieri: Paradiso*. Trans. Allen Mandelbaum. New York: Bantam, 1984.

—. *The Divine Comedy of Dante Alighieri: Purgatorio*. Trans. Allen Mandelbaum. New York: Bantam, 1982.

—. *La Vita Nuova.* Trans. Mark Musa. New York: Oxford University Press, 1992.

Dawson, Christopher. *The Making of Europe: An Introduction to the History of European Unity.* London: Sheed and Ward,1953.

De Man, Paul. *Blindness and Insight.* Minneapolis: U of Minnesota P, 1983.

—. "Semiology and Rhetoric." *Allegories of Reading.* New Haven: Yale UP, 1979: 3-19.

Derrida, Jacques. *Positions.* Trans. Alan Bass. Chicago: Chicago UP, 1981.

Dobrée, Bonamy. "T. S. Eliot. A Personal Reminiscence." *T. S. Eliot: The Man and His Work.* Ed. Allen Tate. London: Chatto and Windus, 1967: 81.

Eco, Umberto. *Travels in Hyperreality.* Trans. William Weaver. New York: Harcourt Brace Jovanovich, 1986.

Eliot, T. S. *After Strange Gods: A Primer of Modern Heresy.* London: Faber, 1934.

—. "The Aims of Poetic Drama." *Adam* (International Review, ed. Miron Grindea) 200 (November 1949): 10-16.

—. "Christianity and Communism." *Listener* 7. 166 (1932): 382-3.

—. *Christianity and Culture.* New York: Harcourt Brace Jovanovich. 1977 [1960].

—. *Collected Poems 1909-1962.* New York: Harcourt, 1963.

—. "A Commentary [Jan. 1932]." *Criterion* 11 (1931-32): 268-75.

—. "A Commentary [Oct. 1937]." *Criterion* 17 (1937-38): 81-86.

—. *Complete Poems and Plays*: 1909-1950. New York: Harcourt Brace, 1952.

—. *Dante.* London: Faber, 1965.

—. *The Elder Statesman: A Play.* New York: Farrar, Straus, and Cudahy, 1959.

—. "In Memory of Henry James," *Egoist* 5.1 (Jan. 1918):[1]-2.

—. "Introduction" to Djuna Barnes, *Nightwood.* London: Faber, 1936.

—. "Introduction" to G. Wilson Knight, *The Wheel of Fire.* London: Methuen, 1962.

—. *Inventions of the March Hare.* Ed. Christopher Ricks. New York: Harcourt, 1996.

—. *Knowledge and Experience in the Philosophy of F. H. Bradley* [1916]. New York: Farrar, Straus, 1964.

—. *The Letters of T. S. Eliot, Volume I: 1898-1922.* Ed. Valerie Eliot and Hugh Haughton. London: Faber and Faber, 2009.

—. *Notes towards the Definition of Culture.* London: Faber, 1948.

—. *On Poetry and Poets*. London: Faber, 1986 [1957].

—. "The Possibility of a Poetic Drama." *Dial* 69: 5 (November): [441]-447.

—. Preface to *Anabasis* by St.-John Perse. Trans. T. S. Eliot. New York: Harcourt Brace, 1938.

—. "A Preface to Modern Literature." *Vanity Fair* (November 1923): 118, 44.

—. Preface. *Transit of Venus: Poems by Harry Crosby*. Paris: Black Sun P, 1931.

—. *The Rock: A Pageant Play*. London: Faber, 1934.

—. *The Sacred Wood. Essays on Poetry and Criticism*. London: Methuen, 1980 [1920].

—. *Selected Essays*. Third enlarged ed. London and Boston: Faber, 1980 [1951].

—. *To Criticize the Critic and other Writings*. London: Faber, 1978 [1965].

—. *The Use of Poetry and the Use of Criticism*. London: Faber, 1975 [1933].

—. *The Varieties of Metaphysical Poetry*. Ed. Ronald Schuchard. London: Faber, 1993.

—. *The Waste Land: A Facsimile and Transcript of the Original Drafts Including the Annotations of Ezra Pound*. Ed. Valerie Eliot. New York: Harcourt, 1971.

Franci, Giovanni. "Dante negli scrittori anglo-americani: Eliot e Pound." *Dante e la cultura anglosassone*. Ed. Alessandro Calzolari et al. Gerione: Incroci Danteschi. 2. Milan, : Unicopli, 2007.

Frye, Northrop. *Anatomy of Criticism*. New York: Atheneum, 1966.

—. *T. S. Eliot*. Edinburgh: Oliver and Boyd, 1963.

Gallup, Donald. "The 'Lost' Manuscripts of T. S. Eliot." *Times Literary Supplement* (November 1968); repr. in *Bulletin of the New York Public Library*, 72 (December 1968): 641-52.

Gardner, Helen. *The Art of T. S. Eliot*. London and Boston: Faber and Faber, 1949.

Gervais, David. "Eliot's Shakespeare and Eliot's Dante." *T. S. Eliot and Our Turning World*. Ed. Jewel Spears Brooker. London and New York: Macmillan/St. Martin's, with Institute of United States Studies, University of London, 2001. 114-24.

Gish, Nancy K. "Discarnate Desire: T. S. Eliot and the Poetics of Dissociation." *Gender, Desire, and Sexuality in T. S. Eliot*. Ed. Cassandra Laity and Nancy K. Gish. Cambridge: Cambridge UP, 2004. 107-29.

Gordon, Lyndall. *T. S. Eliot: An Imperfect Life*. New York: Norton, 1999.
—. *Eliot's New Life*. New York: Farrar, Straus and Giroux, 1988.
Gorman, Herbert. *James Joyce: A Definitive Biography*. New York: Rinehart, 1948.
Grandgent, C. H. *Companion to 'The Divine Comedy'*. Ed. Charles S. Singleton. Cambridge, Mass.: Harvard UP, 1975.
Grob, Alan. *A Longing Like Despair: Arnold's Poetry of Pessimism*. Associated U Presses, 2002.
Gross, Kenneth. "Infernal Metamorphoses: An Interpretation of Dante's 'Counterpass.'" *Modern Language Notes* 100.1 (January 1985): 42-69.
Guenther, Herbert V. *The Tantric View of Life*. London: Shambala Publications, 1972.
Harding, Jason. *The Criterion: Cultural Politics and Periodical Networks in Inter-war Britain*. Oxford: Oxford UP, 2002.
Hargrove, Nancy, "T. S. Eliot and the Parisian Theatre World, 1910-1911." *South Atlantic Review* 66.4 (Autumn, 2001): 1-44.
—. "T. S. Eliot and Opera in Paris, 1910-1911." *Yeats Eliot Review* 21.3 (Fall 2004): 2-20.
—. "T. S. Eliot's Year Abroad, 1910-1911: The Visual Arts." *South Atlantic Review* 71.1 (Winter 2006): 71-131.
Hawkins, Peter S. *Dante: A Brief History*. Oxford: Blackwell, 2006.
Hesse, Hermann. *In Sight of Chaos*. Trans. Stephen Hudson. Zurich: Verlag Seldwyla, 1923.
Hewes, Henry. "T. S. Eliot at Seventy," *The Saturday Review of Literature,* September 13, 1958, 30-32.
Hutcheon, Linda. *Irony's Edge: The Theory and Politics of Irony*. London and New York: Routledge, 1995.
Jain, Manju. *T. S. Eliot and American Philosophy: The Harvard Years*. Cambridge: Cambridge UP, 1992.
Jauss, Hans Robert. "The Alterity and Modernity of Medieval Literature." *New Literary History* 10 (Winter 1979): 181-227.
Jenkins, Nicholas. "More American Than We Knew." [review of T. S. Eliot, *Inventions of the March Hare*], *New York Times Book Review* (20 April 1997): 14-15.
Jarrety, Michel. *Paul Valéry*. Paris: Librarie Arthème Fayard, 2008.
Joyce, James. *The Critical Writings of James Joyce*. Ed. Ellsworth Mason and Richard Ellmann. New York: Viking, 1959.
Julius, Anthony. *T. S. Eliot, Anti-Semitism, and Literary Form*. Cambridge: Cambridge UP, 1995.

Jung, Carl Gustav. *The Spirit in Man, Art, Literature. Collected Works.* Ed. H. Read, M. Fordham, and G. Adler. Trans. R. F. C. Hull. 20 Vols. London: Routledge and Kegan Paul, 1953-1978.

Kearns, Cleo McNelly. "Religion, Literature, and Society." *The Cambridge Companion to T. S. Eliot.* Ed. A. D. Moody. Cambridge: Cambridge UP, (1994). 77-93.

Kenner, Hugh. "Pound and the American Dante." *Dante e Pound.* Ed. Maria Luisa Ardizzone. Ravenna: Longo, 1998. 35-38.

—. *The Invisible Poet: T. S. Eliot.* New York: Harcourt Brace & World, 1969 [1959].

Keyserling, Hermann. *Das Spektrum Europas.* Heidelberg: Niels Kampmann Verlag, 1928.

Knight, G. Wilson. *Neglected Powers: Essays on Nineteenth and Twentieth Century Literature.* New York: Barnes and Noble, 1971.

Lévi-Strauss, Claude. *The Raw and the Cooked.* Trans. J.and D. Weightman. New York: Harper & Row, 1969.

Lewis. C. S. *The Great Divorce.* New York: Macmillan, 1952 [1946].

Lifton, Robert Jay. *The Protean Self.* Chicago: U of Chicago P, 1999.

Lipgens, Walter. *A History of European Integration.* Vol. 1. Trans. P. S. Falla and A. J. Ryder. Oxford: Clarendon P, 1982.

Litz, A. Walton. "Dante, Pound, Eliot : The Visionary Company." *Dante e Pound.* Ed. Maria Luisa Ardizzone. Ravenna: Longo, 1998. 39-45.

Lotman, Y. M. *The Structure of the Literary Text.* Moscow: Iskusstvo, 1970.

Lovejoy, Arthur O. *The Revolt Against Dualism: An Inquiry Concerning the Existence of Ideas.* 1929. LaSalle, IL: Open Court, 1955.

McDougal, Stuart Y., ed. *Dante Among the Moderns.* Chapel Hill: U of North Carolina P, 1985.

Malamud, Randy. "Shakespeare/Dante and Water/Music in *The Waste Land.*" *Time Present and Time Past: T. S. Eliot and Our Turning World.* Ed. Jewel Spears Brooker. Institute of United States Studies/University of London series, vol. 1. London: Macmillan, 2001. 100-112.

Mandelbaum, Allen. "Dante as Ancient and Modern," *The Divine Comedy of Dante Alighieri: Inferno.* Trans. Allen Mandelbaum. New York: Bantam, 1982. 331-340. n.b.: *See also Dante, his works as translated by Mandelbaum.*

Mandelstam, Osip E. "Conversation about Dante." *The Complete Critical Prose and Letters.* Ed. Jane Gay Harris. Ann Arbor: Ardis, 1979. 379-451.

Manganiello, Dominic. "Dante and Wendell Berry's Modern Book of Memory." *Studies in Medievalism* 15 (2006): 115-125.

—. "Literature, Science, and Dogma: T. S. Eliot and I. A. Richards on Dante." *Christianity and Literature* 43:1 (1993): 59-73.

—. *T. S. Eliot and Dante*. London: Macmillan, 1989.

Margolis, John D. *T. S. Eliot's Intellectual Development, 1922-1939.* Chicago: U of Chicago P, 1972.

Marion, Jean-Luc. *Being Given: Toward a Phenomenology of Givenness.* Trans. Jeffrey L. Kosky. Stanford: Stanford UP, 2002.

—. *In Excess: Studies of Saturated Phenomena*. Trans. by Robyn Horner and Vincent Berrand. New York: Fordham UP, 2002.

Marx, Karl. *Surveys from Exile*. Ed. David Fernbach. Harmondsworth: Penguin, 1973.

Miller, J. Hillis. *The Disappearance of God.* Cambridge, Mass.: Belknap P, 1963.

—. *The Cambridge Companion to T. S. Eliot*. Cambridge: Cambridge UP, 1994.

Menocal, Maria. *The Arabic Role in Medieval Literary History: A Forgotten Heritage*. Philadelphia, U of Pennsylvania P, 1987.

Moloney, Brian, "T. S. Eliot's Dante." *Ricerca Research Recherche* 3 (ed. Cleonice Panaro. Lecce: Milella, 1997), 129-47.

Moody, A. D. "*Four Quartets*: Music, Word, Meaning and Value." *The Cambridge Companion to T. S. Eliot*. Ed. A. D. Moody. Cambridge: Cambridge UP, 1994. 142-57.

—. "The Mind of Europe in T. S. Eliot." *T. S. Eliot at the Turn of the Century*. Ed. Marianne Thormählen. Lund: Lund UP, 1994. 13-32.

—. *Thomas Stearns Eliot: Poet*. Cambridge: Cambridge UP, 1979.

Mookerjee, Ajit, and Madhu Khanna. *The Tantric Way*. London: Thames and Hudson, 1977.

Muecke, D. C. *Irony*. London: Methuen & Co Ltd, 1970.

Nelson, Graham. " 'The Waste Land' drafts, 'The Engine' and the sinking of the Titanic." *Notes and Queries* 44. 3 (Sept 1997): 356-358.

Nietzsche, Friedrich. *The Use and Abuse of History.* Trans. Adrian Collins. New York: Bobbs-Merrill, 1957.

O'Connor, Flannery. *Mystery and Manners*. Ed. Sally and Robert Fitzgerald. New York: Farrar, Straus, and Giroux, 1969.

Olson, Charles. *Collected Prose*. Ed. Donald Allen and Benjamin Friedlander. Berkeley: U of California P, 1997.

Ortega y Gasset, José. *The Revolt of the Masses*. Trans. and rpt. London: George Allen & Unwin, 1961 [1930].

Ovid. "The Blinding of Tiresias." Trans. Justus Miller. *T. S. Eliot: The Waste Land*. Ed. Michael North. Norton Critical Edition. New York: Norton, 2001. 46.

Paulin, Tom. *Minotaur: Poetry in the Nation State*. London: Faber, 1992.

Patapievici, H. R. *Cerul vazut prin lentila*. Bucharest: Nemira, 1994.

—. *Omul recent*. Bucharest: Humanitas, 2001.

—. *Los ojos de Beatriz: Cómo era realmente el mundo de Dante*. Trans. Natalia Izquierdo. Madrid: Siruela, 2007.

Perl, Jeffrey M. "A Post-War Consensus." *T. S. Eliot: Man and Poet*. Vol. 1. Ed. Laura Cowan. Orono, ME: National Poetry Foundation, 1990. 343-365.

Plato. "Timaeus." *The dialogues of Plato*. 5 Vols. 3rd ed. Trans. Benjamin Jowett. Oxford: Clarendon P, 1892.

Pound, Ezra. Ezra Pound, *I Cantos*, Ed. Mary de Rachewiltz. Milan: Mondadori, 1985:

—. *ABC of Reading*. New York: New Directions, 1960.

—. *A Lume Spento*. New York: New Directions, 1965.

—. *Canti postumi*. Ed. Massimo Bacigalupo. Milan: Mondadori, 2002.

—. *Carta da Visita*. Milan: Scheiwiller, 1974.

—. *The Cantos*. New York: New Directions, 1989.

—. *Guide to Kulchur*. London: Peter Owen, 1952 [1938].

—. *The Letters of Ezra Pound 1907-1941*. Ed. D. D. Paige. New York: Harcourt Brace, 1950.

—. *Literary Essays of Ezra Pound*. Ed. and introd. by T. S. Eliot. London: Faber and Faber, 1954.

—. *Selected Prose: 1909-1965*. Ed. and introd. by William Cookson. New York: New Directions, 1973.

—. *The Spirit of Romance*. New York: New Directions, 1953.

Praz, Mario, "T. S. Eliot and Dante." *The Southern Review*, 2.3 (1936-37): 525-48.

Raine, Craig. *T. S. Eliot*. Oxford: Oxford UP, 2006.

Rainey, Lawrence. *Revisiting The Waste Land*. New Haven: Yale UP, 2005.

Richards, I. A. *Practical Criticism: A Study of Literary Judgment*. London: Kegan Paul, 1939 [1929].

—. *Principles of Literary Criticism*. London: Routledge, 1995 [1924; 1928].

—. *Science and Poetry*. 2nd ed. London: Kegan Paul, 1935 [1st ed. 1926].

Ricoeur, Paul. *Oneself as Another*. Trans. Kathleen Blamey. Chicago: U of Chicago P, 1992.

Ruebsaat, Susanna, "Taking the Inside View of Art-Making,"

http://www.ierg.net/confs/2003/proceeds/Ruebsaat.pdf Accessed June 12, 2008.

Russell, Bertrand. *Autobiography*. 3 vols. Boston: Litlle, Brown, 1967-69.

Said, Edward. *Orientalism*. New York: Pantheon, 1978.

Sayers, Dorothy L. "Introduction." *The Divine Comedy II: Purgatory (Il Purgatorio).* Trans. Dorothy Sayers. Harmondsworth: Penguin, 1988.

—. *The Letters of Dorothy L. Sayers 1944-1950: A Noble Daring*. Vol. III. Ed. Barbara Reynolds. Swavesey, Cambridge: Dorothy L. Sayers Society, 1998.

Schiller, Jerome. *I. A. Richards' Theory of Literature*. New Haven and London: Yale UP, 1969.

Schuchard, Ronald. "Did Eliot Know Hulme? Final Answer." *Journal of Modern Literature* 27, nos. 1/2, Modern Poets (Autumn, 2003): 63-69.

—. "T. S. Eliot as an Extension Lecturer: 1916-1919." *Review of English Studies: A Quarterly Journal of English Literature and the English Language* 25 (1974), nos. 98 (May) and 99 (Aug.): 163-73, 292-304.

Serpieri, Alessandro. "Eliot e Dante." In *Gli amici per Nando. Giornata di studi in onore di Fernando Ferrara.*,Ed. Lidia Curti and Laura Di Michele. Naples: Apophoreta, 1998. 301-314.

—. *T. S. Eliot: le strutture profonde*. Firenze: Il Mulino, 1985.

Soldo, John J. "Eliot's Dantean Vision, and His Markings in His Copy of the Divina Commedia." *Yeats Eliot Review* 7. 1-2 (June 1982): 11-18.

Solzhenitsyn, Aleksandr. "The Relentless Cult of Novelty and how it wrecked the Century." *The New York Times Book Review*, February 7, 1993, 3, 17.

Spender, Steven. *T. S. Eliot*. Harmondsworth: Penguin, 1976.

Spurr, David. *Conflicts in Consciousness : T. S. Eliot's Poetry and Criticism.*

Stevens, Wallace. *The Collected Poems of Wallace Stevens*. New York: Knopf, 1954.

—. *The Necessary Angel: Essays on Reality and the Imagination*. New York: Knopf, 1951.

Stirk, Peter M. R. *A History of European Integration since 1914*. London: Pinter/Cassell, 1996.

Surette, Leon. *The Birth of Modernism: Ezra Pound, T. S. Eliot, W. B. Yeats and the Occult*. Montreal and Kingston: McGill-Queen's UP, 1993.

Tamplin Ronald, *A Preface to T. S. Eliot*. London and New York: Longman, 1987.

Valéry, Paul. *La Crise de l'Esprit* (1929). *Œuvres* I. Ed. Jean Hytier. Paris: Gallimard, 1957. 988-1014.

—. "Speech" (1922). *Variétés*. Vol 1. Paris: Gallimard, 1998. 33-38.

Voss, Karen-Claire. "Imagination in Mysticism and Esotericism: Marsilio Ficino, Ignatius de Loyola, and Alchemy." *Studies in Spirituality* 6 (1966): 106-130.

Weinreb, Mindy. "A Question a Day: A Written Conversation with Wendell Berry." *Wendell Berry*. Ed. Paul Merchant. Lewiston: Confluence P, 1991. 27-43.

Wilhelm, James J. "Two Visions of the Journey of Life: Dante as Guide for Eliot and Pound." *Dante: Beyond the Commedia*. Ed. Anne Paolucci. Wilmington, DE: Griffon, for Bagehot Council, 2004. 53-61.

Williams, Charles. *The Figure of Beatrice: A Study in Dante*. London: Faber and Faber, 1943.

—. *Outlines of Romantic Theology*. Ed. Alice Mary Hadfield. Grand Rapids: Eerdmans, 1990.

Wright, Charles. *Negative Blue: Selected Later Poems*. New York: Farrar, Straus and Giroux, 2000.

CONTRIBUTORS

Arianna Antonielli earned her PhD in English and American Literature at the University of Florence, where she is Temporary Research Fellow in Anglo-American Studies, Digital Humanities and Multimedia Publishing. She is the head of the Open Access Publishing Laboratory of the Department of Comparative Languages, Literatures and Cultures of the University of Florence. She is also journal manager of the open access journals *LEA—Letterature d'Europa e d'America*, *Studi irlandesi. A Journal of Irish Studies*, and *Journal of Early Modern Studies*, as well as editorial secretary of the open access series "Biblioteca di Studi di Filologia Moderna" and web master of their sites. She is the author of *William Blake e William Butler Yeats. Sistemi simbolici e costruzioni poetiche* (Firenze UP, 2009). She has written essays on T. S. Eliot, William Blake, W.B. Yeats, Althea Gyles, Anatole France, C. A. Smith and Mervyn Peake. She is currently completing an edition on William Butler Yeats's and John Edwin Ellis's *The Works of William Blake: Poetic, Symbolic and Critical.*

Massimo Bacigalupo is Professor of American Literature at the Facoltà di Lingue of the University of Genoa. He has held visiting professorships at Barnard College, New York, research appointments at St. John's College, Cambridge, and at the Institute for the Humanities, University of Michigan, and is on the Academic Board of the Yeats International Summer School, Sligo, Ireland. He is the author of *The Forméd Trace* (1980) and *Grotta Byron* (2001), co-editor of *Ezra Pound, Language, and Persona* (2009), editor and translator of Pound's *Canti postumi* (2002) and of Eliot's *Poesie 1905/1920* (1995). He has contributed essays to *T. S. Eliot and the Idea of Tradition* (CUP, 2007), *The Cambridge Companion to Ezra Pound* (CUP, 1999), *Ezra Pound in Context* (CUP, 2010), and *T. S. Eliot in Context* (CUP, 2011). He is a frequent contributor to *Notes & Queries*, *Journal of Modern Literature*, *American Literary Scholarship*, etc., and is on the editorial board of the journals *Paideuma* and *Leviathan*. Professor Bacigalupo is the author of numerous translations and editions of classic and contemporary writers, from Shakespeare to Wordsworth, Dickinson, and Heaney, and has received many awards, among them the

Premio Viareggio (1982), the *Premio Internazionale Monselice* (1990), and the Italian National Translation Prize (2001).

Richard Berengarten was born in London in 1943, into a family of musicians. After graduating from Cambridge, he went to live in Italy for two years, partly influenced by T. S. Eliot's work on Dante. He has also lived in Greece, former Yugoslavia and the USA. His perspectives combine English, French, Mediterranean, Jewish, Slavic, American and Oriental influences. He has published more than 20 books; his poems have been translated into 22 languages. His latest work is *The Blue Butterfly*, recipient of the Wingate-Jewish Quarterly Award for Poetry (UK) and the Veliki skolski cas Award (Serbia). He has also received the Eric Gregory Award, Keats Memorial Poetry Prize, Yeats Club Prize and the international Morava Poetry Prize. In the 1970's, he founded the international Cambridge Poetry Festival. As a theorist, he is especially interested in poetry universals. He is a Bye-Fellow at Downing College, Cambridge, Preceptor at Corpus Christi College, Cambridge, and a former Fellow of the Royal Literary Fund.

Jewel Spears Brooker is Professor of Literature at Eckerd College where she has received awards for teaching, scholarship, and campus leadership. She has held visiting professorships at Columbia University, Doshisha University (Kyoto), and Colorado School of Mines, and research appointments at Yale, Harvard, and Cambridge Universities. Dr. Brooker has written or edited seven books, including *Approaches to Teaching Eliot's Poetry and Plays* (1988), *Reading* The Waste Land: *Modernism and the Limits of Interpretation* (1990—coauthored with Joseph Bentley), *The Placing of T. S. Eliot* (1991), *Mastery and Escape: T. S. Eliot and the Dialectic of Modernism* (1994), *Conversations with Denise Levertov* (1998), *T. S. Eliot and Our Turning World* (2000), and *T. S. Eliot: The Contemporary Reviews* (2004). She is also co-editor of *T. S. Eliot: The Apprentice Years 1905-1918*, vol. 1 in the forthcoming *Eliot's Complete Prose* (2012).She has also published scores of essays on modern writers. She has received major fellowships from the National Endowment for the Humanities, Knight Foundation, and Pew Charitable Trust. She has lectured widely in Europe and Asia and has served as president of the South Atlantic Modern Language Association and other professional societies. She also served as a member of the National Humanities Council of the National Endowment for the Humanities from 2003-2008.

Stefano Maria Casella is Assistant Professor at Libera Università di Lingue e Comunicazione IULM of Milan/Feltre. He attended Ph.D. courses in American Literature at the University of Venice, was Visiting Fellow (1996) at Clare Hall (Cambridge, UK) and Fellow in Literature (2000) of the Bogliasco Foundation—Liguria Study Centre for the Arts and Letters (Genoa-Bogliasco/New York). He has published essays on Eliot, Pound, Modernism, comparative literature (especially Italian and classical: Latin and Greek vs. Anglo-American) and poetry, as well as translations and reviews. He collaborated with Mary de Rachewiltz on an edition of Pound's letters to his parents. He has contributed a paper on Eliot and Italy in *The International Reception of T. S. Eliot* (Continuum, 2007).

John Xiros Cooper is Professor of English and former Associate Dean in the Faculty of Arts at the University of British Columbia. He has a B.A. from Sir George Williams and was the winner of a Woodrow Wilson Fellowship. His M.A. (1977) and Ph.D. (1984) were earned at U.B.C. where he returned in 1989 after teaching and chairing the department of English at Mount Royal College in Calgary, Alberta. He specializes in twentieth-century literature, with particular interests in poetry, the culture of modernity, and the relationship of literature to the other arts. His books include, *T. S. Eliot and the Politics of Voice: the Argument of The Waste Land* (Ann Arbor 1987), *T. S. Eliot and the Ideology of Four Quartets* (Cambridge 1995), *Modernism and the Culture of Market Society* (Cambridge 2004), and *The Cambridge Introduction to T. S. Eliot* (Cambridge 2006). He has also authored a book-length course guide, *The Modern British Novel* (Vancouver 1998). A long range research project, *Constructing Modernity: A Cultural History of Faber & Faber, 1925-1965*, will examine the cultural impact of one of England's most important publishing enterprises. Cooper is also the editor of *T. S. Eliot's Orchestra: Critical Essays on Poetry and Music* (New York 2000). Other research projects and interests include a grant-funded study of the English poet Lord Byron, titled *Byron and Modernity*, the literature and cultural politics of the 1930s, the writings of M.F.K. Fisher and Elizabeth David and the work of W. B. Yeats, Geoffrey Hill, and Tony Harrison.

Paul Douglass is Professor of English and American Literature at San José State University, where he has been Chair of the English Department and Coordinator of the California Literature Project and of the University's Steinbeck Fellows Program in Creative Writing. He earned his PhD in English and American Literature at UCLA and is the author of

Bergson, Eliot, and American Literature (U P of Kentucky, 1986) and co-editor with Frederick Burwick of *Bergson and the Vitalist Controversy* (Cambridge UP, 1992), and the author and editor of six other books, as well as numerous essays and reviews on topics relating to Pound, Eliot, American and British Literature, film, and philosophy, published in such journals as *Notes and Queries*, *Twentieth Century Literature*, *Social Semiotics*, *Thought*, *Paideuma*, *European Romantic Review*, *Keats-Shelley Journal*, *Modern Language Quarterly*, and *The Wordsworth Circle*.

Nancy K. Gish is Professor of English and women's studies at the University of Southern Maine. She is co-editor, with Cassandra Laity, of *Gender, Desire, and Sexuality in T. S. Eliot* (Cambridge UP, 2004). Her other publications include *Time in the Poetry of T. S. Eliot* (Macmillan, 1981) and *Hugh MacDiarmid: Man and Poet* (Edinburgh UP and National Poetry Foundation, 1992), *Hugh MacDiarmid: The Man and His Work* (Macmillan, 1984) and *The Waste Land: A Poem of Memory and Desire* (Twayne, 1988). She currently holds the University of Southern Maine Trustee Professorship for research on WWI trauma and poetry. Gish also writes extensively on Scottish literature and contemporary women poets.

Temur Kobakhidze is Professor of English at Caucasus School of Humanities, Caucasus University, Tbilisi, Georgia. His research and academic interests focus on twentieth-century American modernist literature and the literary aesthetics of Modernism (mainly T. S. Eliot's poetry and prose writings), with the aim of revealing the principal aesthetic and structural functions of myth in American Modernist poetry, prose, and drama. His publications include *Myth and the Literary Aesthetics of Modernism* (U of Tbilisi P, 1998); *T. S. Eliot: Poetry and Mythos* (U of Tbilisi P, 1991; *Hereditary Poetics: John Donne, W. B. Yeats, T. S. Eliot* (U of Tbilisi P, 1984). He is also the author of numerous articles and chapters in books. He has been a Visiting Fulbright Scholar at San José State University (1994-1995); Fellow, Salzburg Seminar (2000); Foundation Fellow at Clare Hall, Cambridge University (2001-2002); and in 2002 was elected to Life Membership of Clare Hall. He is also a member of various learned and professional societies, including the International T. S. Eliot Society, the T. S. Eliot Society (UK), International Association of University Professors of English (IAUPE), and The Georgian Association for American Studies, Tbilisi. He presently teaches classes for MA students and is writing a book on T. S. Eliot and the culture of Italy.

Randy Malamud is Professor of English at Georgia State University in Atlanta, Georgia. He earned his PhD in English and Comparative Literature at Columbia University. He is the author of *The Language of Modernism* (UMI Research Press, 1989), *T. S. Eliot's Drama: A Research and Production Sourcebook* (Greenwood P, 1992), and *Where the Words are Valid: T. S. Eliot's Communities of Drama* (Greenwood P, 1994). He also edited *The Waste Land and Other Poems* (Barnes & Noble Classics, 2005). In addition to Eliot and modernism, he writes about cultural representations of animals; his publications in the field of human-animal studies include *Reading Zoos: Representations of Animals and Captivity* (NYU P, 1998), *Poetic Animals and Animal Souls* (Palgrave Macmillan, 2003), and *A Cultural History of Animals in the Modern Age* (Berg, 2007).

Dominic Manganiello (B.A. McGill; D.Phil., Oxford), is a Professor of English Literature at the University of Ottawa, where he has taught since 1979. He is the author of *Joyce's Politics* (1980) and *T. S. Eliot and Dante* (1989), and co-author of *Rethinking the Future of the University* (1998). Although he has written extensively on canonical modern authors and the culture of modernism such as T. S. Eliot, James Joyce, and I.A. Richards, his recent work has also focused on a group of writers that includes, among others, G.K. Chesterton, Dorothy L. Sayers, the Inklings (especially Tolkien, Lewis, and Williams), and their return to the Middle Ages as a quest to locate the roots of Western culture. His book-length project, *Making Dante New*, accordingly examines the nature of the high-level reception twentieth-century writers accorded *The Divine Comedy*.

Andrija Matic is Assistant Professor of English and American Literature at the "Alpha" University in Belgrade, Serbia. He earned his PhD in English Literature at the University of Belgrade. His primary critical fields are Anglo-American Modernism and European twentieth-century literature. He has published essays on T. S. Eliot, James Joyce, James Thomson ("B. V."), Gottfried Benn, George Orwell, William Trevor, Ian McEwan and Paul Auster. He is the author of the first Serbian study of Eliot's complete works entitled *T. S. Eliot: Poet, Critic, Playwright* (2007). Besides literary criticism, he writes fiction. He is the author of a collection of short stories *The Museum of Modern Art* (2010) and two novels: *The Disappearance of Zdenko Kupresanin* (2006) and *Manhole* (2009).

Mafruha Mohua has recently obtained her PhD in the Department of English at Queen Mary, University of London. Her thesis has an interdisciplinary element investigating not only the influence of Hindu-Buddhist philosophy in the work of T. S. Eliot, but also the political and cultural implications of such an influence. The issues of race, nationalism, and imperialism constitute key elements in her work.

Viorica Patea is Associate Professor of American Literature at the University of Salamanca (Spain), where she teaches twentieth-century American poetry and nineteenth-century American literature. Her published books include *Entre el mito y la realidad: Aproximación a la obra poética de Sylvia Plath* (Salamanca: Ediciones Universidad de Salamanca, 1989), T. S. Eliot's *The Waste Land* [*La tierra baldía.* (Madrid: Ediciones Cátedra, 2005)], and a study on Whitman (*La apología de Whitman a favor de la épica de la modernidad* [León: Ediones Universidad de León, 1999]). She has coedited various collections of essays, such as *Critical Essays on the Myth of the American Adam* (Salamanca: Ediciones Universidad de Salamanca, 2001), and, in collaboration with Paul Derrick, *Modernism Revisited: Transgressing Boundaries and Strategies of Renewal in American Poetry* (New York and Amsterdam: Rodopi, 2007). At present she is working on a book project on short story theories.

Patrick Query is Assistant Professor in the Department of English and Philosophy at the United States Military Academy in West Point, New York. He earned his Ph.D. from Loyola University Chicago under the direction of David E. Chinitz. He specializes in twentieth-century British and Irish literature and has published articles and chapters on T. S. Eliot, W. B. Yeats, Evelyn Waugh, Graham Greene, and W.H. Auden, as well as numerous reviews. His recently completed book manuscript, entitled *Ritual Returns: British and Irish Writers Imagining Europe, 1919-1939*, deals with the ways in which several major authors of the interwar years used verse drama, bullfighting, and Catholic ritual to explore ideas of European identity. He is currently at work on a new research project, *The Extreme Border of Europe: The Aran Islands and the Irish Mind in the Twentieth Century*.

P.S. Sri is a Canadian of Indian origin and hails from Chennai (Madras), the capital of Tamil Nadu, India. Currently, Sri is a Professor of Comparative Literature in the Dept. of English at Royal Military College of Canada, Kingston, Ontario, with over 36 years of teaching experience. Sri's wide-ranging research includes East-West Literary-Philosophical ideo-synthesis, Post-colonial Multi-cultural Commonwealth Literature, Arabic-Persian Literature as well as Sanskrit and Tamil Literature. Sri is the author of a critical work entitled *T. S. Eliot, Vedanta and Buddhism* (Vancouver: University of British Columbia, 1985), which has been translated into Korean. Sri has also published articles on Bharati Mukherjee, Margaret Laurence, George Bernard Shaw, W. B. Yeats, T. S. Eliot, E. M. Forster, Rumi, Sanskrit myth, Tamil literature and folklore. Sri's most recent publications include his first novel, *The Temple Elephant* (Chennai, India: New Horizon Media Pvt. Ltd., 2007) and his 853-pages trans-*creation* into English of a modern Tamil masterpiece, *Sivakamiyin Sabadam (Sivakami's Vow)* (New Delhi: Sahitya Akademi, 2008). Sri has received many prestigious awards, including the Canadian Federation of Humanities Grant (1984-85), the Social Sciences and Humanities Research Council Grant (1990-91) and the Women and Development program grant (1996-97) of the Shastri Indo-Canadian Institute at the University of Calgary. In 1991, Sri won a prize in an International Essay Contest organized by Washington and Jefferson College, Pennsylvania, USA. In 1993, Sri was awarded the First National Prize for Canada by UNESCO in an International Literary Competition commemorating the 500th Anniversary of Columbus' discovery of the New World.

David Summers is Professor of English, Director of General Education and Assistant Dean of the Division of Humanities at Capital University in Columbus, Ohio. His primary area of academic interest is Shakespeare and the English Renaissance, but he also teaches classical mythology, medieval and early 20th century British literature. He is the author of *Spenser's Arthur*, a study of Spenser's use of the British Arthurian tradition in the *Faerie Queene*, and articles and essays on Shakespeare, Marlowe, Milton, Eliot and David Jones. A native of the Pacific Northwest, he did his Ph.D. work at the University of Washington (1989), and taught at Whitworth College and Seattle Pacific University before coming to Capital University.

INDEX